Center for Basque Studies
Current Research Series, No. 2

Feminist Challenges in the Social Sciences: Gender Studies in the Basque Country

Edited by
Mari Luz Esteban and Mila Amurrio

Current Research Series No. 2

Center for Basque Studies
University of Nevada, Reno

Published in conjunction with the University of the Basque Country
UPV/EHU

Universidad   Euskal Herriko
del País Vasco   Unibertsitatea

Current Research
Selections of the ongoing work done by the faculty of the University of
the Basque Country (UPV/EHU)

Editorial Committee
Amaia Maseda (Chair, UPV/EHU), Arantza Azpiroz (UPV/EHU), Javier
Echeverría (Ikerbasque), Jon Landeta (UPV/EHU), Sandra Ott (UNR), Joseba
Zulaika (UNR), Santos Zunzunegui (UPV/EHU)

Current Research Series, No. 2

Center for Basque Studies
University of Nevada, Reno
Reno, Nevada 89557
http://basque.unr.edu

Cover and series design © 2010 by Jose Luis Agote.
Cover design based on engravings by Eduardo Chillida and Jorge Oteiza.

Library of Congress Cataloging-in-Publication Data

Feminist challenges in the social sciences : gender studies in the Basque
country / edited by Mari Luz Esteban and Mila Amurrio.
    p. cm. -- (Current research series ; no. 2)
  Includes bibliographical references.
  ISBN 978-1-935709-01-5 (pbk.)
  1. Women, Basque. 2. Women--France--Pays Basque. 3. Women-
-Spain--País Vasco. 4. Women's studies. I. Esteban, Mari Luz.
II. Amurrio, Mila.
  HQ1162.F46 2010
  305.48'89992--dc22
                              2010036946

Contents

Introduction

Mila Amurrio and Mari Luz Esteban

Translated by Robert Forstag

The reflections in this book represent different lines of research by feminist academics who teach and research at the Universidad del País Vasco/ Euskal Herriko Unibertsitatea (University of the Basque Country, UPV/ EHU). They mirror the transformations the university has undergone as a consequence of the political transition in the Spanish state following the death of Franco in 1975.

One major objective of the transition was to successfully construct the Spanish nation-state by means of implementing democracy (Moya Valgañón 1984, 215). It was thus necessary to eliminate the previously existent breach in civil society between the victors and the vanquished and to accept and integrate both class inequalities as well as national and regional differences, at once legalizing their organizational forms and their ideological expressions. An amnesty was thus negotiated for opponents of the former regime, political parties were legalized, and a Constitution was promulgated in 1978 that defined the country as a decentralized state comprising seventeen autonomous communities. Within this legislative framework, the unity of the Spanish nation was constitutionally indisputable.

Although the constitution was the product of a consensus on the part of most political groups in the state, when it was submitted to a referendum, moderate and radical Basque nationalism either voted against it or abstained from voting altogether. Nationalist sectors also abstained during the 1979 referendum on Basque autonomy (the Gernika statute). This referendum established that the Comunidad Autónoma del País Vasco/ Euskal Autonomia Erkidegoa (Autonomous Community of the Basque Country, CAPV/EAE) comprising Araba (Álava), Bizkaia (Vizcaya), and Gipuzkoa (Guipúzcoa). In the early 1980s, Navarre also became an autonomous community (not via referendum but instead through a process of *foral* upgrading).[1] The claims of Basque nationalism to all seven territories historically considered to constitute the Basque homeland remained frustrated. These territories—Araba, Bizkaia, Gipuzkoa and Navarre in the Spanish state and Lapurdi (Labourd), Nafarroa Beherea (Basse Navarre), and Zuberoa (Soule), which together with Béarn comprise the Atlantic Pyrenees *département* of the French state, are collectively labeled Euskal Herria in Euskara (the Basque language).

This political process thus encompassed a social reality that included many different territorial and administrative entities, and that represented a range of political and ideological positions. This diversity is also reflected in the chapters that follow, all of whose authors are on the faculty of the UPV/EHU. Thus, some of the chapters transcend an exclusively Basque frame of reference and refer in general terms to the Spanish society as a whole. Others limit their analyses to the CAPV/EAE, or address particular locales within this community. Yet the contributions to this volume share a feminist perspective and one of the purposes of this book is to provide a historical context for this perspective.

The evolution of the feminist movement, in both the Basque Country and in the Spanish state as a whole, can be divided into different phases (Elizondo Lopetegi 1999, 77–81; Zabala González 2008, 21–38): an initial phase of expansion (1975–79); a second phase of fragmentation within the movement (1979–82); a third phase involving the institutionalization of the movement's demands (1982–85); and a final phase of administrative management, which began in 1986 and which continued throughout the 1990s.

The movement began to take shape and acquire organizational form in 1975, when the first Women's Liberation celebrations were held in Madrid. This initial episode saw the coalescence of two distinct viewpoints, with one (more radical) side preferring to maintain its independence from political parties and the other favoring activism in both feminist groups and leftist political parties. There were, however, a series of common demands, such as divorce, the decriminalization of female adultery, the legalization of contraception and abortion, and equal employment opportunity.

---

1. *Foral* derives from the *fueros*, the laws and charters forming a system of common law that had granted the Basque provinces a degree of political autonomy in premodern Spain.

This unity was fractured during the Second Women's Liberation Forum, held in Granada in 1979, which marked the beginning of the second phase of the movement and saw the formation of two different ideological standpoints that were also apparent in international feminism: the more radical "feminism of difference" and the "feminism of equality" that was more consistent with the previously mentioned dual approach.

The defining feature of the third phase was feminist access to official institutions with the general election victory of the Partido Socialista Obrero Español (the Spanish Socialist Workers' Party, PSOE) in 1982. The institutionalization of the feminist movement took two different forms. Initially, Women's Institutes were established, the first of these in Madrid in 1983, with the rest of the autonomous communities following suit; the first Basque Women's Institute—Emakunde—was founded in 1988. Then feminist ideas began to circulate in universities through the creation of different departments and institutes, and the consolidation of women's studies, gender studies, or feminist studies.[2]

Within the Basque context, the First Basque Feminist Forum (1977) emphasized the oppression of women, while the second in 1984 focused on adapting feminist organization and activities to the new circumstances. In 1986, a schism arose within the Women's Assemblies, mainly as a result of both differences between Marxist feminism and "autonomous" or "independent" feminism, and over Basque nationalist positions.

The final stage of the movement, beginning in the late 1980s and continuing through the 1990s, saw a consolidation of institutional and academic feminism. Within this context, the Third Basque Feminist Forum (1994) provided an opportunity to evaluate the movement's successes and to reflect upon its present situation. There have recently been important organizational changes within the movement, with the popular role of many of the early groups having significantly diminished, and some groups having disappeared altogether. At the same time, extensive women's networks have emerged, facilitating joint initiatives and action plans to increase the movement's influence at different institutional levels. These achievements were recognized at the Fourth Basque Feminist Forum (2008).

This book is indicative of not just the diversity of feminist academic production, but of the multifaceted nature of the challenges faced by

---

2. See Ballarín (1995); Ortiz Gómez, Birriel Salcedo and Marín Parra (1998, 1999); and Torres Ramírez (2005).

feminists. There is the challenge of reflecting upon the changes that have occurred in recent decades as regards the presence of women in the job market, in politics, and in public life. These are spheres where feminist activity—in institutional, academic, and professional form—has flourished to a considerable extent, but where inequalities, though often highly sophisticated and therefore difficult to identify, nonetheless remain evident. For this reason debate, reconsideration of issues, and new theories are more necessary than ever.

Yet there is a challenge in another sense as well, because the material gathered here represents a vital contribution to general research in the fields of anthropology, sociology, history, law, economics, political science, and communications sciences. It is a contribution that demonstrates not only the contemporary relevance, but the indispensability of a feminist critique in acquiring a clearer and wider perspective that makes possible a broad understanding of historical changes and a thoroughgoing analysis of social phenomena.

Works Cited

Ballarín Domingo, Pilar, ed. 1995. *Los Estudios de las Mujeres en las Universidades españolas 1975–1991: Libro Blanco*. Madrid: Instituto de la Mujer / Ministerio de Asuntos Sociales.

Elizondo Lopetegi, Arantxa. 1999. *La presencia de las mujeres en los partidos políticos de la Comunidad Autónoma del Pais Vasco*. Vitoria-Gasteiz: Gobierno Vasco/Eusko Jaurlaritza.

Moya Valgañon, Carlos. 1984. *Señas de leviatán: estado y sociedad industrial. España 1936–1980*. Madrid: Alianza.

Ortiz Gómez, Teresa, Johanna Birriel Salcedo, and Vicenta Marín Parra. 1998. *Universidad y feminismo en España (I). Bibliografía de Estudios de las Mujeres (1992–1996)*. Colección Feminae 3. Granada: Servicio de Publicaciones de la Universidad de Granada.

———. 1999. *Universidad y feminismo en España (II). Situación de los Estudios de las Mujeres en los años 90*. Colección Feminae 4. Granada: Servicio de Publicaciones de la Universidad de Granada.

Torres Ramírez, Isabel de, ed. 2005. *Miradas. Desde la perspectiva de género*. Madrid: Narcea.

Zabala González, Begoña. 2008. *Movimiento de mujeres. Mujeres en movimiento*. Tafalla: Txalaparta.

1

The Social Standing of Men and Women in the Basque Country

AINHOA NOVO and ARANTXA ELIZONDO

Translated by Silvia Montero Sanz

The law that created Emakunde, the Basque Women's Institute, was passed in 1988. Amongst this autonomous organization's tasks was the elaboration of an annual report evaluating the situation of men and women in the Comunidad Autónoma del País Vasco/Euskal Autonomia Erkidegoa (CAPV/EAE, Autonomous Community of the Basque Country), to be submitted to the Basque Government and Parliament. Therefore, a periodical review of the inclusion of men and women in different public and private spheres has been available since 1989 in order to measure existent similarities and differences. The main purpose of this is to aid the Basque public authorities in drawing up policies on gender equality.

Since the beginning of the millennium, this analysis has been drafted by the gender studies team in the Department of Political Science at the Universidad del País Vasco/Euskal Herriko Unibertsitatea (UPV/EHU, University of the Basque Country), to which both the current authors belong. This chapter presents a brief synthesis of the most decisive factors used in describing the existing gender gap in the CAPV/EAE, as well as an examination of the methodology used for the general analysis that usually makes up the *Report on the Social Standing of Men and Women in the Basque Country.*

The main sources used for this evaluation are secondary. We consult both public and private studies, reports and research projects, and break them down by the gender variable. The key is to include this variable, when it is both reliable and accessible, in the compilation of information. Despite the approval by the Basque Parliament of the law on gender equality in 2005 that obligated the Basque public authorities to elaborate statistics broken down by gender, still today reports are published by the department without including a gender perspective. This deficiency does not just make it more difficult to compile the annual Emakunde diagnosis to be presented to the parliament; it also hinders the elaboration of reports on the gender impact that specific acts and draft laws must annex since the approval of the aforementioned law on gender equality.

An additional problem is data reliability. Some surveys include the gender variable, but only allow for the cross-analysis of two variables. This data is of considerable significance in fields in which a woman's age may be a determinant of a very different position, in other words, in those social situations with a clear gender-generation gap that would allow for predicting future social transformations. In other circumstances, one's educational level, number of dependent children, or nationality may better explain reality. This type of data is especially significant as regards employment, for example. The existing gender gap in the employment rate may be explained by a cross-analysis using other socioeconomic variables. However, the sample serving as the main source of information—the personal survey on employment carried out quarterly by Eustat (the Basque Statistics Institute)—on the social standing of men and women in relation to productive work does not allow for this type of analysis.

On other occasions, sex-disaggregated data is available but the purpose of the study is not relevant to the purposes of our evaluation. For example, information is collected from time to time on people's sexual habits for its use in preventing the HIV virus. This provides a wealth of information on people's sexual habits, but only those between the ages of twenty and forty-nine. These types of obstacles result in a partial vision of reality.

Last of all, access may be another problem in the drafting of a report based on the use of secondary sources. Despite the major advance represented by the Internet in the transmission and publication of information, not all relevant data from a gender perspective is accessible. Eustat offers a service, available upon demand, for cross-variable analysis that provides access to a wealth of variables, but it is only applicable to those surveys carried out by this institute itself. Information gathered through other Basque Government department surveys cannot be requested via Eustat, making access to such data more difficult and, in some cases, even unfeasible.

For the purpose of providing better access to statistical data broken down by sex, in 2007 Eustat requested that our gender studies team elaborate a plan to improve the dissemination of this information. This resulted in Eustat creating a gender equality section on its website where a selection of the most relevant indicators extracted from its studies on the social standing of men and women in the CAPV/EAE are now compiled.

However, the use of secondary sources is not entirely problematic. One of its main advantages, for example, is the considerable variety of indicators. Therefore, the annual report always includes specific fields, such as population, education, work, health, social inclusion and violence. Other fields that may also be included, depending on the availability of indicators when the report is drawn up, are culture and sports, housing, town planning, transportation, elections, and so on.

The Social Standing of Men and Women by Social Variables

Life expectancy is one of the main demographic indicators that determines the existence of a gender gap. According to the most recently available data, for 2005–6, the life expectancy of women in the CAPV/EAE was 84.3 years and that of men was 77.2 years. There was a difference, then, between the genders of 7.1 years. The effects of life expectancy can be seen in the distribution of the population by age. The population of the CAPV/EAE was 2,147,112, according to data for 2008, with women representing 51.1 percent and men 48.9 percent of this total, respectively. By age groups, the tendency of the last decade was repeated, in that the proportion of women was less than that of men up to forty-five years of age, whereas after the age of seventy women represented over 55 percent of the total population.

In the CAPV/EAE, the constant aging of the population is a growing concern. Specifically, women have progressively delayed having children until they are older. In 2008, women had their first child on average at 32.2 years of age, currently the highest average in Europe. Furthermore, they have also decided to have fewer children than previous generations. Therefore, the total fertility rate—the average number of children per women of fertile age—was 1.5 that same year. Immigration can help boost this rate, but in the CAPV/EAE immigrants accounted for less than 6 percent of the population. Of these, there were equal numbers of women and men as a whole, although there were important differences according to place of origin. Specifically, close to half of the foreign population came from Latin America, and women represented 59.7 percent of this group. The second largest number of immigrants came from elsewhere in Europe, with men representing 57.8 percent of this group. Likewise, most of those who came from Africa were also men (68.1 percent).

Health is also an important social variable, yet its analysis in the CAPV/EAE broken down by gender has been insufficient. The main sources of information on the health of men and women in the CAPV/EAE are health surveys developed by the Spanish National Statistics Institute and the Basque Government's department of health. In general, residents of the CAPV/EAE held a positive perception of their own health. There were no relevant differences between genders in this regard, although men provided slightly higher indicators in more positive responses. Regardless of this slight difference, the general trend during the last few years has been an increasingly positive perception of health among both genders.

The main differences between men and women regarding health matters were the use of health-related services and habits. In this regard, Basque women had a higher frequency of medical appointments than men. Indeed, the proportion of women who had medical appointments more than three times per year was greater than men across nearly all age groups, although the distance between the two decreased considerably among those over the age of sixty-five.

However, according to hospital inpatient survey statistics, Basque men tended to have longer periods of hospitalization as a result of similar diagnoses of disease, with the exception of osteomuscular and locomotor illnesses. The use of health-related services and expenditures is increasingly linked to inadequate health habits. In general, men smoke and drink alcohol more frequently than women; however, an analysis by age groups determined that the difference was greater among the elderly while being practically nonexistent among young people of both sexes.

Abortion was one of the most problematic female health-related issues to control statistically. The number of registered abortions in the CAPV/EAE rose between 1995 and 2007. This incremental evolution was similar in both the CAPV/EAE and the rest of the Spanish state.

Education is one of the most relevant points of analysis in assessing the social standing of men and women in the CAPV/EAE. The chosen level of training, specialty, or field is a determining factor of a person's professional future, economic prospects, and even part of one's social image. The standing of students of both genders in the CAPV/EAE differed in two areas: academic performance and the choice of specialty upon completion of compulsory secondary education at the age of sixteen.

Women achieved a better academic performance both consistently and more generally across all measurement variables: general aptitude, graduating class, repeating student rates, pre-university grade point average, university transcript records, and vocational training. From the 1996–97 academic year on, the percentage of passing students was higher for females than for males at all educational levels.

The second key educational difference is the significant gender gap concerning the choice of studies upon completion of compulsory secondary education, the point at which students opt for differentiated curricula. Here, gender roles play a determining role, specifically as regards the fields of study chosen. For example, almost six out of ten vocational training students were male. According to most recent data, only four out of twenty fields offered as part of vocational training complied with the principle of equality (40/60). In the CAPV/EAE, excessively female-dominated fields in the area of vocational training (with a presence of males under 10 percent) included communications, video and sound production, graphic arts, hotel management, tourism, and the food industry. Meanwhile, males were more likely to choose fields like construction, carpentry and furniture making, mechanical production, electricity and electronics, vehicle maintenance, marine fishing, and maintenance and productive services. This gender gap was a concern for those who sought professionals, resulting in specific studies on the matter as well as publicity campaigns aimed at attracting young women to vocational training.

As to the options for those young people wishing to continue their studies after the age of sixteen as a means of preparing for university entrance, differences by gender were, similarly, particularly notable. The general trend in recent years has been for women to represent between 75 and 80 percent of the total number of students registered in the arts stream, and only between 30 and 35 percent in scientific-technical studies. Likewise, seven out of ten registered students in health sciences, the humanities and social sciences were female. This is the prior stage that explains some of the differences between men and women at the university level.

These qualifications already provide a clue as to the gender gap by major at university. While women represented almost 70 percent of students at the associate degree level, and more than 70 percent at the bachelor's degree level, they represented only around 3 percent in engineering studies in both the upper and lower divisions. The traditionally female role of care-giver was reflected in women's choice of studies with human nutrition and dietary science, nursing, social work, social education, and food science and technology all figuring in the list of major options with more than eighty percent women students.

Teachers make up another significant social group heavily represented by women, especially at the primary and secondary levels. Indeed, men represented less than 20 percent of teachers at these levels. The reverse was true, however, at the vocational training level, where men dominated both student and teacher numbers. In fact, vocational training represented the only preuniversity level where male teachers exceeded their female counterparts.[3]

Contrary to the pre-university level tendencies, at the university level males outnumbered females among professors by a 60-40 proportion. Gender, however, was not the most indicative differential amongst university professors in the CAPV/EAE because there are similar tendencies in both Spanish and European universities as a whole, where female representation decreases as academic position ranking increases. Therefore, only two out of every ten tenured professors were female. At the UPV/EHU, approximately one in five female university professors were tenured, while for their males colleagues that figure was one in two.

Work is another specific field permanently included in the *Statistical Report on the Social Standing of Men and Women in the Basque Country.* It is differentiated between productive and reproductive work: reproductive or domestic work combines tasks required for reproducing the daily routine of the nuclear family as well as for satisfying the physical and psychological needs of its members. Despite recent attempts to establish a market value for this type of work, the means for measuring it are still inadequate and it is updated every five years, as is the case with the household production satellite accounts calculated by Eustat.[4] Other indirect means are likewise available, such as surveys on quality of life or the social

---

3. This information and more can be found at http://www.eustat.es/idioma_i/indice.html.

4. Household production satellite accounts are a calculation of the cost of household production. This calculation was promoted by Eurostat (the statistical office of the European Union) for the purpose of developing a standard method for measuring the impact of this type of work. In the CAPV/EAE it is calculated every five years and its 2008 update was not available at the time of writing this chapter.

use of time, offered by both Eustat and the Spanish National Statistics Institute.

According to the most recent data available (2003) from satellite accounts of household production, women in the CAPV/EAE were responsible for over 70 percent of household production, both in terms of childcare and adult care, and as regards providing food and clothing/laundry services. Women's responsibility for reproductive tasks could not be explained exclusively by men's greater dedication to productive work within the labor market because differences in the time alloted to these tasks occurred both on working days and on Sundays. With the exception of management tasks and repairs, women far exceeded men in carrying out the rest of tasks associated with household production, with the greatest difference evident in tasks such as preparing meals, cleaning the home and doing laundry, without the day of the week implying any notable difference. The general discourse on the evolution of responsibilities concerning domestic work is that men increasingly participate in these tasks, but that their incorporation into the area of household production is quite slow.

In recent years, the presence of women in the area of productive work has grown. From initial data available for the CAPV/EAE in 1985 through to the most recent data from 2008, womens' participation rate in the labor force increased from 32 percent to 46.3 percent. However, this positive evolution falls short when compared to other European countries. A comparative analysis of the labor force participation rate from the gender perspective with other European Union (EU) countries in 2007 did not rank the CAPV/EAE in a high position.[5] In fact, only three other countries showed a greater gender gap in the participation rate: Greece, Italy, and Malta.

The gender gap in labor force participation rate between men and women in the CAPV/EAE exceeded 15 percent. This participation rate in the labor force was reproduced across age groups although the older age group, the greater the difference. If one were to interpret this in generational terms alone, then one might assume that in the future there would be a gradual tendency toward closing the gender gap as regards the labor force participation rate. However, if this tendency is not confirmed, and over the next decade these same differences continue to be reproduced,

---

5. At the time of writing, the most recent data published by Eurostat on the participation rate dated from 2007.

then we would be facing a phenomenon explainable by the life cycle. In any event, the ranking of the CAPV/EAE in this area when compared with the EU was negative: according to data available from 2008, only Malta had a lower female labor force particpation rate.

The most notable differences in the participation rate of women and men were not in relation to their participation in general, but rather to the positions they held within the labor force. There was a more even distribution of employed men in the CAPV/EAE across sectors than that of women, especially in industry and the services sector. However, the proportion of women was greatest in the services sector, at almost 90 percent. Another factor that influenced both one's working conditions and economic independence was whether one worked full time or part time. Employment stability has increased in recent years: between 1998 and 2008 it increased by 10 percentage points for men and 16 percent for women, yet the gender gap between people holding a permanent or open-ended employment contract was 9 percentage points in favor of men.

Some solutions posed for the reconciliation of work and family life have been to reward both a reduction in working time as well as part time employment. These have been options mostly adopted by women, limiting their economic independence and, in some cases, affecting their professional careers. In the CAPV/EAE, the proportion of women among those people employed part time exceeded 80 percent according to the data from 2008, higher than the Spanish state average.

Salary is one of the aspects that has progressed the most when analyzing the labor market conditions. Between 2004 and 2007, the Spanish National Statistics Institute elaborated an annual survey on salary structure that reflected important differences between the sexes. Meanwhile, the survey on living conditions included a variable that also allowed for measuring differences in salary, but without doubt, the most important source of information came from data collected through the personal income tax declarations for 2001 and 2003, published by Eustat. Salary inequality between women and men was not restricted to Spain or the CAPV/EAE. Though the differences vary, average gross salary for men was higher than for women in practically all EU countries. Here, a man's salary may be 47.3 percent higher than a woman's, as in Cyprus, or 38.8 percent higher, as in the United Kingdom. The smallest differences were found in Belgium, Sweden, Hungary, Luxembourg, and Finland. Data on the CAPV/EAE for 2005 taken from the Spanish National Statistics Institute survey on salary structure revealed a difference of 6,233 euros annually, which represented 34.7 percent of the gross annual salary for women.

Differences in salary can be obtained from data used for measuring personal income taken from personal income tax declarations. By observing the personal income derived from the work of employed women according to professional status, one can determine whether differences existed in this regard. The greatest differences were in management positions, workers in the primary sector, and unskilled positions. While personal income for women in management positions was around thirteen thousand euros, for men it was nearly thirty thousand.

Although income derived from work was not the only determining factor of one's personal purchasing power, the position one held at work was linked to personal financial independence. Differences between women and men in the CAPV/EAE based on productive work were also reflected in their distinct socioeconomic status. The proportion of women was significantly higher than that of men at the lowest levels (people without an income or those whose annual income was under 1,500 euros). The inflection point in the proportion of people belonging to each income range occurred at the level of annual incomes between nine and twelve thousand euros. From this amount upward, the proportion of men was greater than that of women.

The gender gap as regards a personal annual income of less than 1,500 euros revealed the growing phenomenon of the feminization of poverty. The Basque Government's Department of Justice, Employment, and Social Security periodically elaborates a series of statistics to measure the poverty level and vulnerability of individuals and families in the CAPV/EAE. In 2008, the twenty-fifth study on poverty in the CAPV/EAE was carried out and because of this, a specific report was published that considered the evolution of its main indicators during this time.

In its analysis of poverty, the study primarily used two related concepts: maintenance poverty and accumulation poverty. Maintenance poverty referred to a situation of insufficient economic resources for covering, in the short term, basic necessities such as food, housing, clothing, and so forth. To the extent that available income is not the only household financial resource and does not include other types of resources like assets or credit, maintenance poverty problems refer more to potential situations of precariousness than to real situations of poverty. By contrast, accumulation poverty was defined as the inability to gain access to the durable goods necessary for sustaining a minimally adequate standard of living in the long term, thus implying a differential degree of precariousness regarding the availability of these types of goods.

Between 1986 and 2004, maintenance poverty indicators revealed a higher incidence of this kind of situation in households headed by women than those headed by men, without any significant variation over time. However, the data from 2008 were more positive, not just because maintenance poverty indicators had decreased in general, but also because this decrease was greater in households headed by women, thus diminishing the gender gap. The reduction of poverty levels was also evident as regarded accumulation poverty. Here, accumulation poverty rate of households headed by women decreased from 10.7 in 1986 to 1.4 in 2008. However, this was still 0.9 points higher than those households headed by men. The survey compiled data based on two other indicators: the risk of poverty and limitations to establishing an independent household. The risk of poverty as a result of personal income was clearly higher among women. In 2008, the risk of poverty rates were 47.1 percent for women and 10.7 percent for men. Therefore, of the total people at risk of poverty by personal income levels, 82.9 percent were women.

Lack of economic resources results in the impossibility of fulfilling one's life objectives. In this regard, the incidence of insufficient economic resources was measured amongst the dependent population that was theoretically able to establish an independent household within one year. Between 1996 and 2008, the percentage of dependent population in the CAPV/EAE due to the lack of economic resources increased considerably. The rate of women in this group grew from 7.2 percent to 41 percent, while for men it increased from 9.3 percent to 29.5 percent. The current financial crisis, dating from late 2008, will lead to important changes in the results of latest surveys on poverty, scheduled for 2010.

Decision-making centers of power are far removed from situations of poverty and social exclusion. The Basque Law 4/2005 of February 18 on the equality of women and men implied an important change in the participation of women in the Basque Parliament. However, women's influence in executive authority, both at the autonomous as well as foral (provincial) levels, was still questionable, as was the case of their leadership roles in political parties. After the approval of the Law on Equality the gender gap in the presence of women and men in the Basque Parliament diminished considerably, and for the first time, during the 2005–9 legislature, the parliamentary presence of women exceeded that of men.

Likewise, Law 3/2007 of March 22 on the effective equality of women and men, passed by the Spanish Parliament, increased the female presence in both the General Councils of the Historic Territories (the *juntas generales*, akin to provincial parliaments in Araba, Bizkaia, and Gipuzkoa) and local city halls. In 1979 women constituted 10 percent of the members of the general councils of Araba, while in Bizkaia and Gipuzkoa this figure did not even reach 5 percent. However, after the 2007 elections women accounted for half the total representation in these same councils in Araba and Gipuzkoa, although not in Bizkaia.

The inclusion of women in executive authority has been even more difficult to implement. Since 2005 the Basque Government has fulfilled the principle of parity, but the *foral* provincial councils (*diputaciones*) still fail to do so, if we consider the provincial leader (*diputado general*) a member of the executive body. The female presence in other high level political appointments, for example in subdirectorates or directorates, was even lower. As regards decision-making levels in the private sector, such as at the management level of large Basque companies that trade securities in the IBEX 35 Spanish stock exchange, the presence of women was merely anecdotal. Despite the important progress made in this area, there is still much work to be done in making for a more equal society, especially within political parties and private companies.

Conclusion

According to the indicators compiled by the annual *Statistical Report on the Social Standing of Men and Women in the Basque Country*, differences continued to exist in the social standing of women and men and their presence in many spheres of both public and private lives was still unequal. Although progress has been made since the turn of the millennium, certain specializations in professional training, university degrees, and different sectors of the economy continue to be dominated by one gender or the other. Likewise, there is still a gender gap as regards working conditions, financial independence and the distribution of time dedicated to reproductive (domestic) work.

The data provided by indicators of the type included in the aforementioned report should be used to guide the development of policies by the public administrations, given that the planning of public programs without taking into account the difference of status based on gender may result in an increase of this inequality. As established by the law on equality, the Basque public authorities should develop even further the systems of sex-disaggregated indicators in order to understand tendencies among the Basque population revealing its social reality, and thereby avoid increasing these gender differences.

References

Departamento de Empleo y Asuntos Sociales, Gobierno Vasco. 2009. *Encuesta de pobreza y desigualdades sociales 2008.* At www.eustat.es/ elem/ele0005200/inf0005277_e.pdf.

Departamento de Justicia, Empleo y Seguridad Social, Gobierno Vasco. 2008. *25 años de estudios de la pobreza en Euskadi.* At www.euskadi. net/r33-2732/es/contenidos/evento/estudio_1_pob/es_pobreza/ adjuntos/EPDS%28Cast%29.pdf. English-language version, *25 Years of Research on Poverty in the Basque Country,* at www.euskadi.net/ r33-2732/es/contenidos/evento/estudio_1_pob/es_pobreza/adjun-tos/EPDS%28EN%29.pdf.

Departamento de Sanidad, Gobierno Vasco. 2006. *Informe sobre la situación de la sanidad pública vasca.* www.osasun.ejgv.euskadi.net/ r52-20726/es/contenidos/nota_prensa/discursosanidad38/es_ds38/ adjuntos/SITUACIONSANIDADPUBLICAPRENSA.pdf.

———. *Encuesta de salud del País Vasco.* 2007. At www.osasun.ejgv.euskadi. net/r52-20726/es/contenidos/nota_prensa/prensasanidad135/es_ np135/prensasanidad135.html.

———. *Programa Salud y Mujeres.* 2009. At www.osasun.ejgv.euskadi.net/ r52-20726/es/contenidos/nota_prensa/prensasanidad160/es_ps160/ adjuntos/osasunaemakumeak.pdf.

Elizondo, Arantxa. 1999. *La presencia de las mujeres en los partidos políticos de la Comunidad Autónoma de Euskadi.* Vitoria-Gasteiz: Gobierno Vasco.

Elizondo, Arantxa, Eva Martínez, and Ainhoa Novo. 2005a *Estudio-Diagnóstico para el conocimiento de la feminización de la pobreza en Vitoria-Gasteiz.* Vitoria-Gasteiz: Ayuntamiento de Vitoria-Gasteiz.

———. *Cifras sobre la situación de las Mujeres y los Hombres mayores en Euskadi.* 2005b. Vitoria-Gasteiz: Emakunde.

———. *Cifras sobre la situación de las Mujeres y los Hombres mayores en Euskadi.* 2005c. Vitoria-Gasteiz: Emakunde.

———. "La integración de la perspectiva de género en la Administración

Pública: Un caso de estudio en el ámbito municipal." 2005d. In *Igualdad de Oportunidades e Igualdad de Género: una relación a debate*, edited by Mª Angeles Barrère y Arantza Campos. Madrid: Dykinson.

———. 2007. "La participación política de las mujeres en la Comunidad del País Vasco." In *Actas del VI Congreso Vasco de Sociología*. Bilbao: Asociación Vasca de Sociología.

———. *Mujeres en la toma de decisión en Euskadi*. 2010. Vitoria-Gasteiz: Emakunde.

Elizondo, Arantxa, Eva Martínez, Ainhoa Novo, and Itziar Casillas. 2005. *Participación social y política de las mujeres y los hombres en Euskadi*. Vitoria-Gasteiz: Emakunde.

Elizondo, Arantxa, Eva Martínez, Ainhoa Novo, and Felix Arrieta. 2005. *Cifras sobre la situación de las Mujeres y los Hombres jóvenes en Euskadi*. Vitoria-Gasteiz: Emakunde.

Elizondo, Arantxa, Eva Martínez, Ainhoa Novo, and Raquel Sanz. 2005. *Cifras sobre la situación de las Mujeres y los Hombres en edad adulta en Euskadi*. Vitoria-Gasteiz: Emakunde.

Elizondo, Arantxa, María Silvestre, and Ainhoa Novo. 2008. "Igualdad entre mujeres y hombres en las universidades españolas: reflexión crítica sobre el Catálogo de indicadores del sistema universitario español del MEC." In *Actas del I Congreso Internacional sobre sesgo de género y desigualdades en la evaluación de la Calidad académica*. Barcelona: Universitat Autónoma de Barcelona, Servei de Publicacions.

Martínez, Eva, and Arantxa Elizondo. 2005. "Luces y sombras del papel político de las mujeres en la Comunidad Autónoma del País Vasco." In the *VII Congreso Español de Ciencia Política y de la Administración*, "Democracia y buen gobierno." Madrid, 21–23 de septiembre.

Novo, Ainhoa, Eva Martínez, and Jaione Almirante. 2008. *Cifras sobre la situación de las Mujeres y los Hombres mayores en Euskadi*. Vitoria-Gasteiz: Emakunde.

2

The Construction of Female Identity through Press Photography: *El País* and *El Mundo*

Flora Marin Murillo and Maria Ganzabal Learreta

Translated by Lauren DeAre

In Spain up until the1960s and 70s, women's presence in the media was practically nonexistent. Their occasional appe,arances were linked to stories that had clearly sexual connotations or in the crime and accident reports as victims. This occurred to such an extent that, "Discrimination against women reached such an extreme that a female press was created that solely featured and was read by women, in order to differentiate it from the press that was typically read by men" (Davara et al. 2009, 131).

Changes in Spanish society since then have given women access to areas that had previously been closed-off to them. These changes stemmed from social developments as well as progress in and increasing sensitivity to equality issues, allowing women to now fulfill traditionally male roles and responsibilities. The most visible elements of government initiatives working toward equality include the redefinition of citizenship, the empowerment of women, mainstreaming the gender perspective, scientific and technological innovations, sensitivity training, and preventative measures to end gender violence. The final objective for all this activity is to close the gap that exists between true equality and legal equality. Within this context, the role of the media cannot be ignored because it constitutes an important tool both for raising awareness in society and for creating and reinforcing certain models.

Studies on the representation of women and the media's treatment of women have gained momentum in Spain since the 1980s. Authors like Concha Fagoaga and Petra María Secanella (1984), Juana Gallego (1990),

Natividad Abril (1994), and Amparo Moreno (1998), among others, have been pioneers in the debate and their contributions are essential for understanding subsequent developments in the field. Along with these authors, others have contributed studies and observations in both the academic and professional realms that have increased the understanding of communicative discourse, including Elvira Altes (2000), Nuria Simelo (2004), and Cristina Fraga (2007). In their analyses, they present the gender dimension as a way "to be aware of what patterns men and women establish amongst themselves and between each other" (Infante 2004, 60–61).

Today, no one questions the importance of the role that the media plays in the construction of female identity. According to María José Sánchez Leyva, "Identity as a means of belonging is constructed and reinforced by various strategies. The same is true for perpetuating stereotypes, sectionalization, language, thematization, bias in public agenda-setting, humor" (2007, 70). Press photography contributes to identity reinforcement because of its documentary aspects, for having its own ontology, and for its ability to be a "footprint of reality" (Dubois 1986), thereby constructing a certain way of seeing.

Consequently, visual resources and codes take over, some specific to photography and others applicable to any type of image like selecting a reality using framing, scale, mise-en-scène or composition. In photography, these codes work together to construct a representation of reality that is no longer portrayed as a faithful reflection, but instead a construction made up of images and symbols that are cultural products. Therefore, when we discuss the construction of the female identity, we understand that "identity is a larger concept that mankind continues to construct, each in their own languages" (Hurtado 2003).

Objectives and Methodology

In this chapter we seek to address several objectives: to specifically identify women's real visual presence by examining press photography from Spain's two most important newspapers; to frame the relevance of women's presence in comparison with the male figure and define the identity of the women represented according to their profession, age, fame or anonymity; to identify gender archetypes (mother, wife, or victim) when applicable; and, through the analysis of visual resources and mise-en-scène, we seek to identify the discursive strategies utilized in the portrayal of images of women.

We chose the two newspapers with the highest daily circulation[1] in Spain, *El País* (401,392 copies) and *El Mundo* (309,995 copies), because we consider them to be the most influential in public opinion and because they are associated with two clearly differentiated business plans and editorial lines. *El País* was first published on May 4, 1976, six months after Franco's death, at a time when Spain was beginning its transition toward democracy. Its founder was José Ortega Spottorno, son of the great philosopher José Ortega y Gassett. It is part of Spain's largest media conglomerate, Grupo PRISA, and defines itself as "a comprehensive, independent, high-quality newspaper and a defender of a pluralistic democracy."[2] It is a center-left newspaper that is most closely aligned with the Partido Socialista Obrero Español (PSOE, Spanish Socialist Workers' Party).

El Mundo first came into print on October 23, 1989, as an initiative of a group of journalists led by Pedro J. Ramírez, who is also its current editor. The newspaper belongs to the Unidad Editorial publishing group, formed by a merger between Unedisa and Recoletos and it constitutes the other leading media conglomerate in Spain. Although defined as liberal, its editorial line is very critical of the PSOE and its positions are closely aligned with the conservative Partido Popular (PP, People's Party).

The material used for this chapter was chosen using a variation of two constructed weeks. According to studies done by Daniel Riffe, Charles F. Aust, and Stephen R. Lacy (1993), Guido H. Stempel (1952) and Iñaki Zabaleta (1997), among others, two constructed weeks form an adequate representation for analyzing the content of a year. However, we decided to increase the amount used for the purposes of our study, given the fact that there are not many photographs depicting females in the Spanish press. Therefore, we have generated a complete month, twenty-eight copies, by selecting four weeks between September, 2009, and January, 2010. Week one includes copies from August 31 to September 6. Week two includes copies from October 5 to October 11, 2009. Week three includes copies from November 16 to 22 and week four includes samples from December 28, 2009, to January 3, 2010. Week four was different because Friday, January 1, was a holiday so its issue was replaced by the issue from Friday, January 8. The total number of photographs analyzed was 821; 420 from *El País* and 401 from *El Mundo*.

---

1. Data from June 2008 to July 2009. See the Spanish Audit Bureau of Circulations (Oficina de Justificación de la Difusión) (OJD), at http://www.ojd.es/.
2. http://escuela.elpais.com/historia-de-el-pais.html.

We employed descriptive and inferential analysis. The descriptive analysis included the identification and classification of the empirical reality subject to our study (press photography). For this analysis, we designed various indexes for data collection including: the number of photos per section, the number of columns allotted to each photo, style of shot, identity of the women represented, and their ages and attitudes in front of the camera.

We were able to draw more detailed conclusions through an inferential analysis of this collected data and by considering in particular "that inferences can be made about the origin, nature, function and the effects of communicative products" (Gaitán Moya and Piñuel Raigada 1998, 284). We also took into account the typology of different photography genres created by Mariano Cebrián Herreros (1992). Regarding visual codes, we considered the following: D.A. Dondis' contributions (1976), Lorenzo Vilches' application of photographic image interpretation, and the methodologies proposed by Javier Marzal (2007).

The Significance of the Image: Quantitative Aspects

John Berger (1974) emphasizes the importance of the gaze when constructing identity. He attributes the power of acting and gazing to men and the ability to appear or to be seen to women. A woman in this situation becomes both viewer and that which is being viewed, the object and subject of her own gaze. Women have been classified as objects to be looked at due to conventions and traditions that have existed for centuries. If, in fact, today these customs are changing, the importance of image in the construction of a subject remains unchanged.

In our analysis, we have taken a close look at these photographs that force us to reflect on our own image. They make women look back at themselves and also be judged by men; the same men who have, for the most part, reproduced the photos. This study not only reveals the percentages of women's appearances in these newspapers, but also how the women were identified and in what subject matter and roles they appeared.

Press photography acts as a reflection or an illustration of content and at the same time it identifies the news' key players and constructs their social representation. To develop a more equal and balanced view, news media professionals must reflect seriously on how a woman is looked at and how that gaze makes her appear. Women's true visibility is difficult to show and is frequently excluded from the public sphere due to its restriction to what we consider soft or hard news and because of the male view of reality.

Our study is primarily separate from the topic of women's under-representation in the media, which is hard to dispute. However, we should clarify some points regarding women's photographic presence in newspapers. We have impartially determined that women, regardless of which print media was chosen or its political slant, barely appeared in these publications: *El País*, 14 percent, *El Mundo*, 11 percent. On the front pages there was an obvious shortage of female subjects. Only three photographs from *El País* were significant enough to be of any value and in *El Mundo* there were only six. On the back pages, the female presence was even more unequal. At *El País*, female writers and reporters contribute to the back page and therefore have attained a certain level of equality with men. However, at *El Mundo*, the ratios are considerably lower and barely reach significant percentages.

Our data revealed a tendency to link women to news sections that deal with society and culture or so-called soft news. In the "Society" and "Culture" sections of *El País*, they attained 29.5 percent, and in *El Mundo*'s "Culture" and "Communication" sections, 36.29 percent. The topics included in these sections—health, education, the environment, and personal and family relationships—are assigned or dismissed to the "Society" section or are politicized and presented as a parliamentary discussion. All of these issues, that are both closely associated with women and that feature women to a greater extent, are attributed less importance because they constitute the ethic of care. Female stereotypes also appeared, including the portrayal of women as sex symbols or as ornamental objects. These images appeared in the society or gossip pages and, in *El Mundo*, they even made it to the front page as a visual ploy or advertisement to attract the reader.

Women are excluded from "hard" news sections and those that deal with subjects considered more important, and therefore any thinking or opinion-making is left to the men. At *El País*, 77.2 percent of the staff are men, and we find similar percentages at *El Mundo*. Most days, *El Mundo*'s "Opinion" section had no female contributors and all editorials were written by men. Our data showed that women are still excluded from certain sections like "Science," "Opinion," "Economy," and "Sports." Women dominated the sections considered to be more frivolous, ordinary, or soft, including the areas of fashion, television, entertainment, and general society.

The lack of images of women was most striking in the Sports section. This complete invisibility of female athletes has been internalized in our society to the point that it is accepted as completely natural that women who practice and compete in sports are not a topic of public interest nor are they newsworthy. When women did appear in this section, it was almost never in connection with female athletic activity. Instead, we found female South African fans dancing in the Soccer City stadium before a game (*El País*, November 20, 2009) or a one-column photograph illustrating the IOC (International Olympic Committee) candidacy of Marisol Casado, president of the International Triathlon Union (*El País*, October 8, 2009). Only one photograph showed the success of a female athlete, Russian pole-vaulter, Yelena Isinbayeva, the winner of a Prince of Asturias Award (*El País* and *El Mundo*, September 3, 2009). At the other end of the spectrum was Natalia Rodríguez, who appeared after her disqualification at the World Athletics Championships in Berlin (*El País*, December 29, 2009).

As we can see, in terms of the news media, women and sports appear in opposition to each other and there are many studies that support this idea. Authors including Ilse Hartmann-Tews and Gertrud Pfister (2003) and Alina Bernstein (2002), among others, have focused on gender and socialization-based exclusion of women and have analyzed the written and audio-visual media coverage of female athletes. In one of the most recent studies carried out in Spain, Marta Angulo completed an exhaustive study of the presence of female athletes in the media. Angulo observed a blatant imbalance and concluded that "all plans of action to improve or increase the presence of female athletes in the media must begin with society's awareness of the issue, and also the awareness of the professionals that manage and work in various media industries" (2007, 7).

Representation of Women: Roles and Stereotypes

Our study showed different results regarding the public representation of women in their roles as politicians, intellectuals or as anonymous figures. We found that female politicians had a considerable presence in the sections devoted to current national and international events: In *El Mundo*, 51 percent, and in *El País*, 24.6 percent. A woman in power tended to be shown in a group or together with a male counterpart, who usually overshadowed her.

Although Spanish female politicians have achieved statistical equality (there are nine female ministers and eight male ministers in the current [2010] Spanish government), they have not obtained equal treatment by photographers. The Global Medial Monitoring Project (GMMP), points out that 49 percent of the world's politicians are female but in the media, only 13 percent of politicians represented are women (Gallagher 2005, 17). Angela Merkel was the most photographed woman in international politics, although others also appeared from time to time, such as Catherine Ashton, high representative for foreign affairs and security policy of the European Union, and other "exotic" women such as Beatriz Paredes, president of the Mexican Revolutionary Party.

Intellectuals constituted a minority in both newspapers and professionals in the fields of law, journalism, education or health were featured more often. In *El País*, however, we found two images of female soldiers. Anonymous women made up 34.4 percent of those appearing in *El País* and 15 percent of those in *El Mundo*. These anonymous women were usually identified as victims, underprivileged, members of a group or association or simply as extras. Meanwhile, immigrant women were almost always and exclusively limited to the roles of victims or the underprivileged. Erika Masanet and Carolina Ripio explain that these cases "only portray the reality of a specific group of women, since they basically only show the most impoverished type of migration" (2008, 183).

Although not high in numbers, the stereotypes portrayed of mothers or wives are significant when compared with the appearance of equivalent male stereotypes, which were practically non-existent. The mother archetype appeared several times, always as a protective and self-sacrificing figure. Fathers did not appear, but mothers fighting to raise their children did: "They took away my daughter and they haven't let me see her in six years" (*El País*, October 11, 2009).

In the national context, wives' roles were featured in stories that dealt with embezzlement attributed to the spouses of politicians or public figures. Wives appeared in international politics as spouses of leaders or rulers, considered relevant because of their charisma, beauty or elegance. Carla Bruni and Michelle Obama are examples of this type of woman. According to Nuria García and Luisa Martínez, "The habit of presenting a woman as a man's companion, as a decorative and/ or sexual object, or as a person that solely enjoys being looked at, is interpreted by the audience as a stereotype that perpetuates gender-based discrimination" (2009, 213).

For that reason, the imagery employed by the media is crucial because it continues to demand greater beauty and youth from women; demands that are not made on men. In fact, middle-aged women comprised the majority of the women photographed and between 26 and 39 percent of the women were young.

We took middle-aged to be from 30 to 60–65 years old and women older than that were considered senior citizens or elderly. Older women were barely represented. There were no portrayals of active women of this age, and those that did appear were generally depicted in groups of retirees or specifically in a grandmother role. However, it is considered normal that men older than sixty-five, for example the president of the European Central Bank, Jean-Claude Trichet (sixty-eight years old in 2010) or the president of the Telefónica company, Cesar Alierta (sixty-five years old in 2010) can appear with relative regularity in the same print media. Young people between eighteen and thirty years old were represented as artists or models and as students, to a lesser extent. Girls were also rarely included and only appeared as victims of some type of violence (*El País*, September 6, 2009).

Although in general, the usage and percentages of female stereotypes employed by both newspapers were similar, *El País* more regularly featured women as fighters or protesters. When these women were part of a group, they appeared in a context of advocacy and protest. This image of an anonymous, organized woman, ready to fight for a number of different causes, caught our attention. A few examples included: female supporters of the Iranian regime (*El País*, August 31, 2009), a rally in support of abortion rights (*El País*, October 8, 2009), and a protest in front of the Iranian embassy in Paris (*El País*, December 29, 2009). *El Mundo* had more of a tendency to trivialize the female image. Its front and back page photographs portrayed women as decorative objects or sex symbols more appropriate for gossip magazines than for news media.

Visual Resources in Identity Construction

Both newspapers primarily used middle shots or group shots, which are the most appropriate compositions for depicting the groups of women and mixed-gender groups that appeared frequently. In both newspapers, half of the women photographed wore a passive expression and were simply posing for the photograph. This is common in institutional photography of press conferences or meetings. In the other half of the photos, the women's postures were much more active: female politicians giving a press conference, professors in a classroom or singers on-stage.

Analyzing it from a gender perspective, we found examples in both newspapers of images of women's gestures, poses or clothing that would never be seen in images of men. These images can be interpreted as examples of Gregory Bateson's "double bind" theory (1976), characterized by the conflict between different contextual orders, and resulting in a paradoxical configuration of communicative sequences. This communication dilemma creates contradictory messages, which cause confusion and do not contribute to women's public image.

Figure 2.1. *El País*, August 31, 2009

Certain photographs stand out, such as those published on September 1, 2009, illustrating the problem of prostitution in Barcelona's La Boquería neighborhood or on August 31, where a cycling tour passes through Spain while a woman in a traditional Spanish dress looks on. The woman here represents an exotic and passive element contrasted with an active, athletic man (See figure 2.1). Another image that attracted our attention shows a young woman pointing to a sign that features soccer forward Thierry Henry, published on November 27, 2009. The photo caption tells us that the woman posing is a journalist, and it has to be spelled out because it would otherwise be impossible to know that she is doing anything related to journalism. Oddly enough, on that day, the same photo was also on the front page of *El Mundo* (See figure 2.2).

Figure 2.2.
El País, November 11, 2009

On September 4, *El Mundo* published a photograph of the Spanish minister of defense, Carmen Chacón, visiting a nursery school. It would be impossible to imagine a man in her position displaying the same motherly manner toward a small girl (See figure 2.3).

Figure 2.3. *El Mundo*, September 4, 2009

Equally as surprising is the inclusion of both a full shot of María Dolores de Cospedal, secretary-general of the PP posing for *Vanity Fair* (see figure 2.4) and an attempt to take photographs at her wedding (*El Mundo*, September 4, 2009). In both of these examples, the woman is represented as an aesthetic object. Her pose and the photo's composition display her body for a masculine gaze.

Figure 2.4.
El Mundo, November 19, 2009

Although we found many examples in both news outlets of clearly stereotypical models and behavior used to identify women beyond the parameters of their professions, we did not find the same treatment of their male counterparts. Frivolousness, flirtatiousness, tenderness and the demonstration of any other emotion was repeatedly associated with images of women, independent of their occupation, thus leaving more serious, introspective and solemn behavior and manners to men.

Conclusion

Women's images in the two newspapers was not representative. There are even days when not one image of a woman appears in *El Mundo*. The representation of women continues to be associated with sections where information is designed for easy consumption and is more playful, light, and informal (in sections like "Society," "Culture," or "Communication").

In terms of public representation, female politicians are the most featured professionals in these newspapers. Even still, real-life equality and equality in representation did not match up. Of the nine female ministers that make up the Spanish government, the newspapers featured only three of them regularly (defense, finance, and health). The others were noticeably invisible.

Spanish newspapers still have certain subjects like science, finance, opinion and sports, that are closed-off to women. The lack of reporting on female athletes was also striking. No coverage existed of any women's team competitions at any level or for any sport, and the small amount of reporting that featured female athletes appeared when their achievements were exceptional.

The women represented in these newspapers were active, young or middle-aged. Representations of senior citizens did not exist. Considering that sixty-five year old women today are often still working professionally, there is no excuse for their absence in the media.

Moreover, certain images published by the newspapers treated women in a discriminatory manner. These photographs featured a catalog of stereotypes that alluded to women's beauty, physical appearance, love lives or maternal instincts.

Both news outlets basically coincided in all parameters analyzed. *El País* was more sensitive to the gender dimension, although it was not consistent. This study again raises the issue of the role the media plays every day in the construction of female identity, whether by omitting the roles women have in public life, silencing women's opinions or representing women so ambiguously that it implicitly undervalues them. The news media contributes to the construction of an image of women in our collective imagination that does not always correspond to reality; a reality that is much more complex.

References

Abril, Natividad. 1994. *Las mujeres en la prensa diaria vasca. Protagonistas, temáticas, tratamiento periodístico: Estudio comparativo de los mensajes publicados en los diarios Deia, Egin, El Correo Español-El Pueblo Vasco y La Gaceta del Norte.* Leioa: UPV/EHU.

Altes, Elvira. 2000. *Imágenes de la mujeres en los Medios de Comunicación: Líneas actuales de Investigación*. Madrid: Instituto de la Mujer.

Angulo, Marta. 2007. "Las imágenes de las deportistas en los medios de comunicación." Madrid: Consejo Superior de Deportes, Ministerio de Educación y Ciencia. At www.csd.gob.es/csd/sociedad/deporte-y-mujer/articulo_imagen_mujer_deportista_en_medios.pdf.

Bateson, Gregory. 1976. "Double Bind" (1969). In *Double Bind: The Foundation of the Communicational Approach to the Family*, edited by Carlos E. Sluzki and Donald C. Ransom. New York: Grunne & Stratton.

Berger, John. 1974. *Ways of Seeing*. London: Penguin.

Bernstein, Alina. 2002. "Is it Time for a Victory Lap? Changes in the Media Coverage of Women in Sport." *International Review for the Sociology of Sport* 37, nos. 3–4: 415–28.

Cebrián Herreros, Mariano. 1992. *Géneros informativos audiovisuales. Radio, televisión, periodismo gráfico, cine, video*. Madrid: Editorial Ciencia 3.

Davara, Francisco Javier, Humberto Martínez-Fresneda, Elena Pedreira, and Gabriel Sánchez. 2009. "Presencia e imagen de la mujer en las primeras páginas de los periódicos españoles." *Comunicación y Hombre* 5: 129–44.

Dondis, D. A. 1976. *La sintaxis de la imagen. Introducción al alfabeto visual*. Barcelona: Gustavo Gili.

Dubois, Philippe. 1986. *El acto fotográfico. De la representación a la percepción*. Translated by Graziella Baravalle. Barcelona: Paidós Comunicación.

Fagoaga, Concha, and Petra María Secanella. 1984. *Umbral de presencia de las mujeres en la prensa*. Madrid: Instituto de Investigaciones Científicas.

Fraga, Cristina. 2007. "Las mujeres y los medios de comunicación." *Comunicación e Cidadanía* 1: 45–52.

Gaitán Moya, Juan Antonio, and José Luis Piñuel Raigada. 1998. *Técnicas de Investigación en Comunicación Social. Elaboración y registro de datos*. Madrid: Síntesis.

Gallagher, Margaret. 2005. *Who makes the news?* London: Global Media Monitoring Project. At www.whomakesthenews.org/images/stories/website/gmmp_reports/2005/gmmp-report-en-2005.pdf.

Gallego, Juana. 1990. *Mujeres de papel. De "Hola" a "Vogue": La prensa femenina en la actualidad.* Barcelona: Icaria.

García, Núria, and Luisa Martínez. 2009. "La representación positiva de la imagen de las mujeres en los medios." *Comunicar* 32: 209–14.

Hartmann-Tews, Ilse, and Gertrud Pfister, eds. 2003. *Sport and Women: Social Issues in International Perspective.* London: Routledge.

Hurtado, José Martín. 2003. "La Identidad." In *A Parte Rei. Revista de Filosofía* 28 (July). At serbal.pntic.mec.es/~cmunoz11/hurtado28. pdf (last updated March 15, 2010).

Infante, Vicente. 2004. "La masculinidad desde la perspectiva de género." In *Perspectiva de Género*, edited by Julia del Carmen Chávez Carapia. México, D.F.: Plaza Valdés.

Marzal Felici, Javier. 2007. *Cómo se lee una fotografía: Interpretación de la mirada.* Madrid: Cátedra.

Masanet, Erika, and Carolina Ripoll. 2008. "La representación de la mujer inmigrante en la prensa nacional." *Papers* 89: 169–85.

Moreno, Amparo. 1998. *La mirada informativa.* Barcelona: Bosch.

Riffe, Daniel, Charles F. Aust, and Stephen R. Lacy. 1993. "The Effectiveness of Random, Consecutive Day and Constructed Week Sampling in Newspaper Content Analysis." *Journalism Quarterly* 70, no. 1: 133–39.

Sánchez Leyva, María José. 2007. "Orientaciones: Comunicación, cultura y sentido." In *Crítica feminista y Comunicación*, edited by María José Sánchez Leyva and Alicia Reigada Olaizola. Seville: Comunicación Social.

Simelo, Nuria. 2004. "La representación de las relaciones entre mujeres y hombres y del recambio generacional en la prensa, de 1974 a 2004." In *Comunicación y Guerra en la Historia*, edited by Alberto Pena. Santiago de Compostela: Tórculo Ediciones.

Stempel, Guido H. 1952. "Sample Size for Classifying Subject Matter in Dailies." *Journalism Quarterly* 29, no. 3: 133–39.

Vilches, Lorenzo. 1983. *La lectura de la imagen: Prensa, cine, televisión.* Barcelona: Paidós Comunicación.

Zabaleta Urkiola, Iñaki. 1997. *Komunikazioaren ikerkuntzarako metodologia: Metodo enpirikoak eta interpretatzaileak.* Bilbao: Udako Euskal Unibertsitatea.

3

Higher Learning and Equality Politics at the University of the Basque Country

JASONE ASTOLA AND MERTXE LARRAÑAGA

Translated by Robert Forstag

The changes taking place in recent decades with regard to equality bet-ween men and women have their roots in the knowledge accumulated within academic feminism.[1] Feminist academics have conducted research in a number of different areas from a different perspective to that of tra-ditional academic knowledge, but their contributions have not yet been assimilated into what we think of as "conventional wisdom." Strange as it may seem, this officially sanctioned knowledge, based on the work of men, continues even today to call into question the validity of studies that incor-porate both women and men as subjects within all fields of knowledge. In other words, those who uphold a partial vision object to those who pro-pose a more complete and academic vision.[2] Taking account of this new knowledge, numerous laws on gender equality, both at the autonomous and state level in Spain, have in recent years played a key role in promo-ting the paradigm change. Legislation related to universities has linked women's, feminist, and gender studies,[3] on the one hand, and regulations regarding what specifically is taught, on the other.[4]

---

1. Regarding this field, see Ballarín Domingo, Gallego Méndez, and Martínez Benlloch (1995); Ortiz Gómez (1999); and de Torres Ramírez (n.d.).

2. See the manifesto of the Feminist Constitutional Law network, initially issued in Bihar (Alicante) on the July 8–9, 2004 and available at www.feministasconstitucional.org/node/25.

3. "Gender studies" here refers to the assignment of different social functions based upon sex. See Tubert (2003) and Bengoechea Bartolomé (2003).

4. This inclusion has not had an immediate effect on the drafting of new study plans by Spanish universities for the purpose of adapting their system to the European Higher Education

The Universidad del País Vasco/Euskal Herriko Unibertsitatea (UPV/
EHU, University of the Basque Country) is currently immersed in this
very process, and has made important strides in recent years. Examples of
such progress include the inauguration of the master's degree programs
"Women and Men: Agents of Equality" (which began in 2001) and "Feminist and Gender Studies," which has recently been relaunched (2010). [5]
In addition, the university has created an equal opportunity office, and a
commission for equality, both of which represent positive steps in terms
of the promotion of equal opportunity among men and women at the
UPV/EHU.

Legislation on the University's Role

The introduction of the principle of equality in education, and the promotion of the inclusion in university courses of the scope and significance of
equality between men and women, have been the subject of many different laws in recent years.

The first explicit reference to the role of the university in this regard
was constitutional law (CL) 1/2004 of December 28, regarding comprehensive protective measures against gender violence,[6] specifically article 4.7, which reads as follows: "Universities will include and will foster
education, teaching, and research regarding gender equality and non-
discrimination across all academic settings." This principle was immediately incorporated into Basque (autonomous) law 3/2004 of February
25, regarding the Basque university system[7] as part of its objectives and
informative principles. Yet undoubtedly the law that best enunciates this
principle within the Comunidad Autónoma del País Vasco/Euskal Autonomia Erkidegoa (CAPV/EAE, Autonomous Community of the Basque
Country) is Basque law 4/2005 of February 18, on the equality between

---

Area (EHEA). More information about this process can be found at www.eees.es/ and www.
educacion.es/boloniaeees/inicio.html.

5. More information at www.sc.ehu.es/sswigual/entrada.htm and www.ikerketafeministak.
ehu.es/p109-1000/es.

6. Constitutional laws are applied throughout the whole Spanish state. The text of this law is
accessible at www.boe.es/aeboe/consultas/bases_datos/doc.php?id=BOE-A-2004-21760. Ventura Franch (2008, 162) describes the parliamentary debates the preceded the enactment of
this law.

7. Available at www.boe.es/aeboe/consultas/bases_datos/doc.php?id=BOPV-p-2004-90003.
This law is one of the first that attempts to use non-sexist language in its text, with specific reference to female teachers and female students (e.g., las profesoras, las estudiantes, etc.).

men and women,[8] article 33 of which includes the following general provisions regarding university teaching:

- Equal opportunity (article 33.1);
- A gender perspective in education and research, and the use of nonsexist language (articles 33.2 and 33.3); and
- The encouragement of research on women, on issues related to equality between women and men (article 33.4), and the establishment of grants for such research (article 33.5).

This last law has had a profound influence on the two constitutional laws referred to below, for which compliance is mandatory throughout Spain: CL 3/2007, of March 22, on the effective equality of women and men, and CL 4/2007, of April 12, which modified CL 6/2001 of December 21 regarding universities.

CL 3/2007 of March 22, on the effective equality of women and men,[9] is the first Spanish regulation that recognizes the importance of an issue that should form a part of every constitutional document, in order to put an end to the old order based on discrimination against women—whether explicit or implicit. Article 1.1 reads: "Women and men are equal in human dignity, and are also equal in rights and obligations." As regards higher education, article 25 of CL 3/2007 includes a weak mandate to include in study plans "when appropriate," the teaching of material regarding the equality of men and women (article 25.2 a).[10] This "when appropriate" has facilitated two different responses: to not propose the equality of women and men as a principle that should govern study plans, either in the structuring of specific courses or in the restructuring of all academic programs; and allowing the possibility for each university to understand that application of this principle is "not appropriate" in nearly all of the degree programs that it offers.

As for the more specific CL 4/2007, of April 12, which modified CL 6/2001 of December 21 regarding universities,[11] in its preamble it expressly refers to the subject that concerns us here: the university as a transmitter

8. A landmark law in equal rights legislation because of its wide-ranging and detailed content. See www.boe.es/aeboe/consultas/bases_datos/doc.php?id=BOPV-p-2005-90002.

9. Available at www.boe.es/aeboe/consultas/bases_datos/doc.php?id=BOE-A-2007-6115.

10. Recall that Article 4.7 of CL 1/2004 of December 28, re comprehensive measures against gender violence, contained the unambiguous wording "will include."

11. Available at http://www.boe.es/aeboe/consultas/bases_datos/doc.php?id=BOE-A 2007-7786.

of values assumes the equality of men and women.[12] For this reason, universities are obliged to establish systems that permit the achievement of parity within their representative bodies, "removing obstacles that prevent women from having a presence in the governing bodies of universities, and at the highest level of teaching and research activity within the civil service, in accordance with the percentage [of women] holding university degrees." This same law also calls for a higher degree of participation of women in research groups. In addition, it vaguely refers to the creation of specific programs regarding equality, an idea that is not further specified in the law.

If we examine the regulations of the different collective bodies that comprise the university, we see that students have the right to equal opportunities and non-discrimination with respect to their access to the university, entering its centers, remaining enrolled in the university, and the exercise of their academic rights (article 46.2 b); as well as to receiving non-sexist treatment (article 46.2 j) and also not to be discriminated against on account of religion, disability, or any other personal or social condition or circumstance. As regards university professors, special emphasis is placed on the balanced representation of women and men, which is regulated with respect to representative bodies (article 13 b), for research groups (article 41.4), and for accreditation and contracting commissions (article 57.1). In order to assure compliance with these requirements, an addition to the twelfth provision establishes that "Universities will include within their organizational structures entities that promote equality, for the purpose of facilitating their proper functioning with respect to the principle of equality between women and men."

At the same time that they were required to comply with this legislation, Spanish universities were also faced with the need to draft new study plans in order to meet the demands of the EHEA, the aim of the Bologna process regarding the standardization of higher education within the European Union (EU), which must be implemented beginning in the academic year 2010–11.

In addition, royal decree 1397/2007 of October 29 establishes the organization of official university teaching materials,[13] and represents an

---

12. Article 27 *bis* 1. e) charges the general committee on university policy to "Coordinate the drafting and follow-through of reports on the application of the principle of equality among women and men in the university."

13. At www.boe.es/aeboe/consultas/bases_datos/doc.php?id=BOE-A-2007-18770.

elaboration of CL 6/2001 of December 21 regarding universities that was subsequently modified by CL 4/2007 of April 12. The decree notes in its preamble that "education within any professional activity must contribute to the knowledge and exercise of human rights, democratic principles, principles of equality between men and women, solidarity, environmental protection, universal access and inclusive design, and a fostering of a culture of peace." Yet article 25 of CL 3/2007 of March 22, with respect to the effective equality of women and men, includes the regrettable expression "as appropriate" when calling for teaching to incorporate such principles of equality. Thus, the final results of this law left much to be desired in terms of realizing the principle of integrating the equality of women and men as a value that the university is required to transmit. This situation is aggravated even further by the fact that the relative circumstances of male and female university professors are not the same within the existing university structure.

The Situation at the UPV/EHU

In the following sections, we will briefly review the most recent steps taken at the UPV/EHU regarding equality of opportunity, and provide a summary overview of the situation of women and men at our university.

The Equal Opportunity Office

The equal opportunity office (EOO) was created by a resolution on June 15, 2006 by the governing council of the UPV/EHU. This resolution specified that the functions of the office would be: to diagnose the current situation; to draft a plan that includes concrete and effective measures aimed at promoting the equality of women and men in its internal functioning, as well as in its external activities; to conduct further assessments and follow-up regarding the contents of both the equality plan previously referred to, and of any other activity aimed at promoting equality.

The creation of the EOO was approved prior to the enactment of CL 4/2007 of April 12, which urged Spanish universities to create entities that promote equality. Thus, the UPV/EHU can rightly be considered a trailblazer14 within Spain in terms of having an administrative body

---

14. There were two forerunners of the EOO at the UPV/EHU: The office of gender equality at the Universidad Complutense in Madrid (created in 2004), and the equality monitoring office at the Universidad Autónoma of Barcelona (2005). Most of the remaining governmental authorities were created following the enactment of CL 4/2007.

responsible for implementing measures that promote equality between men and women.

The EOO was the result of many years of work—especially that of a core of women who were fiercely committed to the cause of equal opportunity within different spheres of Basque society. Just prior to its creation, for example, the Ekimen Feminista (feminist and gender studies network) was established in 2006. This was made up of individuals— mostly women—who worked as professors and researchers, and in the administration and service departments of the UPV/EHU. Ekimen Feminista mainly comprised persons who had worked, or who were working, in leading seminars, groups, workshops, or other initiatives, the main purpose of which was to open up a space to transform knowledge of women—and to transform knowledge itself—and to thus contribute to the transformation of the university and of society as a whole. Prominent among these initiatives was the seminar in women's studies, directed by Professor Teresa del Valle for more than a decade (1981–94).15 One of the objectives of this highly productive seminar was to serve as a catalyst for studies and research on the situation and circumstances of women.

Since its creation, the EOO has undergone important changes. It was launched as an office that reported directly to the rector of the UPV/EHU, yet after a change in university government, the EOO was administratively placed under the office of the vice-rector for social responsibility and university outreach. With the passage of time, the structure of the EOO itself has grown stronger. For example, it currently includes an equality technician on its staff.16

In compliance with the aforementioned legal provisions, the EOO has implemented various measures, especially those involving research (compiling databases of research projects conducted from a gender-based perspective, a call for graduate papers and doctoral theses written from a gender-based perspective), work on enhancing visibility (involving a diagnosis of the comparative situation of women and men at the UPV/ EHU), and outreach (for example, a call for financial aid in organizing workshops and conferences aimed at promoting equality at the UPV/ EHU, and organizing March 8 workshops).

---

15. In addition to this seminar, there were others that were more informal in nature (the Feminism and Law Seminar of the Law School).

16. See www.berdintasuna.ehu.es/.

Currently, the EOO is drafting the first plan for equality between men and women. 17 In the initial design of the plan, the EOO collaborated with an equality commission that represents the three strata of the university (professors, student body, and administrative and service staff), as well as all three campuses of the UPV/EHU. This plan addresses questions related to teaching and research, as well as institutional matters that deal with work and social conditions as well as the university's social outreach. One of the biggest problems with these kinds of plans is that at times they focus on devising ideal strategies that encompass every single objective and every single action that would need to be taken in order to achieve effective equality. Thus, at times they become nothing more than a declaration of intentions. For the purpose of avoiding this, a commitment has been made to a feasible plan consisting of action that can be taken within a specified time frame. Of course, since this is the first such plan, the groundwork is important. It is hoped that this initial plan is approved by the end of the 2009–10 academic year, and that the deadline set for carrying out its ideas will coincide with the end of terms of the current UPV/EHU administrative team.

Men and Women at the UPV/EHU

Having statistics that are broken down by sex is something that is fundamentally important, because in the absence of statistics, there are no problems, and there is no need for policies to change if there are no problems that need to be addressed. Clearly, "what we measure affects what we do" (Stiglitz, Sen, and Fitoussi 2009, point 3), and any decision made on the basis of defective measurement may turn out to be defective as well. Thus, having an accurate picture of the current situation at the UPV/EHU through the collection of systematic data is critically important, because these data allow us to understand the process of its evolution. The EOO has drafted a document diagnosing the situation of women and men at the UPV/EHU[18] based on data for the academic year 2006–7, and it is currently working on another report that will expand (and no doubt improve) upon that first effort.

---

17. Although this will be the first plan to address the entire UPV/EHU, the first equal opportunity plan was drafted in 2004 for the UPV/EHU's School of Labor Relations.

18. Available at www.berdintasuna.ehu.es/. See also the report published by Emakunde (the Basque Women's Institute), Pérez Fuentes and Andino (2003).

The university is not detached from the larger society of which it is a part, and therefore it is highly likely that the inequalities that exist in education and in the labor market are also in some measure reflected at the UPV/EHU; both as an institution dedicated to higher education and research, and as a center of employment for university professors, research staff, and administrative and service personnel.

The labor market is one of the areas in which inequality between men and women is most evident. In economics, one of the arguments most often used to justify inequality in the workplace in general, and salary disparities specifically, has been the unequal level of investment in human capital—meaning the lower level of women's education. However, this argument has gradually lost force in inverse proportion to the gradually increasing levels of women's education. In fact, if we take higher education as an indicator of education in general, women constitute the majority of university students throughout the EU,[19] and are also in the majority at the UPV/EHU. Thus, inequalities in investment in human capital as the basis for the theory of human capital[20] have become incoherent, and the current emphasis is instead no longer on the quantity but rather on the quality of human capital. What this means is that when (to take one factor) the level of education of younger women is equal to or even greater than that of men, then there has been a resort to the different factors to explain the academic choices made by young men and women in order to justify later inequalities within the workplace, and especially disparities in salary.

At the UPV/EHU,[21] from the inception of the series in 1998–99, women have constituted the majority, and the proportion of women has exceeded 55 percent since the 2000–1 academic year. The proportion of women at the university is higher than the percentage of women in both the general population (50.2 percent) and the youth population (49 percent), according to data supplied by Eustat, the Basque Statistics Institute.

---

19. According to the latest data (from 2007) supplied by Eurostat (http://epp.eurostat.ec.europa.eu/portal/page/portal/eurostat/home/), more women graduate with degrees in higher education than men throughout the EU, with the exception of Germany.

20. A widely accepted theory developed mainly by Becker (1964) that has been the basis of many pro-equality measures.

21. All data regarding the UPV/EHU in this section are based on "University Statistics: 2008/2009," available on the website of the UPV/EHU (www.ehu.es), or on information provided by different university services. The figures have been constructed on the basis of information from the same sources.

There remains an inequality that may be rooted in different models of socialization. Yet there have been increasing numbers of women in departments that have been traditionally considered male. The presence of women surpasses 80 percent in health sciences, and they are a clear majority in experimental sciences; social sciences, law and the humanities, while remaining a minority in technical disciplines. Areas of study that are overwhelmingly dominated by women, such as those in education and health, in addition to being arenas that women have concerned themselves with in the absence of remuneration, are today sectors in which there is a high degree of public employment. Meanwhile, technical disciplines tend to supply graduates who are later employed mainly in the private sector, employees whose earnings are generally considerably higher than average.

Studies in which the participation of women exceeds 80 percent are education, nursing, educational theory, translation and interpretation, social work, food science and technology, medicine, nursing, educational psychology, and history. Academic disciplines in which the presence of women is less than 30 percent are generally in fields dealing with technical engineering, marine sciences, as well as physical education and sports sciences.

When it comes to graduate programs, during the academic year 2008–9, women represented 58.8 percent of the student body that had graduated with master's degrees.[22] As regards specific areas of knowledge, the percentage of women ranges from a high of 77.3 percent in health sciences to a low of 42.9 percent in technical disciplines. Thus, the proportion of women is somewhat higher in master's programs than in undergraduate studies, although the disparities in representation among the different fields are somewhat less extreme.

As regards faculty and research staff, where the percentage of women is 42.2 percent, female progress has been unquestionable.[23] Of course, this percentage is almost cut in half when it comes to the highest professional category, because women constitute only 21.7 percent of full tenured university professors at the UPV/EHU.[24] Approaching the data differently,

---

22. Of the dissertations defended during 2005–6, 43 percent were written by women. Women constituted 27 percent of dissertation supervisors and 24 percent of the membership of dissertation review committees.

23. If we do not include the research staff, the percentage of women is 39.6.

24. The number of *sexenios* (six-year periods of assessment of outside research activity per capita of university professors) is similar (3.1 *sexenios* per person).

we see that 14.2 percent of faculty are full professors and that, in the case of women, only 6 percent are full professors. In addition, if we compare the number of full professors with the number of professors in general, we find that, for males, there is 1 full tenured professor for every 1.9 professors in general. Meanwhile, for women, there is one full university professor for every 4.7 professors in general. Thus, it can be said that the so-called "glass ceiling" is in place as regards university employment, and that this phenomenon makes it difficult for women to have access to highest-level positions.[25]

While the presence of women at the highest academic level is clearly unsatisfactory, it should be remembered that in Spain Ángeles Galino Carrillo was the first female tenured university professor, and that she was appointed to a chair in the history of education and the history of educational institutions at the University of Madrid in 1953 on the basis of her performance in an open competitive examination. In addition, according to the ETAN report (European Commission 2000), Spanish universities are in fourth place among EU nations, with women making up 13.2 percent of their full tenured university professors, behind Finland (18.4 percent), Portugal (17 percent), and France (13.8 percent). In the case of associate and assistant professors, Spanish universities are in second place, with women making up 34.9 percent of these positions (European Commission 2000, 10).[26]

Breaking down the data by different disciplines, there are a number of clear disparities when the proportion of women in the student body is compared with their proportion in the teaching and research faculty, for example in the field of health sciences, which is by far the field most heavily represented by women. As regards the student body, in nursing

---

25. The limited number of female tenured university professors is typically explained by the fact that the mass entry of women into universities occurred much later than that of men, so it is "logical" that there would now be fewer women than men in such positions. This is an argument that continues to be brought up for the purpose of explaining the generally scant presence of women in positions of high responsibility. However, many studies have shown that, when men and women of the same generation who have taken positions with companies at the same time are compared, after a lapse of X years, the number of men who have earned promotions is greater than that of women.

26. Thus, even though the information mentioned above is not up to date, when more recent data are consulted regarding various Spanish universities, one sees that the percentage of women holding degrees and professorships at the UPV/EHU is higher than the mean for Spain as a whole. See Dirección Para la Igualdad, UPV/EHU (2008) and the Unidad de Mujeres y Ciencia (UMYC) (2007).

schools, women form the clear majority (67.8 percent), and in medicine and dentistry, they are the overwhelming majority among students and yet a minority among teaching and research faculty (32.6 percent). This might be a legacy of the past, since nursing was long considered a generally female discipline, while the heavy female presence in medical studies is much more recent. The most balanced among the large departments at the UPV/EHU (defined here as those having more than two hundred professors), is the Faculty of Economic and Entrepreneurial Sciences. There is also a relative balance between students and faculty in engineering, even though the percentage of female students and professors is less than 30 percent.

When it comes to the governmental bodies at the UPV/EHU, the current governing board is balanced because it is composed of eight men and seven women. However, both in terms of the highest position of responsibility at the UPV/EHU as well as in its various departments, men are in the clear majority, comprising 75 percent of deans and directors of advanced technical schools.[27]

However, the presence of women in the highest representative bodies of the university is very recent. The first female dean in Spain was Carmina Virgili Rodón, who was named dean of the Department of Geological Sciences at the University of Madrid in 1977. In addition, since 1982, when Elisa Pérez Vera was named rector of the Universidad Nacional de Educación a Distancia, there have been very few women at the helm of a university.[28]

Finally, very few women have been awarded honorary doctoral degrees: Of sixty such degrees awarded by the UPV/EHU since 1970, only two were conferred on women, meaning that women have earned just 3.3 percent of honorary doctoral degrees:[29] the first to Micaela Portilla, a historian and anthropologist from Araba, in 1993, and the second (and thus far the last) to Carmen Codoñer, a philologist from Salamanca, in 2003. Judging by such data, and by data regarding other forms of recognition,

---

27. In the case of university departments, the male majority is significantly less because, in some 40 percent of cases, women hold leadership positions.

28. Flecha García (1996) analyzes this pattern beginning in the year 1872, the year that the first woman student was officially admitted to the Universidad de Barcelona, and ending in 1910, when the royal orders regulating the equitable admission of men and women to university were published.

29. The extremely low percentage of women who have been awarded honorary degrees is not peculiar to the UPV/EHU, but is a general tendency among all Spanish universities.

it appears that there continues to be resistance within the university to recognizing the work of women in different areas.

Gender and Feminist Studies at the UPV/EHU

The struggle for equality within the university has been evident since at least the 1970s. However, the 1980s saw the real beginning of a concerted effort on the part of academic feminists to advocate that scientific data regarding the inequality between men and women be incorporated into the university system (Campos 2007), and this process of institutionaliza-tion has accelerated in recent years.

As regards undergraduate studies, we are currently witnessing a time of important transition, since the new study plans that have been adapted to the EHEA will begin in the 2010–11 academic year. As noted, this new era might well have served as a propitious time to consolidate gender studies. Unfortunately, we fear that this field will enjoy a limited pres-ence, and that it will likely be restricted to those departments traditionally devoted to these studies, or that have professors on their faculties who specialize in feminist and gender studies. It will thus be important to see what place gender studies has on the new map of degrees at the UPV/ EHU, and this will undoubtedly be a focus of the first equality plan for women and men.

Focusing on graduate studies, recent decades have witnessed very valuable contributions from feminist studies, gender studies, and/or women's studies, an academic field of knowledge that has been consol-idated at an international level, and that encompasses practically every discipline, although its presence is especially important in social sciences and the law.

The UPV/EHU is no exception.[30] Since 2001, it has offered a graduate degree program—the master's program in "Women and Men: Agents of Equality."[31] The purpose of this is to educate qualified specialists capable of advocating for equality between women and men. Due to this program's

---

30. The information in this section has been collected from the following websites: berdinta-suna.asmoz.org/ and www.ikerketafeministak.ehu.es/.

31. There was a short-lived precursor to this: a Master's program in Co-education in 1993. From its very inception, the "Women and Men: Agents of Equality" program has enjoyed the collaboration of Emakunde. Moreover, during the academic year 2009–10, it became an online program managed by the UPV/EHU in collaboration with Eusko Ikaskutza, the Society of Basque Studies. The faculty of this program is composed of seventy-three university employees, and of professionals from various areas.

multi-disciplinary and comprehensive focus, its graduates have enjoyed considerable success in advocating equality within a wide range of arenas, including education, culture, employment, sociopolitical participation, and sports.

More recently, the official university Master's program in Feminist and Gender Studies, taught by forty male and female professors representing eleven university departments and five centers of UPV/EHU. These men and women are specialists in a wide range of disciplines within the field of social sciences and the law (anthropology, political science, communication and journalism, law, economics, history and sociology). It was taught for the second time during the academic year 2009–10, and it has been quite successful, judging by the high student demand.[32]

It is an unprecedented program in that, for the first time, it provides formally endorsed academic instruction that is interdisciplinary, broad-based, and specifically research-oriented. The fact that the UPV/EHU has a large number of specialists with long and extensive university teaching experience (undergraduate, graduate, and specialized studies) has been a very positive influence in its successful launching and subsequent development. These specialists have wide experience in writing and supervising doctoral dissertations; conducting research; editing and publishing both individual and collaborative works; organizing conferences and workshops; teaching courses and seminars, and organizing a variety of other activities related to promoting equality between men and women.

Conclusion

Recent years have witnessed undeniable changes in society with respect to equality between men and women. Women have made progress in every area, including that of the university, and these changes are evident in the recent legislation promoting equality noted above.

In the university sphere, a certain institutionalization of knowledge has occurred within the field of feminist and gender studies, especially at the graduate level. Similarly, structures within the university itself that promote equal opportunity have become progressively more entrenched, one example being the EOO at the UPV/EHU. These steps have been

---

32. In addition to the two master's programs, gender-specific subjects are also taught in other master's programs such as International Development and Cooperation, Globalization and Development, Community Participation and Development; Psychoeducation, Psychology of Education and Specific Learning Strategies, and Contemporary History.

taken thanks to the work—that in many cases has received little academic recognition—of men and especially of women, without whose efforts they would never have been possible.

Despite these achievements, effective equality remains a chimera in nearly every sphere of society—including the university. We need to continue to think of ways to increase the number of women professors, and to call for qualified women be considered for leadership positions within academia as well. We need to deepen our understanding of the reality of universities, to design new measures, and to make specific diagnoses regarding issues like violence; balancing personal, work, and family life; and other vital issues.

Finally, we are living through an important transition as regards teaching at the university level, with launching of the EHEA. Beginning in the academic year 2010–11, the offerings of undergraduate courses should be closely examined to determine which degree programs have finally deemed it "appropriate" to include teaching material related to equality between women and men.

References

Ballarín Domingo, Pilar, Mª Teresa Gallego Méndez, and Isabel Martínez Benlloch. 1995. *Los estudios de las mujeres en las universidades españolas 1975–91. Libro Blanco*. Madrid: Ministerio de Asuntos Sociales; Instituto de la Mujer.

Becker, Gary S. 1964. *Human Capital: A Theoretical and Empirical Analysis, with Special Reference to Education*. New York: National Bureau of Economic Research; distributed by Columbia University Press.

Bengoechea Bartolomé, Mercedes. 2003. "El concepto de género en la sociolingüística, o cómo el paradigma de la dominación femenina ha malinterpretado la diferencia." In *Del sexo al "género": Los equívocos de un concepto*, edited by Silvia Tubert. Madrid: Cátedra.

Campos, Arantza. 2007. "Estratexias para a integración dos estudos feministas no ámbito univeritario." In *O reto da igualdade: Feminismo, xénero, universidade*, edited by María Jesús Fariña Busto, Purificación Mayobre Rodríguez, and Beatriz Suárez Briones. Translation by Marta Gil González. Vigo: Universidade de Vigo.

De Torres Ramírez, Isabel. "Los recursos informativo-documentales para los Estudios de las Mujeres. Panorámica breve desde Europa." At www.nodo50.org/mujeresred/isabel_de_torres.html.

Dirección Para la Igualdad, UPV/EHU. 2008. "Mujeres y hombres en la UPV/EHU." At www.berdintasuna.ehu.es/p234-content/es/contenidos/informacion/ikasketak/es_ikasketa/txozten_upv.html and www.berdintasuna.ehu.es/p234-content/es/contenidos/informacion/ikasketak/es_ikasketa/adjuntos/diagnostico.doc.

European Commission. 2000. *Science Policies in the European Union: Promoting Excellence through Mainstreaming Gender Equality*. Report from the ETAN Expert Working Group on Women and Science. Brussels: European Commission.

Flecha García, Consuelo. 1996. *Las primeras universitarias en España: 1872–1910*. Madrid: Narcea.

Ortiz Gómez, Teresa. 1999. *Universidad y Feminismo II. Situación de los estudios de las mujeres en los años 90*. Granada: Universidad de Granada.

Pérez Fuentes, Pilar, and Susana Andino. 2003. *Las desigualdades de género en el sistema público universitario vasco*. Vitoria-Gasteiz: Emakunde/Instituto Vasco de la Mujer.

Stiglitz, Joseph, Amartya Sen, and Jean Paul Fitoussi. 2009. *Report of the Commission on the Measurement of Economic Performance and Social Progress*. Executive summary at www.stat.si/doc/drzstat/Stiglitz%20report.pdf.

Tubert, Silvia. 2003. "La crisis del concepto género." In *Del sexo al "género": Los equívocos de un concepto*, edited by Silvia Tubert. Madrid: Cátedra.

Unidad de Mujeres y Ciencia (UMYC). 2007. *Universidad pública en cifras*. At www.igualdad.us.es/pdf/Universida%20p%C3%BAblica%20en%20cifras%202007.pdf and www.berdintasuna.ehu.es/.

Ventura Franch, Asunción. 2008. "Normativa sobre estudios de género y universidad." *Feminismos* 12 (Diciembre): 155–84.

4

Demythicizing, Unveiling, Challenging: A Review of Twenty-five Years of Feminist Academic Production (1985–2010)

JONE M. HERNÁNDEZ AND ELIXABETE IMAZ

Translated by Robert Forstag

This book is being published in 2010, twenty-five years after the publication of *Mujer Vasca. Imagen y Realidad* (Basque Women: Image and Reality) a collection of essays edited by Teresa del Valle. This chapter is a tribute to that work, which constituted a landmark in Basque feminist and gender studies (Fernández Rasines and Hernández García 1998, 47–60), a remarkably vital movement that subsequently developed along three separate fronts: as a social movement; in academia; and in institutional activity. As regards the current state of Basque academic feminism,[1] we propose the use of three concepts: demythification, unveiling and challenging.

Feminism in the Immediate Aftermath of Franco's Dictatorship

The Basque feminist movement began to take on an organized structure in 1976 (Zabala 2008, 26). One year later, the first Women's Forum was orga-

---

1. This chapter will center on academic feminism, although we recognize the contribution to the development of feminist knowledge and teaching of various public bodies (Emakunde-the Basque Women's Institute, the Ombudsman's Office for Sexual Equality, EUDEL-Berdinsarea, the Navarre Institute for Equality, *diputaciones* or provincial governments, and city halls) through their sponsorship of research, publications, and their launching of educational initiatives; the continuing work of multiple and diverse feminist collectives; of associations (especially the work of IPES, the Institute for the Promotion of Social Studies, and the Center of Feminist Documentation and Studies in Bilbao); and even of private companies (consultancies or research institutes).

nized in Leioa (Bizkaia),[2] in the context of a boom in feminist activity in the Spanish state after 1975 (Pérez 1987). In academic circles, meanwhile, a feminist research project received the first Joxe Miguel Barandiaran grant, awarded by Eusko Ikaskutza (the Society of Basque Studies) in 1981. This eventually led to the creation of the Seminario de Estudios de la Mujer / Emakumeari Buruzko Ikerketarako Mintegia (SEM/EBIM), the Women's Studies Seminar.[3] Its founding purpose was to conduct research and provide consultation facilities, organize forums, diffuse feminist analyses beyond university settings, create a widely accessible documentation resource, and publish material.

Demythification: Foundations of Feminist Knowledge

The methodology employed in *Mujer Vasca* represented a break with previous analyses that, in the case of the social sciences, were inspired by authors such as Joxemiel Barandiaran and Julio Caro Baroja. For Barandiaran, considered to be the founder of Basque anthropology, women are found generally confined to two spheres: the rural environment and the mythological world. He stressed the importance of women within the socioeconomic unit of the household (where women were in charge of everything having to do with domestic organization, the care of minors, fostering socialization, and transmitting the language), as well as their importance with regard to religion—especially in reference to rites of passage (birth, death, and so forth).

This led to a hypothesis of women's importance in Basque society on the basis of their (supposed) equality in reference to men. Caro Baroja who, in *Los Pueblos del Norte* (Peoples of the North, 1977), even suggested a possible Basque matrilineal society (del Valle 1985, 28). These hypotheses were strengthened by the analyses of Mari, an important female figure in pre-Christian Basque mythology. This theorizing reached its height in the 1980s when Andrés Ortiz de Osés posited "the existence of a Basque matriarchal society" in conflict with later rationalist and individualist patriarchal influences (Del Valle 1982, 280).

---

2. At the Leioa campus of the Universidad del País Vasco/Euskal Herriko Unibertsitatea (UPV/EHU, University of the Basque Country).

3. The results of this subsidized project, which was conducted in eleven coastal communities, in both rural and urban environments within the Basque Country, were also presented in *Mujer Vasca*.

These initial studies on the role of Basque women held a special place witchcraft. In Barandiaran's work, "the witch is a genie that inhabits the Basque mythological world, in addition to representing an actual person which serves as the vessel within whom the myth is incarnated, who engages in evil actions of various kinds, and who attends ceremonies presided over by the devil" (Del Valle 1985, 28). Caro Baroja expanded on this, analyzing the historical process in which the Inquisition burned witches (Del Valle 1985, 30).

In line with these images of rural women and of the power of female mythological figures, classical Basque nationalism has also consolidated an "idyllic" representation of Basque women. In the words of Del Valle (1985, 229):

> In nationalist writing and theorizing, women are systematically associated with images of mother, Earth, the Virgin, and the Motherland. Thus, we see *ama* (mother), Amabirjiña (the Virgin), Ama Aberria (the Motherland), and Ama Lur (the Earth). Women were thus identified with the figure of the mother, with everything that was pure and elevated— and in this way given a superhuman status. On another level, women were considered to be fundamentally important to perpetuating the race, to transmitting the language, and to maintaining the family.

Indeed, one of the contributors to the anthology *Mujer Vasca*, Begoña Aretxaga (1988) examines funeral rituals for the purpose of analyzing the functions that had been "imposed" upon Basque women on the basis of a particular world view or ideology. She points out that there is the important element of condensing symbols involving the family—especially as regards the function of women as biological mothers and mediators.

Unveiling: Road Maps of Feminist Knowledge

Following the publication of *Mujer Vasca*, feminist academic production focused on a new dual objective: unveiling those elements that perpetuated inequality and reconstructing those cultural mechanisms involved in making the structures responsible for such inequality invisible. This revealing of invisible structures quickly became an indispensable element of feminist literature, and many studies in the 1980s exposed a gender structure, much like the power structure in general. This new turn dates to the publication of *La mujer y la palabra* (Women and Words, 1987), a work that was jointly authored by some of those who had contributed to *Mujer Vasca*. It included reflections on the influence of religion in the lives of women, the process of modernization and the changes it had wrought, as experienced by Basque women; and the relationship between gender and art (Del Valle et al. 1987).

In general, the 1980s constitute a high point of the Basque feminist movement—a time when reflection, the quest to define new values, and feminist criticism all began to yield important results. The Second Leioa Forum was held in 1984,[4] and in the late 1980s lines of research became more sharply defined. The main concern was no longer the deconstruction of myths, but rather the definition of a positive agenda involving the identification of contemporary issues.

We will now briefly discuss some of those areas that originally emerged in the 1990s and that continue to be developed today. The examples here are presented for illustrative purposes,[5] and are intended to draw attention to some of the important contributions of those working in different disciplines and areas of interest.

History has been an important discipline within gender studies in Basque academic institutions. Pilar Pérez-Fuentes (1993, 2003) examines the industrialization of the Basque Country and draws attention to the "genderization" of labor markets at the beginning of the modernization process, as well as the formalization of women's invisibility within these markets. Lola Valverde (1994) explores the evolution of Basque family systems, focusing specifically on childhood and women. Meanwhile, Mercedes Ugalde studies women's activity in the Basque nationalist movement. Her doctoral thesis (Ugalde 1993) considers the discourse and practices of early twentieth-century Basque nationalism through the prism of gender.

Moreover, a new generation of historians includes Nerea Aresti (2007), who explores the ideals of femininity and masculinity in recent times, and debates regarding gender identity. Mercedes Arbaiza (2003) applies a cultural perspective to the field of economic phenomena (such as work and social choice). In addition, Miren Llona's work (2002) incorporates oral sources to address the interconnected themes of gender, class, and nation, offering a comprehensive view of the process of contemporary identity formation. Finally, within the field of ancient history, the work of Ana Iriarte Goñi (2002) constitutes an indispensable reference for the study of classical antiquity from a gender-based perspective.

---

4. The Leioa Forum was subsequently convened in 1994, and again most recently in 2008.

5. We apologize for any unintentional oversights in our subsequent discussion of the disciplines and subject areas.

A second area of feminist academic development concerns a critical evaluation of Basque culture from a feminist perspective in cultural anthropology. Carmen Larrañaga (1994) examines *bertsolaritza* (improvised oral poetry) as a stronghold of masculinity. Meanwhile, Jone M. Hernández (2007) explores the relationship between language and identity from a perspective grounded in feminist theories from linguistic anthropology. Carmen Díez has worked on varied issues in Basque society and culture (such as the labor market, maternity and caregiving, sports, and socialization). Yet a constant in her work are questions related to myths and traditions as fundamentally important elements in the reproduction of gender inequities: for example, her article inspired by a model of adrogyny in which she reinterprets the myth of Mari (1999).

Tradition and ritual are recurrent themes in the work of Maggie Bullen. Since 1997, she has been analyzing the conflict surrounding the *alardes* (annual festivals based around military-style parades). Other researchers have also explored the space and time of holidays and festivals, and the role assigned within them to women (Andreu and Vázquez 1988). Similarly, Kepa Fernández de Larrinoa (1997) examines festivals, dances, and *carnaval*, exploring women's roles in various events and holiday celebrations. Finally, Sandra Ott (1992) reflects on the concept of *indarra* (implying a range of qualities such "force," "power," "strength," "energy" and "authority") in a traditional Basque sheepherding community and her conclusions were later applied in various feminist research studies.

Feminist anthropology has, since the 1990s, incorporated new theories related to the body, such as health, sexuality, and reproduction, as well as subjects dealing with emotions and love. For the purpose of synthesizing some of the principal axes that orient these works, there are two prominent tendencies.

The first of these is a type of research in which the body is observed and analyzed as a locus of social practices, and as a point of departure for the construction of social discourses and images related to the construction of identities and practices. One example of this is the work of Mari Luz Esteban dealing with health (1993, 2004), which is especially important because of the extent to which it has influenced the development and consolidation of a feminist anthropology of health in the Spanish state. Other examples are work on maternity (Imaz 2008) and sports (Díez and Hernández, 2008).

The second tendency concerns the relationship between the body and arts and esthetics—a topic addressed by both Lourdes Méndez (2002) and

Teresa del Valle (1997a). This tendency attempts to link the theory of the body to an argument that makes the body not so much an *object*, but rather a *subject* of research, and which sees it as a "conscious, experiencing, acting, and interpreting entity."[6] This perspective attempts to transcend an analysis that exclusively concerns health, sexuality, and identity, and that instead attempts to address relationships between social structure and practice. It is the kind of approach that requires both epistemological as well as methodological revisions of the social sciences in general and of anthropology specifically.[7] This new tendency has also been influential in the emergence of another line of research—that of the emotions and love (see the work of Esteban).[8]

Finally, two anthropologists—Paloma Fernández-Rasines and Beatriz Moral—conduct fieldwork outside the Basque Country (Ecuador and Micronesia respectively), and have made interesting contributions to the study of blood relations, maternity, the body, and sexuality on the basis of feminist theory and criticism (Fernández-Rasines and Hernández García 1998; Moral 1999).

Sociology has also been a key part of Basque academic feminism from the 1990s on. Begoña Arregi is a pioneer who, since the 1980s, has focused on population sociology (Arregi and Dávila 2005). To her name we might add a new generation of researchers such as Marta Luxán and Unai Martín Roncero (Arregi, Larrañaga, Luxán, and Martín Romero 2008; Luxán 2006). Meanwhile, since the 1990s, Mila Amurrio has researched two specific areas: theorizing on key concepts in feminist thinking such as "gender" (Amurrio 1995) and studying the role of women in Basque nationalism; specifically, women's role in education (Amurrio 2003). Education has also been a central focus of other social scientists such as Idoia Fernández (1994). Within the general field of sociology, the work of Txoli Mateos, Ana Irene del Valle, Ane Larrinaga, and Elisa Usategui deserves mention. These women have collaborated on a more or less regular basis with Mila Amurrio on research and publications, such as their

6. Esteban, chapter 13 in this work, quoting Margot L. Lyon and Jack M. Barbalet.
7. This is the way that concepts such as "corporeal ethnography" and "corporeal itineraries" are referred to, and Esteban (1993, 2004) employs this methodology.
8. The analysis of corporal, emotional, and ritual practices allows a specific examination of changes, continuities, and conflicts in gender relationships among young people (a project being carried out by a team comprising Bullen, Díez, Esteban, Hernández, and Imaz). Another study dealing with changes in gender relationships was conducted by a team led by Teresa del Valle (2002).

recent work on gender stereotypes among Basque adolescent males and females (Amurrio et al., 2008a, 2008b). A Basque working group has also been established that focuses on the sociology of health. This group analyzes various issues concerning women's health such as social inequities in health through the prism of gender and the quality of life of caregivers (Arregi, Larrañaga, Luxán, and Martín Roncero 2008).

Political science began to assume a leading role in feminist research in the 1990s, through the contributions of academics such as Arantxa Elizondo and Eva Martínez (1995). They also collaborate with Ainhoa Novo, as part of the "Gender Studies Team of the Department of Political Science and Administration of UPV/EHU." Moreover, this team produces a series of reports published by Emakunde (the Basque Women's Institute) on the situation of young men and women in the Basque Country (1995; see also, for example: Novo, Martínez and Almirante 2008).

Concern about the presence of women in the public sphere has assumed a number of different forms, such as the use of public and especially urban space (Larizgoitia 1986; Vázquez 1986). The notion of space has also been a constant in del Valle's work and her treatment of urban planning (1997) is an important reference text in the field.

Another area of emerging interest has to do with the sphere of communication. Natividad Abril (1994), who in the 1990s had begun studying the presence of women in the Basque press, was a pioneer in this area. She continues to explore the representation of women in print media. Similarly, María Ganzabal and Flora Marín have focused on an examination of the women's press and the way it serves as a vehicle of particular gender stereotypes (Marín, Armentia, and Ganzabal 2010). Rosa Martín, on the other hand, has concentrated on gender inequities that affect male and female television and radio journalists in the Basque Country, collaborating with Mila Amurrio (Martín and Amurrio 2003, 2006). Notable works within the area of audiovisual studies include those of Casilda de Miguel, who has collaborated with other researchers on various projects that have attempted to analyze the creative work of female movie directors in the Spanish state (1995–2005) and gender identity in film images (De Miguel, Olábarri and Ituarte 2004; De Miguel, Olábarri, Ituarte and Siles 2005).

Economics has in recent decades incorporated a feminist analysis into its theoretical arguments. Initially Felisa Chinchetru (1988) and then later authors such as Arantxa Rodriguez (whose primary research later became urban planning), Mertxe Larrañaga, Yolanda Jubeto, Idoye Zabala, María José Martínez, Elena Martínez, and María Luz de la Cal (all working within the area of applied economics) critically analyze different aspects of the economic dimension of Basque society (Rodríguez and Larrañaga 1999; Larrañaga 2005; Jubeto 2007; I. Zabala 2005).[9] Areas explored include productive and reproductive work, a gender-focused exploration of public budgets, reconciliation strategies, and politics and/or practices having to do with development. As regards development, the demand for inclusion of a gendered perspective in NGOs' and public entities' programs and strategies is worthy of mention. Within the Basque context, the work of Clara Murguialday, who began her research in this area in the late 1980s, is of particular importance (Murguialday and Hernández 1992).

Beginning in the late 1990s, research began on the social exclusion of female collectives, with a prominent example being Amaia Barandica's study on immigrant women in Navarre (1996). Another important study was conducted in the late-1990s by a research team (Equipo Barañi 2001), which included Elixabete Imaz, and that conducted research about criminal recidivism among Roma (Gypsy) women.

Regarding Navarre, we should also mention the work carried out by the Equipo de Investigación de Género del Departamento de Trabajo Social de la Universidad Pública de Navarra /Nafarroako Unibertsitate Publikoa (2001) from 1997–99, led by the sociologist Blanca Fernández Viguera. The aim of this study was to gain a comprehensive understanding of the situation of women in Navarre.[10]

Law is another field that has enhanced academic feminism. Here, authors such as Arantza Campos (whose approach is philosophical) and María Angeles Barrère (who focuses on anti-discrimination law) have contributed much to the understanding and definition of some of the central concepts of feminist theory, such as the notions of discrimination, equal opportunity, affirmative action, and violence against women (Campos and Méndez 1993; Barrère and Campos 2005). Further, Jasone Astola (2005) offers an interesting feminist revision of constitutional law to this line of critical research. Finally, the work of Itziar Alkorta (2006) initially focused on civil rights, but in more recent years has addressed women's reproductive rights.

---

9. In 2005, the Department of Applied Economics at the UPV/EHU held the First Conference on Feminist Economy in Bilbao.

10. This project was taken upon once again two years later with the development of a new analytical approach (Equipo de Investigación de Género del Departamento de Trabajo Social de la Universidad Pública de Navarra 2005), once again led by Blanca Fernández Viguera.

Turning to the humanities, Paloma Rodríguez Escudero (1987) and especially Lourdes Méndez (2002) were among the first to address issues involving the artistic sphere. But it was not until the 1990s that more researchers began to work in this area and expand its horizons. María Teresa Beguiristain (1996) and Xesqui Castañer (1993) are two key figures for understanding the world of art from a gendered point of view. In the case of literature, the work of both Linda White (1996, 2003) and Maria José Olaziregi (1999) represents an important contribution to the analysis of Basque women writers.

Finally, another interesting area of study in recent years has to do with the presence/absence of women in the world of science. Teresa Nuño (2000) insists on the need to recognize the many contributions made by women to scientific progress, and calls for a greater female presence in the sciences. Within this area, male and female researchers such as Victoria Fernández, Edurne Larraza, Txelo Ruíz and Kepa Sarasola examine the relationship between gender and new technologies, focusing especially on stereotypes that tend to steer women away from careers in information technology (Fernández, Larraza, Ruíz and Maritxalar 2008; Larraza et al. 2008).

In closing, we would especially single out work that has involved a broader analysis of feminist theory. It seems particularly appropriate to mention here the contributions of those authors working within disciplines with a stronger feminist tradition, such as anthropology, philosophy, and sociology. We would therefore cite the work of del Valle; Méndez (2008), who in the 1990s began publishing a series of reflections on feminist theory that has continued to the present day; and Amurrio, who has also addressed the concept of gender (1995, 2003). At the end of this admittedly cursory review of feminist academic production during the 1990s, one can appreciate the diversity of feminism—not only as a movement, but also as a space of intellectual reflection.

Challenging: Tomorrow's Genealogies

By way of conclusion, our final point is directly related to the consolidation of feminist theory in the university teaching curriculum. This represents a genuine challenge for many of the feminist theorists affiliated with the UPV/EHU and who in some measure saw their efforts rewarded with the launching in 2001 of the university's first Master's degree program in Male/Female Equality.[11]

---

11. This graduate program was preceded during the years 1992–94 by a Master's program at the UPV/EHU (with classes at the SEM-EBIM) in "Women's and Gender Systems." The program

This Master's program[12] represented the dawning of a new era. Nearly one decade later, the prospects for feminist and gendered education have improved considerably, and there are now two additional graduate programs: Since 2003, the University of Deusto has offered a Master's program in Intervention in Violence Against Women. And in the academic year 2008–9, the UPV/EHU launched a Master's program in Feminist and Gender Studies.

Previously, there had been other significant accomplishments, such as the introduction of an undergraduate degree program in social anthropology that included three required courses involving feminist and gendered subject matter. In addition, the undergraduate program in sociology included an optional course on "Gender Sociology" which will be required beginning in the 2010–11 academic year.[13]

The official presence of feminism and gender studies in universities will offer new perspectives on feminist work, research, and even activism. An important change has taken place between the older and newer generations of feminist academics with respect to interests, perspectives, and theoretical approaches—and also between professors and their students. But changes are also being promoted as regards the kinds of questions to be focused on, and different ways of approaching various issues.

Thus, if we take as an example some areas of research presented by students at the end of various graduate programs, the following are all potential areas of future research: the labor market, caregiving, reconciliation processes, sports/physical activity, the body, health, maternity, new models of the family, sexual diversity and gender identities, emotions and love, violence against women, women's political activity and general social participation, immigration, social exclusion of particular women's groups, the analysis of equal opportunity policies, the development of the feminist movement, feminist theory and its most recent ramifications, and masculinity.

---

only graduated a single class of students, and its directors were Teresa del Valle and Carmen Díez.

12. Beginning in the academic year 2009–10, this program also began to be offered online.

13. The UPV/EHU has been offering an undergraduate program in social and cultural anthropology (2nd cycle) since the 1995–96 academic year. Beginning in 2010–11, this will become a four-year undergraduate degree program through the implementation of the "Bologna Process," an educational reform program to create a standard system for all universities in the European Higher Education Area (EHEA). There are other degree programs that offer courses involving feminist and gender studies classes, such as a Master's program in "Comparative Literature and Literary Studies" that includes a course on "Gender Studies."

As we can see, there are many elements of continuity. But at the same time, there is a sense of renovation and change as a result of a new era of feminism characterized by approaches, methodologies, and practices in line with the current social context. In the face of this, perhaps the most intelligent course of action is to move forward, taking advantage of the momentum gathered during the past twenty-five years of the feminist academic tradition; to learn to build bridges between generations and lifestyles; and to share our knowledge with one another.

References

Abril, Natividad. 1994. *Las mujeres en la prensa diaria vasca: Protagonistas, temáticas, tratamiento periodístico: Estudio comparativo de los mensajes publicados en los diarios Deia, Egin, El Correo Español-El Pueblo Vasco y La Gaceta del Norte*. Leioa: UPV/EHU.

Alkorta, Itziar. 2006. "Los derechos reproductivos de las mujeres vascas en el cambio de siglo: de la anticoncepción a la reproducción asistida." *Vasconia* 35: 345–71.

Amurrio, Mila. 1995. "Jenero Konzeptuaren inguruko hausnarketak." *Uztaro* 13: 89–98.

———. 2003. *Genero, nazio eta nazio hezkuntza: Ikastoletako irakasleria*. Bilbao: UPV/EHU.

Amurrio, Mila, Ane Larrinaga, Elisa Usategui, and Irene del Valle. 2008a. *Violencia de género en las relaciones de pareja de adolescentes y jóvenes de Bilbao. Informe cualitativo*. At www.bilbao.net/castella/ mujer/violencia_genero/informe_violencia_adolescentes_jovenes/ informe_cuanlitativo.pdf.

———. 2008b. *Violencia de género en las relaciones de pareja de adolescentes y jóvenes de Bilbao. Informe cuantitativo*. Bilbao: Área de la Igualdad, Cooperación y Ciudadanía, Ayuntamiento de Bilbao; Universidad del País Vasco-Euskal Herriko Unibertsitatea.

Andreu, Rosa, and Karmele Vázquez. 1988. "Mujeres, fiestas y reivindicaciones." *Kobie. Serie Antropología Cultural* 3: 73–85.

Arbaiza, Mercedes. 2003. "Orígenes culturales de la división sexual del trabajo en España (1800–1935)." In *¿Privilegios o eficiencia? Mujeres y hombres en el mercado de trabajo*, edited by Carmen Sarasúa and Lina Gálvez. Alicante: Universidad de Alicante.

Aresti, Nerea. 2007. "The Gendered Identities of the 'Lieutenant Nun':

Rethinking the Story of a Female Warrior in Early Modern Spain." *Gender & History* 19, no. 3: 401–18.

Aretxaga, Begoña. 1988. *Los Funerales en el nacionalismo radical vasco.* Donostia: Primitiva Casa Baroja.

Arregi, Begoña, and Andrés Dávila. 2005. *Reproduciendo la vida, manteniendo la familia: Reflexiones sobre la fecundidad y el cuidado familiar desde la experiencia en Euskadi.* Bilbao: UPV/EHU.

Arregi, Begoña, Isabel Larrañaga, Marta Luxán, and Unai Martín Roncero. 2008. "La experiencia demográfica: Teoría, estrategia y realidad." In *Textos y pretextos para repensar lo social: Libro homenaje a Jesús Arpal,* coordinated by Ignacio Mendiola. Bilbao: UPV/EHU.

Astola, Jasone. 2005. "Mujeres y hombres en el ordenamiento jurídico del País Vasco." In *Género, constitución y estatutos de autonomía,* coordinated by Teresa Freixes Sanjuán and Julia Sevilla Merino. Madrid: Instituto Nacional de Administración Pública.

Barandica, Amaia. 1996. *Mujeres inmigrantes en Navarra.* Pamplona: SOS Racismo-Ipes elkartea.

Barrère, María Angeles, and Arantza Campos, eds. 2005. *Igualdad de oportunidades e igualdad de género: Una relación a debate.* Madrid: Editorial Dykinson.

Beguiristain, María Teresa. 1996. "Arte y mujer en la cultura medieval y renacentista." *Asparkia* 6: 135–46.

Bullen, Margaret, and José Antonio Egido Sigüenza. 2004. *Tristes espectáculos: Las mujeres y los Alardes de Irún y Hondarribia.* Bilbao: UPV/EHU.

Campos, Arantza, and Lourdes Méndez, eds. 1993. *Teoría feminista: Identidad, género y política. XI. Cursos de Verano de San Sebastián 1992.* Leioa: UPV/EHU.

Caro Baroja, Julio. 1977. *Los pueblos del norte.* San Sebastián: Txertoa.

Castañer, Xesqui. 1993. *La imagen de la mujer en la plástica vasca contemporánea (s. XVII-XX): Aproximación a una metodología del género.* Bilbao: UPV/EHU.

Chinchetru, Felisa. 1988. *Mujer y realidad social.* Bilbao: UPV/EHU.

De Miguel, Casilda, Elena Olábarri, and Leire Ituarte. 2004. *La identidad de género en la imagen fílmica.* Bilbao: UPV/EHU.

De Miguel, Casilda, Elena Olábarri, Leire Ituarte, and Begoña Siles. 2005.

La identidad de género en la imagen televisiva. Madrid: Servicio Editorial Instituto de la Mujer.

Del Valle, Teresa. 1982. "La problemática de los estudios de la mujer: una aproximación al caso vasco." In *Actas de las primeras jornadas de investigación interdisciplinaria. Nuevas perspectivas sobre la mujer.* Volume 2. Madrid: Universidad Autónoma de Madrid/Seminario de Estudios de la Mujer.

——, dir. 1985. *Mujer vasca. Imagen y realidad.* Barcelona: Anthropos.

——, et al. 1987. *La Mujer y la Palabra.* Donostia: Primitiva Casa Baroja.

——. 1997a. "La memoria del cuerpo." *Arenal* 4, no. 1: 59–74.

——. 1997b. *Andamios para una nueva ciudad.* Madrid: Ediciones Cátedra.

——, et al. 2002. *Modelos Emergentes en los sistemas y las relaciones de género.* Madrid: Narcea.

Díez, Carmen. 1999. "Mari, un mito para la resistencia feminista." *Ankulegi* 3: 63–72.

Díez, Carmen, and Jone M. Hernández. 2008. "¿Acaso no hay diosas en el Olimpo? Práctica deportiva y sistema de género: apuntes de una investigación en marcha." In *Actualidad en el deporte: Investigación y aplicación,* coordinated by Luis Cantarero, F. Xavier Medina, and Ricardo Sánchez. Donostia: Ankulegi.

Elizondo, Arantxa, and Eva Martínez. 1995. "Presencia de mujeres y políticas para la igualdad entre los sexos: El caso de las instituciones políticas vascas (1980–1994)." *Revista de Estudios Políticos* 89: 345–68.

Equipo Barañí. 2001. *Mujeres gitanas y sistema penal.* Madrid: Ediciones Metyel.

Equipo de Investigación de Género del Departamento de Trabajo Social de la Universidad Pública de Navarra. 2001. *Situación social de las mujeres en Navarra, 1975–1996:Evolución y tendencias de cambio.* Pamplona: Gobierno de Navarra, Departamento de Bienestar Social, Deporte y Juventud; Instituto Navarro de la Mujer.

——. 2005. *Situación social de las mujeres en Navarra, 2003: Evolución y tendencias de cambio.* Pamplona: Departamento de Bienestar Social, Deporte y Juventud; Instituto Navarro de la Mujer.

Esteban, Mari Luz. 1993. "Actitudes y percepciones de las mujeres respecto a su salud reproductiva y sexual. Necesidades de salud percibidas por las mujeres y respuestas del sistema sanitario." Ph.D. Diss., Universitat de Barcelona.

———. 2004. *Antropología del cuerpo. Género, itinerarios corporales, identidad y cambio.* Barcelona: Ediciones Bellaterra.

Fernández, Idoia. 1994. "Emakumea, hezkuntza eta nazioa Euskal Herrian." *Jakin* 83: 29–48.

Fernández, Victoria, Edurne Larraza, Txelo Ruíz, and Montse Maritxalar. 2008. "Una aproximación a la situación de la mujer en los estudios universitarios de informática." *Arbor: Ciencia, pensamiento y cultura* 733: 877–87.

Fernández-Rasines, Paloma, and Jone M. Hernández García. 1998. "Crítica feminista en Ciencias Sociales. Algunas teorizaciones sobre el género en el contexto de Euskal Herria." *Inguruak* 22: 47–66.

Fernández de Larrinoa, Kepa. 1997. *Mujer, ritual y fiesta: género, antropología y teatro de carnaval en el valle de Soule.* Iruñea: Pamiela.

Hernández García, Jone M. 2007. *Euskara, comunidad, identidad. Elementos de transmisión, elementos de transgresión.* Madrid: Ministerio de Cultura.

Imaz, Elixabete. 2008. "Mujeres gestantes transitando los espacios públicos. Algunas reflexiones acerca de la dimensión externa del cuerpo embarazado." In *La materialidad de la identidad*, edited by Elixabete Imaz. Donostia: Ariadna Editorial.

Iriarte Goñi, Ana. 2002. *De amazonas a ciudadanos: Pretexto ginecocrático y patriarcado en la Grecia antigua.* Madrid: Akal.

Jubeto, Yolanda. 2007. "Aurrekontu publikoek sexurik ote dute? Generoaurrekontuen osagai eta erronka nagusiak." *Uztaro* 61: 25–44.

Larizgoitia, Arantza. 1986. "Utilización del espacio público por la mujer. Caso práctico del Casco Viejo de Bilbao." In *El uso del espacio en la vida cotidiana. Actas de las cuartas jornadas de investigación interdisciplinar. Actas de las IV Jornadas de investigación interdisciplinarias*, edited by Aurora García Ballesteros. Madrid: Seminario de Estudios de la Mujer, Universidad Autónoma.

Larrañaga, Carmen. 1994. "El bertsolarismo: Habitat de masculinidad." *Bitarte* 4: 29–50.

Larrañaga, Mertxe. 2005. "Mujeres y mercado de trabajo en la CAPV." *Lan harremanak* 13: 13–34.

Larraza, Edurne, Montse Maritxalar, Txelo Ruiz, Kepa Sarasola, and Victoria Fernández. "Ingeniería en informática y género: Un estudio cuantitativo." In *Estudios iberoamericanos de género en ciencia, tecnología y salud: GENCIBER*, edited by Consuelo Miqueo, Mª José Barral and Carmen Magallón. Zaragoza: Universidad de Zaragoza, 2008.

Llona, Miren. 2002. *Entre señorita y garçonne: Historia oral de las mujeres bilbaínas de clase media, 1919–1939*. Málaga: Universidad de Málaga.

Luxán, Marta. 2006. "Cambios generacionales en los procesos de formación familiar: La fecundidad en las generaciones de mujeres y hombres a lo largo del siglo XX." *Vasconia* 35: 331–32.

Marín, Flora, José Ignacio Armentia, and Maria Ganzabal. 2010. "La publicidad en las revistas femeninas y masculinas: Reflejo de los estereotipos de género." *Doxa Comunicación* 10: 35–56.

Martín, Rosa, and Mila Amurrio. 2003. "¿Para qué sirven los periodistas? Percepciones de los y las profesionales de radio y televisión en la CAPV." *Zer* 14. At www.ehu.es/zer/zer14/periodistas14.htm.

———. 2006. "Euskal irrati eta telebistetako kazetarien soslai soziologikoa." *Uztaro* 58: 29–52.

Méndez, Lourdes. 2002. "Cuerpo e identidad: Modelos sexuales, modelos estéticos, modelos identitarios." In *Pensando el cuerpo, pensando desde un cuerpo*, coordinated by Carmelo Blanco Mayor, Aurora Miñambres, and Tomás Miranda Alonso. Albacete: Popular Libros.

———. 2008. *Antropología feminista*. Madrid: Síntesis.

Moral, Beatriz. 1999. "Cuerpo de hermana, cuerpo de mujer. Sexualidad, pudor y tabú del incesto en las Islas Carolinas." *Ankulegi* 3: 81–88.

Murguialday, Clara, and Teresita Hernández. 1992. *Mujeres indígenas, ayer y hoy: Aportes para la discusión desde una perspectiva de género*. Madrid: Talasa, D.L.

Novo, Ainhoa, Eva Martínez, and Jaione Almirante. 2008. *Cifras sobre la situación de las Mujeres y los Hombres mayores en Euskadi*. Vitoria-Gasteiz: Emakunde. At www.emakunde.euskadi.net/u72-20010/es/contenidos/informacion/cifras_ant/es_emakunde/adjuntos/cifras_2008_es.pdf.

Nuño, Teresa. 2000. "Género y ciencia." *Revista de psicodidáctica* 9: 183–214.

Olaziregi, Mari Jose. 1999. "Intimismoaz haraindi: Emakumezkoek idatzitako euskal literatura." *Oihenart* 17: 1–77.

Ott, Sandra. 1992. "*Indarra*: Some Reflections on a Basque Concept."

In *Honor and Grace in Anthropology*, edited by J.G. Peristiany and Julian Pitt-Rivers. Cambridge: Cambridge University Press.

Pérez-Fuentes, Pilar. 1993. *Vivir y morir en las minas: Estrategias familiares y relaciones de género en la primera industrialización vizcaína (1877–1913)*. Bilbao: UPV/EHU.

———. 2003. *"Ganadores de pan" y "amas de casa": Otra mirada sobre la industrialización vasca*. Bilbao: UPV/EHU.

Pérez, Carmen. 1987. "Historia y actualidad del movimiento feminista en Euskadi." *Inguruak* 3: 53–59.

Rodríguez Escudero, Paloma. 1987. *Arte y Mujer. V. Cursos de Verano de San Sebastián 1986*. Leioa: UPV/EHU.

Rodríguez, Arantxa, and Mertxe Larrañaga. 1999. "El tiempo de trabajo y su distribución por sexos en la Comunidad Autónoma Vasca." *Lan harremanak: Revista de relaciones laborales* 1: 193–219.

Ugalde, Mercedes. 1993. *Mujeres y Nacionalismo vasco: Génesis y desarrollo de Emakume Abertzale Batza (1906–1936)*. Bilbao: UPV/EHU.

Valverde, Lola. 1994. *Entre el deshonor y la miseria: Infancia abandonada en Guipúzcoa y Navarra, siglos XVIII y XIX* Bilbao: UPV/EHU.

Vázquez, Karmele. 1986. "Concepción de la mujer: Concepción del espacio público." In *El uso del espacio en la vida cotidiana. Actas de las cuartas jornadas de investigación interdisciplinar*, edited by Aurora García Ballesteros. Madrid: Seminario de Estudios de la Mujer, Universidad Autónoma.

White, Linda. 1996. "Emakumeen hitzak euskaraz = Basque Women Writers of the Twentieth Century." Ph.D. Diss., University of Nevada, Reno.

———. 2003. "Language, Love, and Lyricism: Basque Women Writers Urretabizkaia, Mintegi, and Oñederra." In *Amatxi, Amuma, Amona: Writings in Honor of Basque Women*, edited by Linda White and Cameron Watson. Reno: Center for Basque Studies, University of Nevada, Reno.

Zabala, Begoña. 2008. *Movimiento de mujeres. Mujeres en movimiento*. Tafalla: Txalaparta.

Zabala, Idoye. 2005. "Claroscuros de género en la globalización neoliberal." *Lan harremanak: Revista de relaciones laborales*, 12: 139–66.

5

"Be Cautious, Not Chaste!"
Gender Ideals and Sexuality (1920–1936)

Nerea Aresti

Translated by Eric Heuberger

Gender relations are constantly changing and marked by moments of especially critical development. In the past century, the 1970s witnessed the emergence of a defiant brand of activism in the feminist movement; and the no less turbulent 1920s was a period marked by feelings of uncertainty over the future of the "sexual order." In the aftermath of World War I, early-twentieth-century feminism provided an agitated context that also affected those countries that remained neutral throughout the war. The crisis had an immense impact on Spanish society, transforming the ideas and ideals that been the guiderail for the sexual life of women and men. In fact, it meant nothing less than the total collapse of the traditional and seemingly unexpungeable sexual mores of the times.

The framers of progressive liberal ideology played a fundamental role in shaping the sexual principles of the times. Among middle class professionals, there were those who were determined to accelerate the modernization of gender relations and the secularization of the discourse about sexuality. These modern moralists proposed to substitute the dictates of the Catholic Church, which considered chastity to be its most emblematic ideal, in favor of a new ideal based on moderation and rational control over sexual impulses. Slogans such as "Be cautious, not chaste!" reflected the spirit behind those modernizing crusaders. This chapter analyzes the main features of the intense and ambitious sexual reform campaign and what it spelled for the men and, more poignantly, for the women of that age.

I will examine the reshaping of sexual attitudes, from the discursive strategies used to discipline women's (and men's) physical lives to the new technologies employed for controlling pleasure and regulating lifestyles. Both the more orthodox Catholic discourse, as well as that of the new secular moralists who legitimized their discourse through scientific principles, held common views on sexual instincts and impulses as natural forces that required channeling. Nevertheless, both sides adopted very different views about how human beings should go about such strictures. More conservative opinion did not believe in strong willpower as an agent of control over the onslaught of the body. Only the church could act as a restraint and thus safeguard the divine will. However, modern theoreticians specializing in the "sexual question" believed in rational will, assisted by education. Both would see to the civilized taming of instincts and passions.

Catholic Views on Sexuality

In the early twentieth century Catholic discourse on sexuality, marriage and chastity represented two crucial concepts. The required attitude was highly exacting, not only for women but for men as well since they were required to conform to an ideal model of sexual restraint that few men actually adhered to. The permissive attitude toward male excess and the condemnation of female lapses were constant features of sexual politics in the Catholic Church. Tolerance toward moral double standards with regards to men always belied an otherwise hardline dogma. Total sexual abstinence was the church's dictum to the faithful who remained unmarried, and this sometimes also applied to couples who had been married a long time as well (Blanc y Benet 1905, 10–11). Catholic intellectuals would often remind the faithful that the body's sexual organs and desires had not been granted to human beings for the purpose of pleasure seeking, but rather for the sake of procreation (González Blanco 1903, 105), while claiming, simultaneously, that it was possible to reduce the pleasure felt during the reproductive act to a minimum (Castro Calpe 1927, 19; also see Blanc y Benet 1905, 7).

Despite these views, the Catholic Church considered the institution of marriage to be a fundamental social element, a sacred and inviolable sacrament (Monreal 1931, 84, 86).[1] Marriage was a bulwark against the chaos of natural instincts and their disastrous consequences for moral and social order. Yet this was not tantamount to an endorsement, from the

---

1. For a study of the changing significance of marriage throughout history, see Coontz (2005).

standpoint of a religious life, of the condition of mother and wife. These were not deemed to be the most acceptable nor even the most prized state because chastity and spiritual purity, symbolized by the Virgin Mary, represented a superior female ideal. As a consequence, Lutheranism was condemned because the church accused it of staining the image of the Virgin, which it had cast down from celestial heights into our sinful world. The ultra conservative thinker Alejandro Pidal y Mon referred to Luther as an apostate monk, guilty of barbarism and jealousy because he had expulsed "the Virgin from the Lord's cloister to consort with her in heinous and sacrilegious union" (1902, 17). Dogmatic Catholics accused Luther of having made the sacred figure sexual because, having prostituted her, he had criminally robbed her of her virginal veil in order to "cast her out, alone and forlorn into gutter" (20).

Despite its erstwhile importance, marriage was often represented as a means to an end rather than a goal in itself. As the jurist Quintiliano Saldaña stated, Saint Paul gave married couples the right to live together; he did not demand it of them, rather, he forgave those who did so (Saldaña 1929, 157). Marriage fell into the category of *"ex genere permissorum"* (Montero y Gutiérrez 1927, 20), a status granted as a divine indulgence. God dealt thus with the cowards, the pusillanimous, the timid, those with little willpower and incapable of controlling themselves, for whom marriage was due because "it is better to get married than embrace the fire of impurity" (Bayo 1930, 42). Orthodox Catholics were against abandoning the doctrine promulgated at the Council of Trent, which pronounced the following: "If any one saith, that the marriage state is to be placed above the state of virginity, or of celibacy, and that it is not better and more blessed to remain in virginity, or in celibacy, than to be united in matrimony; let him be anathema."[2] This idea survived on and off within the Church, and cohabitated there with the glorification of the institution of marriage, which was still necessary to perpetuate the order of things.

The Catholic Church, despite its deserved reputation for resisting any progress in its purview and its attendant high toned opposition to change of any sort, did not renounce its mandate to rule over the private life of its subjects, controlling their desires and actions. As the scientific community's intellectual and social authority grew, Catholic religious thought incorporated systems meant to combine science with dogma. Religious

---

2. Council of Trent 1563, Twenty-fourth Session, Tenth Canon. Campión (1936, 21) erroneously cites this as the Sixth Canon of the Council of Trent.

arguments in defense of chastity changed apace. If the Church's theorists had hitherto underscored the necessity of opposing sexual impulses with reason and faith, rather than on considerations of health, they now used views of hygiene to argue that abstinence was not unhealthy or dangerous (Blanc y Benet 1905, 10, 14; Blanc y Benet 1901, 231–32; also, see Castro Calpe 1927, 5). Another attempt at doctrinaire renewal by the Church consisted in the gradual abandon of the traditional silence reserved for sexual topics. With the explosion of sexual discourse in the years following World War I, the Church was forced to respond to secular and materialist visions that were inundating society. The traditional silence, imposed for so many years that it had become a matter of sheer inertia, was now an obstacle when it came to attempting a defense of religious arguments on the ideological battlefield. When Pope Pius XI wrote his famous *Casti Conubii* encyclic (1931) to explicate the current position of the Church on such matters, he was himself prompted to claim that he would have preferred not write about such things "in fitting with the saints," but he had been obliged to do so "for the good and the salvation of souls" (21).

The Catholic Church's efforts to adapt to the new times in a changing society were always few and far between, and insufficient for any success at handling an imminent crisis in ideological authority. Meanwhile, less rigid and more tolerant views on sexuality were becoming popular. Some observers even dared to say that atheism and irreligious sentiments had swept away all Christian precepts on sexuality in the aftermath of World War I (Gómez Ocaña 1919, 127). At a time when modern existence's temptations and "attacks of passion" seemed to be stronger than ever, few seemed to rely on the salvation proffered by the Catholic faith (Sánchez de Rivera 1929, 311). Despite the alarmist tone and the exaggeration contained in these statements, such perceptions of reality were not uncommon. It seemed obvious that the Church did not know how to respond to the demands of those critical times and some observers said that the sermon had become the least practical form of all to win over souls (M. 1926, 15).

Toward a New Sexual Morality

Decades of relative silence were shattered by a "fever of publishing," conferences and debates on "sexual questions" in Spain in the 1920s.[3] The

---

3. Raquel Álvarez Peláez (1985, 112) concludes that of seventy publications in the Morata publishing house catalogue, forty-five were about sexual topics.

differences between the sexes, marriage, prostitution, venereal diseases, sexual pathologies, Malthusianism and eugenics were the subjects of predilection for the authors of hundreds of articles, books and speeches. New milestones in this area of public thought included the popular writings and lectures of Gregorio Marañón, a campaign in favor of abolishing prostitution by the psychiatrist César Juarros, and the work of the medical doctor Antonio Navarro Fernández, designed to provide a popular venue for ideas about sexual hygiene and eugenics. These authors were professionals, doctors, journalists, lawyers and social theorists whose aim was an ideological renewal of society.[4]

The increase in discourses was part of a process that Michel Foucault (1990) defines as the salient characteristic of modern Western societies and one that brought the exercise of power into the realm of the body's internal workings. The creative focus of these new attitudes was centered away from the apparatus of state, which perpetuated rhetorical motifs reinforcing traditional views on sexuality more in line with the stipulations of the Catholic Church. Yet the new modes of discourse were not powerless. On the contrary, they showed a great ability to engage the public mind. By the end of the 1920s new ideas had been widely accepted in the fields of natural sciences and medicine. Furthermore, in their popularized forms these theories reached a wide audience and were later to inspire government policy on these same issues after 1931 during the Second Spanish Republic.

In the opinion of the modern moralists it was none other than the Catholic Church that bore the responsibility for the ideological stagnation on "sexual questions." The Church, they claimed, had enjoyed a monopoly on providing sexual education for the people, and had by the same token been responsible for perpetuating absolute ignorance on such subjects. Critics narrowed their criticism to the concept of chastity. The Church had tried to impose a model of such perfection that it could only be applied to certain individuals, rather than aspire to be a universal ideal. The renowned jurist Quintiliano Saldaña observed ironically that for those who had known how to resist "the ambitious temptation of becoming a saint," the chastity model was simply over the top. In his opinion, prohibiting what is lawful in order to foment perfection was unfair to common mortals (Saldaña 1929, 156–60). Furthermore, given that this ideal

---

4. For an analysis of the growing inroads of the medical sciences into the discourse on sexuality, see Vázquez García and Moreno Mengíbar (1997).

was not really practical, it spelled a clandestine and hypocritical double
sexual morality, which was singularly strong in Spain (Noguera 1930,
50). Religious intolerance had always been accompanied by a climate of
inequality, deception and injustice, congenital infidelity and the "art of
dissimulating" (Juarros 1926, 83). In the new rhetoric, abstinence and so-
called sexual perversions were two faces of the same coin. The effects of
abstinence was comparable to uncontrolled lust (Martín de Lucenay 1933,
51), the irrational proscription being no less than at fault for a supposed
proliferation of "sexual perverts and libertines" in Spanish society at that
time (Torrubiano Ripoll 1926, 3). The sexual impulse was an irrepress-
ible force of nature that, if repressed, would not only fail to disappear but
would manifest itself in pathological symptoms. Sigmund Freud's theories
had exercised a considerable influence on the scientific literature exploring these issues, and explicit references to his work were not uncommon.

The ideological battle between Catholics and secular moralists not
only affected the issues that each defended. The confrontation also called
into question their respective ideological authority. They were claiming
the lead position in providing guidance on sexual issues in the coming
decades.[5] Doctors and biologists defended their propensity to act as the
new advisors on sexual and family life. In fact, religious and secular notions
of sexuality were not so different. Rather, it was possible to find significant
connections between the two. They held different views on what the social
and moral order should be, but both recognized the need to control and
to civilize natural individual impulses. Both positions were necessary to
establish a standard version of sexuality, although what was "normal" had
a different meaning in each case.

The definition of a sexual normalcy was a central motif for the reformers. It was important to draw a new line delineating this normalcy. As
they claimed, "we shouldn't condemn Sexuality. Rather, we should ensure
that the masses understand its real meaning" (Editorial 1926, 2). Age and
civil status were two important criteria when it came to differentiating the
respective categories of "good sexuality" from "deplorable habits." Most
sexual reformers were against sex before marriage. On the other hand,
they changed their views with regard to prostitution,[6] in that they con-

---

5. On the conflict of jurisdiction during the dictatorship of Primo de Rivera, see Díaz Freire
(1999).

6. Guereña (2003) examines prostitution in Spanish society from the end of
the eighteenth century on.

fronted the widely held view that it was an initiation rite and educational ritual for young single men. In fact, this topic became a fundamental pillar of the new program. Likewise, homosexuality, which was systematically linked to feminism and called the "third sex," proved fascinating to social theorists. A new concept of homosexuality came to substitute the religious perception, particularly in progressive, liberal and socialist circles. No longer considered a sin, homosexuality became a medical pathology.

"Divided Love" and the New Sexual Woman

For many years, thinkers from diverse ideological backgrounds agreed on the paramount place of religious piety as the defining trait of Spanish women. In 1901, Henry Havelock Ellis described Spanish women as consistently cold and reserved. He wrote of the impression of chastity that they cast off, which fit their extreme sobriety and religiosity most perfectly (279–80). The defining traits of the female character referred to by both secular and religious social theorists were almost always in regard to women from middle and upper class backgrounds. These writers were therefore rendering a distorted portrait of the female half of society, exaggerating women's observance of Catholic rules of chastity. Furthermore, the so-called *señoritas* purposefully painted themselves in prudish and modest colors, a useful tactic to distinguish themselves from poor and working-class women. Theorists of femininity themselves reinforced this exclusionary construct of identity depicting two opposing models of womanhood: one "pure," which they identified with women from comfortable social classes, another "immodest," usually associated with poorer women. Of course this did not mean that women from modest social backgrounds were in fact normally "impure" and impious. The powerful antithesis of pure versus sexual was nothing more than an ideological instrument meant to interpret and shape society at a discursive level.

For most women sexuality was a still more complex aspect of life, where their own desires coexisted with a power bias and a normative discourse. Contact between middle and upper class *señoritas* with men from the same social background was relatively "safe." The fiancés of these *señoritas* did not generally harbor any ambition of maintaining sexual relations with them prior to marriage. As for married women, everything seems to indicate that, should they wish so, they could opt to minimize sexual contact with their spouses, appealing to the dominant female ideal of their social class and the dictates of the Church on such matters. If women from a privileged background remained unmarried, then religious piety was there to provide a decorous and respectable alternative to live by. All in all, despite the fact that voluntary sexual abstinence among *señoritas* could sometimes be wielded in self defense and provide a mainstay for their self-esteem, it was at root nothing more than an ironclad and violent imposition: any dubious conduct could endanger the future prospects and marriage strategies of young marriageable women.

Numerous sources point to the difficult conditions faced by poorer women with regard to their sexual relationships, in circumstances where pleasure and danger coexisted side by side.[7] They often had to bear insistent pressures from their fiancés to maintain "intimate relations" before marriage. These pressures sometimes took on the form of a plea for a "token of their love." Both possible responses these women could offer were problematic: rejecting sexual contact could endanger the relationship itself, since the fiancé might not be disposed to wait any longer, while ceding to the demand was also a risky move. It might satisfy the fiancé's short-term expectations but not without weakening the women's future marriage prospects and the risk of pregnancy was ever present. In fact, a difficult mixture of love, passions, pressure, fear, beliefs and social convention shaped many young women's experience of sexuality above and beyond any particular sexual impulse.

For the new generation of secular moralists and sexual reformers however, the principle problem threatening women's intimate lives was chastity as imposed by the Catholic Church. From their perspective, women from comfortable social circumstances were the principle victims of this traditional outlook. This view reflected their perception of women from modest social classes, whom they deemed more sexual that those of their own class. They contributed to perpetuating the legend of an idealized woman of the people, free in her sexual conduct, an image that was not short of an important dose of male fantasy. Jaime Torrubiano Ripoll, for example, stated that poor women were always ready to satisfy his sexual desires: "They know how to satisfy one's appetites, both night and day, unconstrained, without hang-ups, in pleasure-filled collaboration, voluptuously and indulgently . . . ; these adorable little women are priceless treasures" (Torrubiano Ripoll 1921, 223). Given that such experiences of middle class men with "the other" women were normally based

---

7. Concerning strategies for treating the female body in this context, see Llona (2007).

on extramarital relations, they tended to adhere to traditional perceptions dividing the female population into two categories: the sexual, as represented by prostitutes and illicit affairs, and the chaste, the fiancées and spouses (Jiménez de Asua 1984, 28).

At the end of the 1920s, the term "divided love" became popular as a way of describing the male experience of sexuality and its double standards. The reform "experts" were against both the chastity dictum of the Church and "divided love," which they saw as intimately linked. In their opinion, the inflexibility of Catholic doctrine reinforced the male double standard and divided women into two classes: the victims of absurd social conventions and the "flowers that adorn the temple of sin" (Terrádez 1926, 1). They preached a full and harmonious womanhood created by nature, a harmony that men had defiled and segregated into two parts, the body and the soul. And they claimed that "Love is never complete" (Juarros 1927, 65). It was necessary to overcome a form of love that always tended to "sterile contemplation or unbridled sensuality" so as to reunite both parts into a wholeness. In this way, they would unite the various fragments of femininity and a "whole woman" would be recovered.

Male infidelity was the constant backdrop for the old division of love and femininity, and any attempt to lead sexual reform required a change in male behavior. Male adultery thus received constant criticism and became a basic part of the sexual re-education program. Male hypocrisy was denounced in its constant demand for women's virtue while at the same time it conspired constantly against this same virtue (Francos Rodríguez 1920, 309). Likewise, the abolition of prostitution was at the heart of the reformists' agenda. The commonplace idea that prostitutes were the saviors of virtue for "honest" women, protecting them from the unstoppable sexual impulses of men, was also attacked. The feminist press of the time celebrated the fact that science was now reproving such erroneous ideas while simultaneously calling for the abolition of what it considered a "villainous slavery" (Doña Equis 1931, 2).

For sexual reformers, women also needed to change their behavior. In order to solve the problem of "divided love" it was necessary to reduce the gap between the way women of different social classes experienced sexuality. The reformist theologian Torrubiano Ripoll, in an openly classist tone, framed the problem as follows: "You need to learn one form the other: first and foremost you from *them*, the lower ones, about how to be women; lastly, though it is perfection, they from you the upper ones . . . on

how to be Christian women" (Torrubiano Ripoll 1921, 16).[8] In its attention to the lives of working class women, the reformist agenda focused on
abolition and contraception, which was considered an essential part of the
quest for "conscientious maternity." The question of sexuality itself in the
reformist agenda was especially meant to impact middle and upper class
women and their "unnatural" chastity.

This preoccupation was part of these men's personal interests in relationships with women of their own classes, and in their hostility toward
religious control over private life. The rejection of sexual pleasure by the
Church, while not in itself a threat to male authority within the family
structure, did in fact chip away at the legitimacy of husbands' demands for
sexual practices not strictly meant for reproductive purposes. In the more
secular version of conjugal obligations, women lost some of their power
in exchange for a veto on the frequency and timeliness of sexual relations
with their husbands, thereby managing their own sexual desires. "Do not
forget that this is not advice," remonstrated Jaime Torrubiano Ripoll "but
rather, a duty of utmost seriousness" (1921, 84). For men, this was the only
way to avoid having recourse to adultery and prostitution: "Your husband
must always see, delightful and vehemently passionate, your sexual passion, always ready for pleasure" (106). Anything less would wound the
husband's sexual pride and drag him down into infidelity. The wife must
emulate "the other" and compete with her in sexual ardor (41).

The impact of modernization on sexual mores was full of contradic-
tions. Women would obtain the right to be recognized as sexual beings,
while being deprived at the same time of specific power mechanisms
affecting day-to-day decision-making. Even Torrubiano Ripoll suspected
that his words might be particularly harsh for the women he was directing
his proclamations at. He expressed this concern in a hypothetical reaction
of a priest to his writing: "You are stricter with women than we are . . .
women have nothing to thank you for; you are extremely cruel with them"
(1921, 45–46). Ripoll answered his imaginary priest by affirming that no
genuine duty was difficult to carry out nor did it make sense to avoid duty
when there is love.

I have already drawn attention to renewal in relation to the conjugal
duties facing the new "sexual *señorita*," clearly delineating the recognition of female sexual pleasure as a positive counterpart. Not all the doc-

---

8. The reference to Christianity should not obscure the secular nature of Ripoll's argument
regarding women of his own social class.

tors, sociologists and writers concerned with these issues showed such enthusiasm in this respect, yet the defense of female pleasure was a recurrent theme among the modern moralists. Even Gregorio Marañón, with his renowned austerity, chose to emphasize this aspect of the new sexual morality. His colleague, the gynecologist Vital Aza expressed this right in clear and direct style, stating that women had a right to "enjoy the pleasure of participation in the sexual act" (Aza 1934, 25). Of course, most doctors thought that female sexual impulses were weaker and easier to master than those of men. And in fact, women who did have pronounced sexual impulses such as those typically attributed to men were treated like pathological cases and classified as nymphomaniacs. Such cases were generally considered the pernicious outcome of enforced chastity (Martín de Lucenay 1933, 53–60).

It is very difficult to assess the impact of these new attitudes on women's actual experiences. We do know that the inroads made by gynecologists filled their waiting rooms with middle class women who were not satisfied with their sexual lives. If we are to believe the testimony of the doctors themselves, many of these problems were rooted in the inconsiderate and selfish attitude of their husbands. In the case of working-class women, for whom pregnancy, delivery and raising children could be harsh experiences, sexual relations were still fraught with understandable fears.

In the final analysis, the 1920s and 1930s constituted a turning point in evolving attitudes toward sex. Modern reformers wanted to make rational will the force regulating sexual impulses, according to criteria derived from the laws of nature and defined by science. Their efforts thus turned into a normative program that abandoned a view of sex as sin, imposing instead new dictates and duties that also required adherence. This sexual reform agenda, whose most far-reaching influence was felt during the Second Republic, led to complex and contradictory consequences that affected women's capacity to manage their sexual life, a process that was also to affect men's sexual life and gender privileges as well.

References

Álvarez Peláez, Raquel. 1985. "Introducción al estudio de la eugenesia española (1900–1936)." *Quipu* 2, no. 1: 95–122.

Aza, Vital. 1934. *Derechos y deberes biológicos de la mujer.* Madrid: Imp. Rot.

Bayo, Lázaro. 1930. *Luchas de la castidad*. Cádiz: M. Álvarez.

Blanc y Benet, José. 1905. *La moderación de la libídine*. Barcelona: Imprenta de la Casa Provincial de Caridad.

——. 1901. "Los principios de la moral y la práctica médica. IV. Excesos venéreos." *Criterio Católico en las Ciencias Médicas* 44: 231–32.

Castro Calpe, Antonio. 1927. *Deontología médica en las tendencias sexuales de los célibes*. Madrid: E. Maestre.

Coontz, Stephanie. 2005. *Marriage, A History: From Obediente to Intimacy, or How Love Conquered Marriage*. New York: Viking.

Council of Trent. 1563. *The canons and decrees of the sacred and oecumenical Council of Trent*, edited and translated by J. Waterworth. London: Dolman, 1848, available at history.hanover.edu/texts/trent.html. Quoted in Leo Campión, "Temas sexuales," *Estudios*, no. 158 (1936): 21.

Díaz Freire, José Javier. 1999. "La reforma de la vida cotidiana y el cuerpo femenino durante la dictadura de Primo de Rivera." In *El rumor de lo cotidiano. Estudios sobre el País Vasco Contemporáneo*, edited by Luis Castells. Bilbao: UPV/EHU.

Doña Equis [pseud.]. 1931. "Infame esclavitud." *Mundo Femenino* 77 (July): 2.

Editorial. 1926. "Sexualidad." *Sexualidad* 47 (April 11): 2.

Ellis, Henry Havelock. 1901. "In Modern Spain: The Women of Spain." *Argosy* 75, no. 15: 279–80.

Foucault, Michel. 1990. *The History of Sexuality*. Volume 1. *An Introduction*. Translated by Robert Hurley. New York: Vintage Books.

Francos Rodríguez, José. 1920. *La mujer y la política española*. Madrid: Pueyo.

Gómez Ocaña, José. 1919. *El sexo, el hominismo y la natalidad*. Madrid: Moliner.

González Blanco, Edmundo. 1903. *El feminismo en las sociedades modernas*. Volume 2. Barcelona: Imp. de Henrich y Cª.

Guereña, Jean-Louis. 2003. *La prostitución en la España contemporánea*. Madrid, Marcial Pons.

Jiménez de Asúa, Luis. First edition 1928; reprint 1984. *Libertad de amar y derecho a morir*. Buenos Aires: Depalma.

Juarros, César. 1926. *De regreso del amor*. Madrid: Mundo Latino.

———. 1927. *El amor en España. Características masculinas.* Madrid: Páez.

Llona, Miren. 2007. "Los otros cuerpos disciplinados. Relaciones de género y estrategias de autocontrol del cuerpo femenino (primer tercio del siglo XX)." *Arenal. Revista de Historia de las Mujeres* 14, no. 1: 79–108.

M., A. de. 1926. "La sexualidad en la calle." *Sexualidad* 80 (28 de Noviembre): 14–16.

Martín de Lucenay, Ángel. 1933. *La abstinencia y la moral.* Madrid: Fénix.

Monreal, Porfirio. 1931. "El Sacramento y el rito del matrimonio." In Pío XI, *El matrimonio cristiano. Comentarios y glosas a la Carta Encíclica de S.S. sobre el matrimonio cristiano.* Madrid: Razón and Fé.

Montero y Gutiérrez, Eloy. 1927. *El matrimonio y las causas matrimoniales.* Seville: Eulogio de las Heras.

———. 1932. *Neomalthusianismo, eugenesia y divorcio.* Madrid: Juan Bravo.

Noguera, Enrique, and Luis Huerta, eds. 1934. *Genética, eugenesia y pedagogía sexual. Libro de las Primeras Jornadas Eugénicas Españolas.* Volume 2. Madrid: Javier Morata.

Noguera, Joaquín. 1930. *Moral. Eugenesia y Derecho.* Madrid: Tip. Artística.

Pidal y Mon, Alejandro. 1902. *El "Feminismo" y la cultura de la mujer.* Madrid: Tip. Artística.

Pío XI. 1931. *El matrimonio cristiano. Comentarios y glosas a la Carta Encíclica de S.S. sobre el matrimonio cristiano.* Madrid: Razón y Fé.

Saldaña, Quintiliano. First edition 1918; reprint 1929. *Siete ensayos sobre sociología sexual.* Madrid: Mundo Latino.

Sánchez de Rivera, Daniel. 1929. *La ruta del matrimonio.* Madrid: Imp. Helénica.

Terrádez, Vicente. 1926. "Libertad y responsabilidad sexuales." *Sexualidad* 63 (August 1): 1.

Torrubiano Ripoll, Jaime. 1921. *¿Son ellos adúlteros? Para mujeres casadas y casaderas: Y para gente de sotana.* Madrid: Suc. de Rivadeneyra.

Vázquez García, Francisco, and Andrés Moreno Mengíbar. 1997. *Sexo y razón: Una genealogía de la moral sexual en España (Siglos XVI–XX).* Madrid: Akal.

6

Patriotic Mothers of Basque Nationalism: Women's Action during the Spanish Second Republic in the Basque Country

Miren Llona

Translated by Robert Forstag

In this chapter,[1] I will focus on one concrete example of women's leadership—the conduct of female Basque nationalist activists as regards "the rhetoric of motherhood" during the Second Spanish Republic in the Basque Country. By examining this particular experience, and employing a theoretical approach that focuses on an interpretation of subjective experiences and life stories, I will attempt to enter into the phenomenology of an individual subject and her idiosyncratic awareness. My goal is to gain an understanding of how social and gender identities are constructed, and how it is that human endeavors come to transform reality.

Satya Mohanty suggests placing emotions at the center of the process by which one learns about the world (1997, 210).[2] This way, the impact absorbed by the body as a result of emotional experiences, and the individual's understanding and interpretation of such experiences,

1. Research for this article was carried out thanks to a postdoctoral grant from the Basque Government during the period 2005–7, and the help of the Department of Equality of Opportunity in the office of the Chief Representative of the Provincial Council of Bizkaia. This is an updated and expanded version of "Polixene Trabudua, historia de vida de una dirigente del nacionalismo vasco en la Vizcaya de los años treinta," *Historia Contemporánea* 21 (2000), 459–84.
2. Mohanty's notion of an identity that is constructed as a result of a process involving both cognitive and emotional effort is influenced by the novelist Toni Morrison, whose works include *The Bluest Eye* (1970), *Song of Solomon* (1977), and *Beloved* (1987).

come to constitute the genesis of a cognitive-emotional process in which one's subjective world takes shape and is subject to ongoing modification (Anzaldúa 1987).

My case study is in fact a practical example of this constant process of redefining the limits of one's identity. As a result of this redefinition, it is possible to reformulate the hegemonic discourses of gender. Here, I will utilize written documents and oral recollections pertaining to the life of one of the most important Basque nationalist propagandists, Polixene Trabadua (born in 1912 in a small village near Bilbao), in order to explore the evolution of both her subjective experience and her personal interpretation of that experience. Specifically, I employ a method that explores the possibilities of Cherry Moraga's "theory in the flesh" (1983, 23). This theory understands the construction of identity as something inseparable from both physical experience and the impact of that experience on the human body. In keeping with this approach, I have identified two key experiences in Trabadua's life during the Second Republic in the 1930s: her arrest and imprisonment in 1933 at the age of twenty-one and her becoming a mother in 1934–35.

The second part of Moraga's approach underlines the importance of language and narratives that are accessible to the subject for the interpretation of his or her emotions. In line with this approach, I have conducted research regarding both the Basque nationalist movement's rhetoric with respect to women, and its foundational myths concerning women. On the basis of the stereoscopy resulting from the fusion of both perspectives, we will come to see the possibility of understanding the process of identity construction among Basque nationalist women during a given historical period, and the importance of that identity in the construction of the Basque nation.

Transcending the Limits Imposed on the "Mothers of the Nation"

Before exploring the role of Basque nationalist women as "mothers of the nation," I will first discuss a number of contextual elements that allow us to reconstruct the social and ideological climate into which these women were born, and in which they came of age.

The Partido Nacionalista Vasco (PNV, Basque Nationalist Party) was founded in the 1890s. It constructed a nationalist ideology that defended the notion of a distinctive Basque people, and of its political independence from the Spanish state. The context of expanding industrialization and of rapid economic transformations in the Basque Country during the last quarter of the nineteenth century and the beginning of the twentieth century was a decisive factor in the emergence of this new ideology. Basque nationalism confronted this modernization process with a steadfast defense of tradition and a reaffirmation of Basque uniqueness. In the early twentieth century, the PNV succeeded in making the "imagined community" (Anderson 1983) its political lodestar. It was on the basis of this imagined community that the PNV claimed a separate legal status within the framework of the Spanish state. For the purpose of constructing a national identity, the PNV consciously went about becoming a mass political party and expanding its ideology to embrace a broad range of social classes, despite its initially middle-class nature. This transformation led to the emergence of a modern political organization in which women also came to play an important part.[3]

During the Second Republic, the relationship between Basque nationalists and the Spanish government was extremely tense. The estrangement between the PNV and central authority was evident in the rejection by the Spanish government of various proposals for an autonomy statute in the Basque Country. Basque nationalists viewed the impediment of an autonomy statute as an obstacle to nation-building. This perception of the nation as a living entity whose existence was imperiled led to a groundswell of popular support, and provided the impetus for the inclusion of women in the nationalist cause during the 1920s and 1930s. Yet Spanish government approval of an autonomy statute for the Basque nation would not occur until October, 1936, following the outbreak of the Spanish Civil War.

One modern aspect of the PNV was its inclusion of Basque women in the process of nation building.[4] In 1908, following the introduction of the iconic party slogan *"Jaungoikoa eta Lagi Zarra"* (literally "God and the Old Laws," the latter a reference to the tradition implied by the old

---

3. On gender-based national construction, see Aretxaga (1997); Condren (1995); Yuval-Davis (1997); Altan-Olcay (2009); Vickers and Vouloukos (2007); and Patriarca (2005).

4. Díaz Freire (1993, 206–58) has drawn attention to the fact that the beginnings of the PNV as a mass movement was the result of a conscious effort to construct a constellation of group identity symbols that would be capable of imposing a decisive influence on the subjective identity of existing Basque society. On the development of Basque nationalism as part of the general process of modernization in Spain as a whole, see de Pablo and Mees (2005); de la Granja (2007); and Núñez Seixas (1999).

foral system), Basque nationalism defined the role and the limits of female participation. In accordance with the term *"Jaungoikoa"* ("God"), women were charged with the preservation of religious tradition: it was expected that they would conserve the moral welfare of the nation through their involvement in charitable institutions and Sunday schools. In reference to the term *"Lagi Zarra,"* (the tradition implied by the *foral* system), women were expected to embrace a commitment to ensure the continuity of tradition, the most critical component of which was the Basque language, Euskara. Thus, the task of transmitting what Basque nationalism identified as one of the key symbols of Basque identity was placed in the hands of the "mothers of the nation."

In 1922, the first organization for Basque nationalist women, Emakume Abertzale Batza (EAB, the League of Nationalist Women), was created, along with other women's associations devoted to charitable work, the home, and education. At that same time, a propaganda commission was created that solicited the active involvement of women in spreading nationalist thinking and sentiment.[5] In fact, it was as a participant in this propaganda campaign that Polixene Trabadua first appeared on the political scene in 1931, at the age of nineteen, thus beginning her long career as a propagandist in the service of the cause of Basque nationalism, holding meetings in towns and villages throughout the Basque Country. As a result of her speechmaking, Trabadua was brought to trial twelve times, and was imprisoned in 1933 for not having paid a fine imposed upon her for the radical content of her speeches. For Trabadua (1997, 88):

> As a result of a political gathering, where we advocated independence with particular vehemence, both the famous speaker Haydée de Aguirre and I were arrested and taken to the Larrínaga Prison, where we were held for fifteen long days. We were very young—barely nineteen years old. We were village girls who had been brought up in the strict social environment that prevailed during the 1930s.... That prison, with its enormous bolted doors and keys and, above all else, the different areas and corridors that kept us penned in ... made us feel like we were martyrs to the cause.

This incarceration, along with her interpretation of that experience as a kind of martyrdom, seems conducive to the notion of "theory in the flesh."

---

5. For a study of the EAB, see Ugalde Solano (1993). For the specific history of nationalist women in their role as mothers, see Llona (2002, 159–99).

In Basque or Spanish society, the term "martyrdom" is clearly associated with Catholicism. Martyrs evoke a time when saints willingly gave their lives in order to defend the Christian faith. By reviving this term and using it to apply to her own circumstances, Trabadua is trying to put herself in the category of those who are capable and fortunate enough to defend their nation. Her choice of language suggests that she is conferring upon herself the status of a soldier. In order to appreciate the extent to which discursive elements that promote such identification are present in her words, we might consider the possible discourses available within the dominant nationalist ideas of the time that associated prominent women with the idea of sacrifice for the Basque nation.

The most prominent woman in Basque nationalist thinking was the literary character Libe, a creation of Sabino Arana, the founder of Basque nationalism. Between the early twentieth century and the 1930s, Libe's symbolic meaning underwent an important transformation. Where originally she symbolized the Immaculate Virgin Mary, by the 1930s she came to be identified with Our Lady of Sorrows.

Libe, a play written by Arana in 1902, concerns the romance between the Basque girl Libe and a Castilian count (Arana 1980).[6] The symbolic referent implicit in Libe is that of the Immaculate Conception, an archetype of female purity. The message—in dramatic code—transmitted by this character to women was that the best way for women to defend the Basque nation was to eschew mixed marriages and love relationships with foreigners and to dedicate themselves to preserving Basque racial purity.[7] Such a connection aside, there is no reason to believe that Libe has the capacity to make any sacrifice for the nation. In fact, she shows herself to be a woman incapable of becoming involved in political matters and of

6. The scene takes place in 1471during the Battle of Mungia (Munguía), where the Basques fought against Castile and Leon. Libe decides to prepare herself to marry a Castilian count and rejects a young Basque suitor. When the Basques and Castilians go to war, the count supports his king and joins forces with the enemies of the Basques. Upon hearing this news, Libe finds herself torn between her country and the man she loves, but is incapable of making a decision. In the heat of the battle, a horrified Libe is able to do nothing more than pray to the Immaculate Virgin Mary for the protection of her people. Finally, in the face of a Basque defeat, Libe climbs upon a rock and unfurls and waves a flag in order to exhort the Basque soldiers engaged in battle. Severely wounded, Libe is taken to the house of the suitor whom she had rejected and there, surrounded by his family, who forgives her, succeeds in redeeming herself for the infamy of her past betrayal of the nation with her death.

7. On Libe's function in preserving the myth of Basque racial purity, see Díaz Freire (2002, 79–85).

taking sides. This foundational female myth of Basque nationalism discouraged women from taking part in political causes and instead relegated them to their familial roles as mothers of future Basque generations.

Yet three decades later, Manu Sota, an influential nationalist politician, introduced a series of important changes in this protagonist (Sota 1934).[8] In Sota's version, Libe symbolizes Our Lady of Sorrows, represented traditionally as *Pièta*, with a meaning that is completely different from that of the Immaculate Virgin. The fact that Our Lady of Sorrows bears witness to Jesus's crucifixion gives her a place of honor in the context of the Passion—the martyrdom—of Jesus Christ. Here, in accompanying her son in his suffering, the mother comes to suffer the exact same torments as he himself has endured (Warner 1976). The female role model that appears associated with this divine figure is a woman who participates in—and who earns the right to share in—not only the suffering but also the glory of the men who give their lives for the homeland. This revised discourse allowed Trabadua to reinterpret her captivity as (paradoxically) a liberating experience. In fact, the model of the ideal woman evoked in her recollections has elements in common with the prototype represented by the reconstructed Libe. In the words of Trabadua:

> Manu Sota, in writing Libe, stimulated women's involvement [in the Basque nationalist cause]. He had a very human appreciation of women and of their possible role. . . . [His Libe] is a strong woman—someone who struggles shoulder to shoulder with men—even on the battlefield itself if necessary. She is not a passive creature who sits in the kitchen weeping or piously reciting the rosary, but an active woman who ventures out into the real world. For the first time, women propaganda workers went out and about with the men following meetings. There were sometimes problems: beatings, being chased down in the streets. I think that was a small

---

8. The revised plot is as follows: When the Castilian count decides to join the troops that are going to attack Bizkaia (Vizcaya), Libe immediately breaks her engagement to him, putting the love of her country first and thus learning the painful lesson that there is no way one can both love one's country and love its enemies. She voluntarily and actively throws herself into the battle, placing her faith in Our Lady of Sorrows, and taking on her very form in a symbolic reenactment of the Pietà when she holds the lifeless body of a wounded Basque soldier in her arms. The bravery that Libe inspires in the Basque soldiers is decisive for their victory. Thanks to her intervention, women are promoted to the status of soldiers, and the following cry is heard: "Oh women of Bizkaia; fearless soldiers of the Basque hearth!" Shortly before dying, Libe declares, "Father, I alone am to blame. . . . I courted death so that Basque women would learn how to die for the glory of God and for freedom—the true legacy of their children." Libe is then honored with a soldier's funeral (Sota 1934, 100).

window of opportunity [pause]—an opening up of minds regarding the proper role of women in a future society (Trabudua 1998–99).

The 1930s Libe represented an enormously powerful symbolic discourse that proved useful to nationalist women at the time who were testing the limits of the female role in political activity, and who did not even have a vocabulary to describe such activity. Thus, paradoxically, even though a rhetoric centered on motherhood continued to be invoked, the fact that they had also been identified with the Sorrowful Mother allowed a redefinition of what it meant to be a woman—in a liberating sense involving the expansion of the social space it now became possible for women to occupy within society.

However, this ideal of woman was not shared by the majority of PNV leaders. Pressure to return women to their traditional roles and maintain the divide between patriotic activity and political action was soon apparent. As a result, after Trabadua and Aguirre were released from jail, they were not treated as soldiers, as prisoners, or even as patriotic comrades. Instead, the party tried to redefine their activities within the framework of "mothers of the nation." For this purpose, a mass reception for them was held on February 5, 1933 at the Euskalduna *frontón* (handball court) in Bilbao under the banner of "Tribute to Basque Motherhood." At this gathering, the two women gave speeches that employed rhetoric in keeping with Sota's notion of Libe—taking their inspiration from Our Lady of the Sorrows as a symbol of women's involvement—through sacrifice and pain, in the salvation and rebirth of the Basque nation. Trabadua declaimed to the assembled crowd:

> The childhood of your daughters will not be darkened by the clouds of persecution, fines, and the prisons of those who are the enemies of Euskadi. Instead these daughters have risen up and joined forces in the struggle—a struggle of idealists, of those of noble character. They stand ready to forsake their homes if necessary, and to leave behind those whom they hold most dear, because their minds are capable of clearly discerning the bright star of truth that is the Basque nation (Trabudua 1933, 7).

The experiences of these two women in prison and following the homage bear witness to the fact that the boundaries imposed by the nationalist movement on women's political activity were at times questioned and transgressed. But the circumstances also reveal the difficulties that existed during the 1930s within the nationalist movement when it came to characterizing women's political action in a manner that transcended the discursive bounds of woman as mother. The idealization of the Basque woman as mother whose task was to preserve the Basque race and traditions constituted a heavy ideological burden that impeded any recognition of an active political role for women, who could only take on such a role through identifying with Our Lady of the Sorrows.

Trabudua herself, in a retrospective examination of the effect of her participation in the "Tribute to Basque Motherhood," recaptured the meaning of her iconoclastic stance:

> We were not mothers—that idea was a kind of smokescreen of what the tribute really was about. It was really a tribute to daring, courageous, and involved women—to women who fought side by side with men. In reality, that was what the tribute was all about—and it was deliberately given a different kind of character that was more conservative . . . more in keeping with the ideas of the Basque Nationalist Party. . . .They associated it with Basque motherhood precisely because it really had nothing to do with Basque mothers. Instead, it was a tribute to us foolish women who were dedicated to the cause, and who struggled and went around shouting and swearing (Trabudua 1998–99).

The political activity of the women propaganda workers, although characterized by a symbolic rhetorical frame of reference in which women were represented as mothers, was perceived by the workers themselves, and by the social environment in which they functioned, as something that in practice represented a radical break with the rules that had traditionally been imposed by the nationalist movement on women's participation in the cause. Embracing new spheres of activity, nationalist women contributed to challenging traditional differential gender roles. The new breed of nationalist woman, such as Trabadua, modernized the public image of women during the 1930s. Their characterization in the Spanish press as women who represented a new kind of female ideal is a measure of the distance that separated them from traditional notions of the passive woman.[9]

9. In a report on the growing politicization of Spanish women, Josefina Carabias wrote: "In Bilbao, all the women wear political buttons on their coat lapels or their hat ribbons. It is a curious thing that surely is not seen in any other Spanish capital. Yet it is not surprising because Bilbao is perhaps the only place where women have thrown themselves into political struggle in such a dedicated and militant way." In this same report Carabias profiled other Basque women propagandists, such as the socialist Aurora Arnaiz, the traditionalist María Rosa Urraca Pas-

Disobedience Within the Private Sphere

In 1933, the same year that she was released from prison, Polixene Trabadua married José Mandaluniz.[10] Even though Trabadua remembers the early years of her marriage as being happy, the fact that she became pregnant meant that she would have to experience firsthand a series of conventional restrictions—specifically, the condescension toward motherhood and the pregnant woman—that ran counter to the rhetorical exaltation of motherhood at the public level.[11] The pregnant female body was perceived as an expression of sin, and this view justified attitudes that promoted both the isolation of, and the repulsion toward, pregnant women—attitudes typical of traditional misogyny. Catholic tradition had succeeded in transmitting the notions of Eve as a sinner, as well as the Aristotelian view of the female body as a defective male (Laqueur 1990). The Biblical story was used to promote the notion of the female body, and specifically of female sexuality, as a symbol of human weakness and as the origin of evil. Following the Council of Trent, the Catholic Church took a more decidedly negative stance toward the biological processes involved in motherhood: pregnancy and giving birth.[12] Yet the fact that on December 8, 1854, Pope Pius IX proclaimed the dogma of the Immaculate Conception in the Papal Bull *Ineffabilis Deus* represented a turning point in the traditional misogyny of Catholic thought. This dogma signaled a sea change in the traditional identification of womanhood, replacing Eve the original sinner, with the purity of the Virgin Mary. Pope Leo XIII's proclamation of the dogma of the Virgin as co-redeemer of humanity was the supreme expression of this more favorable view of woman, which was responsible for creating an expanded social space for women in the Catholic-dominated societies of the nineteenth century, and which in the early twentieth century would be

---

tor, and the communist Dolores Ibárruri. But she especially emphasized the public activities of nationalist women. Photos of Haydée Aguirre and Polixene Trabadua leaving Larrínaga Prison, as well as illustrations of nationalist meetings depicting women propagandists standing on the podium accompanied the report. See Carabias (1933).

10. José Mandaluniz was the center-forward for the Athletic Club de Fútbol soccer team, as well as a fiery militant of the organization Juventud Vasca (Basque Youth). He was a man who represented the most radical element of Basque nationalism.

11. On the discourse regarding motherhood and its conversion into the principal characteristic of female cultural identity during the late nineteenth and early twentieth centuries, see Nash (1993) and Morata (2003).

12. As Ibero (1994, 103) argues, during the Baroque Period, the disappearance of the Lactating Virgin and the scarcity of religious birth scenes—and their replacement by the icon of Virgin and Christ Child or the Holy Family—represented the redefinition of a new ideal of motherhood that concealed the physical reality of reproduction.

the driving force behind the creation of Acción Católica de la Mujer (the Catholic Women's League).[13]

Polixene Trabadua's life story enables us to appreciate the difficulties involved in the process of the gradual replacement, within the Catholic Church, of the traditional identification of women with sin by new more dignified discourses. In this regard, it is important to note how deeply rooted misogynist conceptions were still rooted in Basque society during the 1930s, with traditional attitudes continuing to function as bulwarks against the new modernizing discourses that exalted motherhood.

Trabadua remembers as particularly unfair the relegation of pregnant women to domestic duties—an attitude that she herself confronted with outright rejection:

My husband said to me: "What's all this? So now you're married, with a huge belly . . . But what terrible sin have you women committed for God to punish you like this?" And he never went out with me when I was pregnant. He was ashamed. All the men were very sexist. . . . All of them.

My brother-in-law, Valentín Mandaluniz, came one day looking for my husband so that they could go together to see a very popular movie that was showing. I said: "Take me as well."

"How can we take you there with a belly like that! You'd better stay home."

And my brother-in-law was . . . , since he was still single . . . [he said], "Let Polixene come."

"No, she'd better stay home."

And the two of them went off to Bilbao. And my mother said to me: "You know what I would do, Polisetxu. I would doll myself up really good, with that nice big coat—I had a very large coat to cover my belly— and I would go to the movies as well. They [my husband and brother-in-law] will see you when you leave, and they'll have quite a fright."

And this is what I did. It was on the Gran Vía [the main street of Bilbao] and I went to the cinema by myself, all by myself, something that was highly unusual . . . and I went to sit [in the balcony], and I saw the two of them sitting down below. During one of the intermissions, I did this [waved at them]. And the two of them definitely had a fright (Trabudua 1998–99).

---

13. For a study of the ambivalence of Catholic thought and its capacity to mobilize women's involvement in the Church, see Blasco Herranz (2003).

There are two important subversive elements in this story: the explicit disobedience of a woman toward her husband and the defiance of social norms still expected from a woman in the 1930s in going to a public place by herself. Taking the train by herself, going into town, strolling along the Gran Vía and sitting in the theater by herself—these were highly unusual things for a woman to do in those days, especially if she was noticeably pregnant. The story also shows the reaction of Trabadua's mother, whose advice to go to the city alone and thus break the chains of submission to her husband suggests that nonconformist attitudes regarding deeply rooted sexism were shared by older generations of Basque women as well. The confinement of pregnant women that persisted into the 1930s was a sign of the ongoing vitality of traditional misogynist views, and was also evidence that new discourses that glorified motherhood and the human body had not yet taken root.

This attitude was part of a generalized male superiority that was common in those days (Aresti 2007). This dominant position within the marriage also allowed husbands to preserve the same degree of freedom that they had had when they were single. In this regard, women seem to have been more accepting of new ideas regarding intimacy, the home, and family relations within the home than men. The need to share private space and child-rearing duties—as well as leisure time with children—with one's husband seemed a realistic aspiration for many women during the 1930s who no longer found the partying and carefree attitude of their husbands acceptable. As Trabadua recalled:

> Then again, you see, there was the open-air dances in Lujua [Loiu in Basque] and my husband had been out partying all day, while I stayed home with the children. By then, my mother had passed away. So I fixed myself up really nicely—I remember putting on a dress I had made for my wedding, a velvet dress, with a Brussels lace neck and some artificial violets pinned here [on the lapel]—really nice. Just think: How ridiculous was it to go to a dance? Really ridiculous. The little carriage was all decked out with bunting. I was with the kids. And then the journey to Asua—and then from Asua to Lujua in the little carriage. And when I got to where the dance was going on, I saw Joseba [José, her husband] dancing a *paso doble* with some girl. [He said to me:]
>
> "What's going on!, Why did you come here?"
>
> And he went on dancing [laughs]. And I got back in the little carriage and cried all the way home—to Asua and then from Asua to Sondika. These are important experiences, you know. . . . This was the kind

of thing that happened all of the time. It didn't seem right to me. It made me angry, but this is how things were: the woman stayed at home and the husband went off with his friends. He may not have done anything especially exciting, but at least he had his freedom (Trabudua 1998–99).

Given her rebellious nature, Trabadua tried to confront inequities inherent in the differential roles of men and women with respect to their family obligations. Her nonconformity with the traditional male custom of leaving the family at home and going out and having a good time in settings where there was no place for their wives and children reveals women's changing values and attitudes toward the components of male identity. Paternal responsibility, tenderness, and providing care for children were coming to be seen by women as newly desirable male qualities (Llona 2007).

In conclusion, this brief examination of part of Polixene Trabadua's life tells us something of what it was like to be a woman in the Basque Country during the 1930s. Her experience as a nationalist propagandist shows that a wide range of social conventions was dominant during that time that minimized the political work of women like her. In this regard, the "Tribute to Basque Motherhood" that was held following the release of Trabadua and Aguirre from prison is an example of how the use of the "rhetoric of motherhood" in the service of nationalism served the purpose of masking the transgressive nature of the public activity that nationalist women were engaged.

Similarly, Trabadua's resistance toward the imposition of particular expectations upon women in their roles as wives and mothers, and unconditional obedience of their husbands, shows the distance between female and male ideals within the private sphere. Trabadua rebelled against both male misogyny and the prevailing social mores of the Basque Country in the 1930s—mores that looked down upon motherhood, and that ran counter to women's own reappraisal of their roles as mothers. The enjoyment of motherhood, as well as the desire to share childrearing duties and other aspects of private life with their husbands, was something that in the 1930s constituted a female ideal. Throughout the course of the twentieth century, this ideal gradually gained widespread social acceptance.

In light of Trabadua's recollections, the 1930s emerge as a complex period as regards the reconciliation of diverse gender ideas with respect to women. Women were faced with the task of reconciling two highly disparate attitudes: one in which maternity was exalted within the public sphere, and another in which they were subject to misogynist expectations regarding gender roles—expectations that undervalued the actual experience of being a mother, and that were far removed from women's own experience as mothers and from the importance that they attributed to this role. In daily life during the 1930s, this disparity in how motherhood was differentially valued by men and women was one of the most salient social issues. Trabadua's defiance of both of these attitudes suggests the emergence of a new structure of feelings on the part of women— as regards both the true public importance of their political activities, and the value of motherhood and child rearing.

References

Altan-Olcay, Ozlem. 2009. "Gendered Projects of National Identity Formation: The Case of Turkey." *National Identities* 11, no. 2: 165–87.

Anderson, Benedict. 1983. *Imagined Communities: Reflections on the Origin and Spread of Nationalism.* London: Verso.

Anzaldúa, Gloria. 1987. "La conciencia mestiza." In *Borderlands/La Frontera: The New Mestiza.* San Francisco. Spinsters/Aunt Lute.

Arana, Sabino. 1980. "Libe." In *Obras completas.* Tomo III. Donostia: Sendoa.

Aresti, Nerea. 2001. *Médicos, Don Juanes y mujeres modernas: Los ideales de feminidad y masculinidad en el primer tercio del siglo XX.* Bilbao: UPV/EHU.

———. 2007. "Shaping the Spanish Modern Man: The Conflict of Masculine Ideals through a Court Case in the 1920s." *Feminist Studies* 33, no. 3: 606–31.

Aretxaga, Begoña. 1997. *Shattering Silence. Women, Nationalism and Political Subjectivity in Northern Ireland.* Princeton: Princeton University Press.

———. 1996. "¿Tiene sexo la nación? Nación y género en la retórica política de Irlanda." *Arenal* 3, no. 2 (July–December): 199–216. English-language version: 2005. "Does the Nation Have a Sex?" in *States of Terror: Begoña Aretxaga's Essays.* Reno: Center for Basque Studies, University of Nevada, Reno.

Blasco Herranz, Inmaculada. 2003. *Paradojas de la ortodoxia: política de masas y militancia católica femenina en España (1919–1939),* Zaragoza: Universidad de Zaragoza.

Carabias, Josefina. 1933. "¡Mujeres a votar!" *Estampa* 27 (April 22).

Condren, Mary. 1995. "Work-in-Progress. Sacrifice and Political Legitimation: The production of a Gendered Social Order." *Journal of Women's History* 6, no 4/7, no 1 (Winter/Spring):160–89.

De la Granja, José Luis, 2007. *El nacionalismo vasco. Claves de su Historia.* Madrid: Grupo Anaya.

De Pablo, Santiago, and Ludger Mees. 2005. *El péndulo patriótico: Historia del Partido Nacionalista Vasco.* Barcelona: Crítica.

Díaz Freire, José Javier, 2002. "Cuerpos en conflicto. La construcción de la identidad y la diferencia en el País Vasco a finales del siglo XIX." In *El desafío de la diferencia: Representaciones culturales e identidades de género, raza y clase,* edited by Mary Nash and Diana Marre. Bilbao: Universidad del País Vasco.

———. 1993. *La República y el Porvenir. Culturas políticas en Vizcaya durante la II República.* Donostia: Kriselu.

Ibero, Alba. 1994. "Imágenes de maternidad en la pintura barroca." In *Las mujeres en el Antiguo Régimen, Imagen y realidad,* edited by Isabel Pérez Molina, Mayte Vicent Valentín. Barcelona: Icaria.

Laqueur, Thomas. 1990. *Making Sex: Body and Gender from the Greeks to Freud.* Cambridge: Harvard University Press.

Llona, Miren. 2002. *Entre señorita y garçonne. Historia oral de las mujeres bilbainas de clase media (1919-1939).* Málaga: Universidad de Málaga.

———. 2007. "Los otros cuerpos disciplinados: relaciones de género y estrategias de autocontrol del cuerpo femenino (primer tercio del siglo XX)." *Arenal* 14, no. 1: 79–108.

Mohanty, Satya. 1997. *Literary Theory and the Claims of History: Posmodernism, Objectivity, Multicultural Politics.* Ithaca, NY: Cornell University Press.

Moraga, Cherry. 1983. *This Bridge Called My Back: Writings of Radical Women of Colour.* Albany, NY: Kitchen Table/Women of Color Press.

Morata, Eva. 2003. "La imagen de la maternidad en la España de finales del siglo XIX y principios del XX." *Arenal* 10, no. 2: 163–90.

Nash, Mary. 1993. "Maternidad, maternología y reforma eugénica en España 1900-1939." In *Historia de las mujeres en Occidente,* edited by Georges Duby and Michelle Perrot. Madrid: Taurus.

Núñez Seixas, Xosé Manuel. 1993. *Los nacionalismos en la España Contemporánea (siglos XIX y XX)*. Barcelona: Hipòtesi.

Patriarca, Silvana. 2005. "Indolence and Regeneration: Tropes and Tensions of Risorgimento Patriotism." *American Historical Review* 110, no. 2: 380–408.

Sota, Manu. 1934. *Libe*. Bilbao: Juventud Vasca.

Trabudua, Polixene. 1933. "Discurso en el Homenaje a la Madre Vasca," *Euzkadi* (Feb. 7).

———. 1997. *Crónicas de amama*. Bilbao: Fundación Sabino Arana y Emakunde.

———. 1998–99. Interviews by Miren Llona, October 10, 1998 and January 17, 1999. Ahoa: Ahozko Historiaren Artxiboa/Archivo de la Memoria, collection "Mujeres de las clases medias."

Ugalde Solano, Mercedes. 1993. *Mujeres y nacionalismo vasco. Génesis y desarrollo de Emakume Abertzale Batza (1906–1936)*. Bilbao: UPV/EHU.

Vickers, Jill, and Athanasia Vouloukos. 2007. "Changing Gender/Nation Relations: Women's Roles in Making and Restructuring the Greek Nation State." *Nationalism and Ethnic Politics* 13, no. 4: 501–38.

Warner, Marina. 1976. *Alone of All Her Sex: The Myth and the Cult of the Virgin Mary*. New York: Knopf.

Yuval-Davis, Nira. 1997. *Gender and Nation*. London: Sage Publications.

7

Spanish Cinema through its Women Directors: 1995–2005

CASILDA DE MIGUEL, LEIRE ITUARTE, and KATIXA AGIRRE

Translated by Robert Forstag

Feminism has always been interested in the way that women have been represented in different cultural texts. Cinema is no exception. For more than a century, the imaginaries created for the big screen have helped make sense of both immediate and future reality. Yet from a sociocultural standpoint the stature of movies as the most important audiovisual medium was eclipsed some time ago by television, and has lost still further ground in recent years with the arrival of new media. Surfing the web, interactive media and multimedia in its various forms within popular culture have all emerged as new entertainment options that share the stage with movies and television. Thus, the construction and transmission of images and messages regarding meanings of "being a man" or "being a woman" no longer occur exclusively through movies. Media influence has diversified, resulting in an accompanying diversification of the stereotyped patterns and models that shape modes of representing identity. Feminist film studies have both served as a platform for, and have contributed notably to developing the study of modes of representation as a means of understanding how sexual difference, gender identity, and the notion of subjects-spectators are each constructed. In an ever-changing society, these modes of representation derive from past certainties to a far greater extent than from the contemporary context surrounding their construction.

The decade between 1995 and 2005 was a period of profound transformations in the world of Spanish cinema. In an increasing number of films, women gave voice to sociocultural changes and renegotiated the terms of gender-representation politics.[1] While gender inequality is the inescapable reality of our research, we recognize the achievements of women who have attempted to break new ground in an arena that, until a very short time ago, was the exclusive domain of men. According to Fátima Arranz (2008), only 7 percent of Spanish films made between 2000 and 2006 were directed by women. Similarly, in 2006, women occupied only 24 percent of managerial positions in the media (*Informe* 2006). This extends to Spanish academic research on film theory—a field where, even in 2010, an attitude of androcentrism persists that is reluctant to consider either the creative contributions of a new crop of women filmmakers or the methodological emphases of feminist film theory. We agree with Susan Martín-Márquez's assessment that Spanish critics have paid scant attention to feminist film theory, and that Spanish film criticism in general continues to be characterized by androcentric attitudes—such as that exemplified in the denial or omission of the contribution of women to the national film industry (1999, 10).[2]

The entire notion of "Spanish cinema" remains controversial. Far from wishing to impose any rigid definition upon what the term constitutes, we prefer to embrace a more dynamic conceptualization along the lines of Burkhard Pohl and Jorg Turschmann. They contend that "any attempt to categorize Spanish cinema according to a single exclusive label would not do justice to the wide diversity represented by more than one hundred feature films per year. What continues to be described today as Spanish cinema is a mixture of traditions, strategies, and interactions of production and reception" (2007, 21).

At the level of production, to speak of "Spanish cinema" during the era of globalization is difficult, not just because the infrastructure necessary for many productions is only available outside our borders but because, in the specific case of our sample, 46 percent of the films made during the period under study have involved the participation of more than one country and, of these, 42 percent involve a Spanish component that does not exceed 30 percent. In this regard, at times the term "Spanish cinema" should be limited to either a film's setting—to its narrative

---

1. See, for example: Camí (2001); Heredero (1997, 1998, 1999); Irazabal (1996); Merino (1999); Martin-Márquez (1999); Jordan and Morgan-Tamosumas (1998); Pohl and Türschmann (2007); and Arranz (2008).

2. Nevertheless, we should still recognize the steps that are gradually being taken in this direction, including De Miguel, Olábarri, and Ituarte (2004); De Miguel, Olábarri, Ituarte, and Siles (2005); Ituarte (2007); Siles (2006a, 2006b); and Parrondo (1996).

and iconographic potential to construct imaginaries that reflect a Spanish sociohistorical and cultural specificity—or to where the film was released (to the position of the filmgoer insofar as his or her reaction to the film).

Our criterion for selecting films has generally followed the 2007 Spanish film law, which provides that in order to be a "Spanish" film: the production and creative teams must comprise 75 percent Spanish or European Union nationals; preferred language of Castilian or another official language of the Spanish state; shooting, postproduction, and laboratory work done either in Spain or an affiliated country by agreement; and films can be coproduced with foreign companies (*Boletín* 2007). We followed these guidelines, but excluded coproduced films that involved a Spanish participation of less than 30 percent and other films that—even though their length met the criterion for a feature film—were in fact collections of short films organized around a common theme.

The popular view of "Spanish cinema" has been that it has generally been reviled to the extent that critics are ignorant of its content; that despite international awards and recognition it is not widely viewed outside of the country; that films are professionally produced yet not released as they should be; and that it is unable to compete for box office receipts with American films—despite Hollywood studios mining its veins for high-budget remakes of, for example, Alejandro Amenábar's *Abre los ojos* (*Open Your Eyes*, 1997) and Nacho Vigalondo's *Los cronocrímenes* (*Time-crimes*, 2007).

Despite the difficulty in characterizing Spanish cinema, we agree with Jo Labanyi (1995, 397) that, "the postmodernist deconstruction of identity does not mean that one has to abandon all attempts at definition: rather, it means recognition of the fact that 'Spanishness' is a shifting concept, encompassing plurality and contradiction. And, above all, that identities are strategic constructions: neither inherent nor imposed, but negotiated." We therefore ask: What possible contribution does the female imaginary make to the distinctive nature of Spanish cinema? and, To what extent is a distinctive woman's perspective able to renegotiate time-worn identity landscapes?

Our focus is on the feature film production of women directors during a period when they had grown weary of "being invisible agents of the industry, of filming with lower budgets, of being relegated to obscurity, and of having to overcome more obstacles than their male colleagues" (CIMA, n.d.). An important milestone of the era studied was the creation of the Asociación de Mujeres Cineastas y de Medios Audiovisuales (CIMA, Association of Women in Film and Audiovisual Media)—in order to ameliorate the effects of gender inequality that women confront within the world of audiovisual media.

In the history of the Spanish film industry, women were practically invisible in the role of filmmaker until the late 1970s; it was this latter period that marked the beginning of a halting of this trend, and gradual increase in the output of women filmmakers. Yet the real turning point took place in the mid-1990s, with a marked rise in women directors: our research shows that the ratio of men to women directors for the 1970s was 187:1, falling to 60:1 in the 1980s, and then to 10:1 in the 1990s, while in the period 2000–5 it was 8:1. As we can see, then, while women's involvement in the Spanish film industry reached unprecedented levels in the 1990s and beyond, there is still no parity in terms of the comparative output of men and women.

Less than 3 percent of feature films produced during the history of Spanish cinema have been directed by women, and 20 percent of these cases involved a woman codirecting a film. When women have codirected a film, they have generally done so in collaboration with a man. These occasions were sometimes exceptions to a general pattern while, at other times, collaboration occurred only in one's first feature film. There are several instances of women who have worked exclusively with male partners, but who never directed a picture by themselves; for example, Margarita Alexandre (with Rafael Torrecilla) and Dunia Ayaso (with Felix Sabroso). There are many possible explanations for this: complicity, insecurity, the need to gain experience, difficulty, lack of confidence, and so on. Undoubtedly, however, during the period cited, women who both codirected and exclusively directed a film represent exceptions to the general pattern (for example, Cecilia Bartolomé, Yolanda García Serrano, and Nuria Villazán).

As regards viewership of films directed by women, there is a general lack of awareness. In fact, when typical filmgoers are asked to name Spanish female directors, only three or four names are spontaneously and repeatedly mentioned, and the names of actresses are typically much better known. Using data taken from the Spanish Ministry of Culture (www. mcu.es) on the history of women's involvement in films, however, we would suggest a reconceptualization of the role of women directors in Spanish cinema. What we see is a continuum divided into various stages, beginning with a complete absence of women directors, progressing to a small but gradually increasing presence and ending with a an ever-increasing visibility during the latter half of the 1990s.

Between the origins of Spanish cinema and the late 1940s women were largely absent from directing films. This was clearly something seen as the province of men, with some isolated exceptions such as Rosario Pí during the 1930s and the single appearances of Helena Cortesina and Jeanne "Musidora" Roques as codirectors in 1922.

From the 1950s through 1972, it is interesting to note the emergence of Ana Mariscal as perhaps the only Spanish woman director who could be considered to have had a continuous career in film, directing ten feature films between 1953 and 1968. Another pioneer who shared the spotlight with her during this period was Margarita Alexandre who, between 1953 and 1957, co-directed three feature films with Rafael Torrecilla. Women's invisibility in the role of film director during this period was an emblematic reflection of the silence and ostracism to which women were subjected in public, intellectual, and artistic life during Franco's dictatorship.

The period from 1973 to 1983 is notable for the appearance of the first class of women graduates of the Escuela Oficial de Cinematografía (Official School of Cinematography): Josefina Molina, Pilar Miró, and Cecilia Bartolomé. Molina made her directorial debut with *Vera, un cuento cruel* (*Vera, A Cruel Story*, 1973), Miró with *La petición* (*The Request*, 1976), and Bartolomé with *Vámonos, Bárbara* (*Let's Go, Barbara*, 1978). The emergence of these three directors marks the true beginning of women's efforts to project their own cinematic vision from a place behind the camera.

From 1983 to 1995, there was a gradual increase in the number of female directors. In addition to those who had already established their careers, individuals of diverse backgrounds appeared on the scene, and their emergence provided additional momentum to women's increasingly important role. Among the most notable of this new generation were Isabel Coixet, Ana Diez, Pilar Távora, Rosa Vergés, Chus Gutierrez, Gracia Querejeta, Arantxa Lazkano, Maite Ruiz de Austri, and Mirentxu Purroy. This marked increase can be traced to the appointment of Pilar Miró as general director of cinematography by the new socialist government in 1983. This lead to what is known as the "Miró decree," which proclaimed a preference for quality over quantity, and the further professionalization of production. This logically resulted in a decrease in production (919 films were made throughout the 1980s compared to 1,140 in the 1970s), but at the same time it lent support to new filmmakers, and resulted in a considerable increase in the number of women who made their feature-film directorial debuts—including some who appeared as directors for the first time in any capacity whatsoever.

These precedents helped lay the groundwork for the relative explosion of women directors during the period 1995–2005, when women directed no less than 124 feature films. Equally unprecedented was the range of directors represented. Some of these—such as Miró, Bartolomé, and Vera Belmont—already had three or more feature films under their belt prior to 1995. Others who had had some previous experience came of age as directors during this time, including the aforementioned Coixet, Diez, Vergés, Querejeta, Gutierrez, and Ruiz de Austri, as well as Marta Balletbó, Azucena Rodríguez, Iciar Bollain, Dunia Ayaso, Yolanda García Serrano, María Ripoll, Laura Maña, and Patricia Ferreira. Yet the majority of women directors represented during this period made their directorial debuts.[3]

A number of factors help explain this surge of new women directors. Start-up grants designed to finance new directors's projects provided a strong incentive for relatively new and first-time directors. Moreover, the new Escuela de Cinematografía (ECAM, School of Cinematography), established in 1995, provided a suitable educational framework for the development of the profession. In addition, the period witnessed the proliferation of university communications programs that attracted large numbers of students who wanted to break into the film industry. The percentage of women who received training in these departments was only slightly less than that of men, and thus the increasing incorporation of women into the industry was a logical consequence.

The flourishing of women's involvement in film production after 1995 therefore appears to be the logical result of a slow and gradual evolution that paralleled the progressive improvement in women's social conditions in general. The history of Spanish cinema reflects the historical burden

3. Directing debuts were made by Dolores Payás, Mireia Ros, Eva Lesmes, Manane Rodríguez, Pilar Távora, Pilar Sueiro, Daphna Kastner, María Miró, Lisa Alessandrini, Nuria Villazan, Charlotte de Tuckheim, Helena Taberna, Judith Colell, Isabel Gardela, María Novaro, María de Medeiros, Susana Seideman, Beatriz Flores Silva, Inés Paris, Daniela Fejerman, Lidia Zimmermann, María Lidon, Angeles Gonzalez Sinde, Silvia Munt, Silvia Quer, Dominique Abel, Margarita Ledo, Teresa de Pelegri, Mary McGulkian, Ana Pérez, Mata Arribas, Susana Koska, Lucrecia Martel, Mercedes Segovia, Mercedes Alvarez, Julia Solomonoff, Elisabeth Cabeza, Lola Salvador, Dolores Payás. Ana Murugarren, Ariadna Pujol, Lola Guerrero, Julia Montejo, Mar Targarona, Mónica Laguna, Eugenia Kléber, Cecilia Barriga, Jana Bokova, Nely Reguera, and Farida B. Amor.

of Spanish society's patriarchal culture—a culture in which women were initially relegated to invisibility and then allowed to work in the shadows, before being granted a limited presence and then gradually emerging as a true force to be reckoned with in the film industry.

The result of this is a cinema where women representing different generations and of varying backgrounds and education all have a place, and there is no one specific "school" or grouping. Some of these women have combined academic and practical experience. Others have burst onto the scene during economically favorable times. Still others are more or less established directors, some of them protégées of figures who are widely renowned within the industry.[4] What they have in common is their role as women directors.

There is, however, one remarkable common denominator among the widely diverse spectrum of films that comprises "women's cinema" within the period under consideration: the tendency to portray female subjectivity as a central and differential element of cinematographic narration. This is an element as logical as it is revealing if we take account of the fact that that the conventional cinematographic narrative (and "conventional" is here synonymous with "male") typically constructs female identity on the basis of a representation of women as "objects" rather than "subjects" of cinematographic depiction. To the extent to which, in many of these films, female discourse and the representation of women as subjects (as active constructors of their own stories) takes center stage, it is the male universe that becomes identified as "the other." There is a role reversal, and men come to occupy the discursive space traditionally reserved for women. We would therefore expect that, despite the enormous diversity of stories and the disparity among the different narrative and esthetic depictions characterized by the group of films in question, there would remain a number of constants—a leading female role in the cinematographic narrative, a portrayal of female subjectivity, desire, and fantasy as part of the narrative discourse, a predominance of female characters' perspectives, and female activism—that all transgress the cinematographic narrative conventions of patriarchal discourse.

But what exactly do we mean when we refer to "women's cinema"? This is a difficult question to answer, and one that has generated a fair

---

4. This is the case, for example, for *A mi madre le gustan las mujeres* (My Mother Likes Women), by Daniela Fejerman and Inés París. The film was produced by Pedro Almodóvar, who was credited as director of the film in Italy and other countries. See París (2007).

amount of debate throughout the course of feminist film theory. In order to properly frame the complexity of the term and the debate it has raised, Alison Butler contends that "women's cinema is a notoriously difficult concept to define. It suggests, without clarity, films that might be made by, addressed to, or concerned with women, or all three. It is neither a genre nor a movement in film history, it has no . . . filmic or aesthetic specificity, but traverses and negotiates cinematic and cultural traditions, and critical and political debates" (2002, 1).

Without losing sight of either the complexity or the difficulty implicit in the term, the label "women's cinema" we employ here primarily concerns a sample of films directed by women but designed for a wide audience. The term as we use it therefore clearly represents an inversion of Mary Ann Doane's notion of the "woman's film," understood as a subgenre of films belonging to the traditional category of melodrama, and designed primarily for female audiences while generally being directed by men (1987, 3). Despite this terminological discrepancy, our example continues to share with the general categorization of "women's cinema" one important characteristic: a kind of cinema that, to some extent, tends to transgress the habitual mechanisms of point of view, fascination, and spectacle of the active traditional cinematographic narrative, which is designed to gratify the erotic expectations of the male filmgoer.

What definitely appears beyond question is the fact that our notion of "women's cinema" in no way consists of films that are designed for an exclusively female audience. It is clear that neither critics nor distributors use this label, and it is equally clear that neither places any special emphasis on the fact that a film has been directed by a woman. This may be owing to purely commercial considerations. Women directors themselves have stated that what they strive for is a personal kind of film that retains a commercial appeal; a kind of film that generally gives pride of place to women's stories—not from a combative feminist perspective, or from any intention to create a kind of auteur cinema, but rather within the very context of commercial cinema. Women directors further contend that they have sought to appeal to the interests and values of filmgoers. Still, within the diversity that characterizes the filmography of the period under consideration, there are isolated cases of very personal films that seem to fall within the tradition of auteur cinema. In any event, the directors in question do not seem to be overly preoccupied with labels. In the words of Inés Paris, director, screenwriter, and CIMA president, "What is important is that there is film and that there are images created by women, and that each woman says whatever she wants to without fear of being excluded because of the fact that she is a woman" (2007).

We also need to get away from the kind of mindset that attempts to impose a single perspective. It would be a mistake to study the woman director as some sort of generic category and thus neglect the individuality of each filmmaker. Such a framework has in the past been both confusing and unfair: confusing because it ignores the contributions of individuals and unfair because it reduces the complex role of women in the production of films to a relatively small number of names.

Women directors also do not identify with a "national cinema." Instead, they defend their right to tell the stories that they want to tell. In the words of Isabel Coixet, "My films, whether Spanish or American, are my own, and that is that. . . . I like my country. I like my city—Barcelona. But through the films that I make, I am not expressing this or that specific language or the reality of a particular country, but rather my own vision" (Agencia EFE 2003).

With women now having achieved visibility, the time has arrived to begin the struggle for parity, for while it is true that there are now more women directors than ever making films (González Sinde 2008), they continue to constitute a small proportion of directors as a whole.[5] Directing films in Spain is complicated for everyone, but it is especially difficult for women. Salary disparities that affect women in other professional fields are also a feature of the film industry. It is harder for women to carry out their projects, and to obtain high budgets for the films that they want to make. It appears to still be the case that women directors inspire less confidence than their male counterparts. For this reason the film law includes a section that reads: "In addition, it will be determined whether a project has applied measures related to gender equality with respect to the creative activities involving the direction and the screenplay" (*Boletín* 2007, section 3a, article 25). The application of the equality law within the audiovisual sector, promoting rights to equal access for women, has brought about opportunities for women on boards of directors, committees, and other decision-making bodies. In this context, 1995 represented a turning point in the heightened visibility of women, but in 2005 it remained to be seen whether these advances would turn into full equality.

---

5. In 2006, 150 feature films were produced. Only seven were directed by women and, of these seven, four represented directorial debuts.

References

Agencia EFE. 2003. "Isabel Coixet presenta en la Berlinale la producción hispano-canadiense *Mi vida sin mí*," in *El País Digital,* February 10.

Arranz, Fátima. 2008. *Mujeres y hombres en el cine español (2000–2006).* Estudio realizado para el Instituto de la Mujer.

Boletín Oficial de las Cortes Generales. 2007. Congreso de Diputados. Vlll Legislatura, serie A: proyectos de ley, June 8, 2007, no. 138-1.

Butler, Alison. 2002. *Women's Cinema: The Contested Screen.* London and New York: Wallflower. Short Cuts Collection.

Camí, Vela M. 2001. *Mujeres detrás de la cámara. Entrevistas con cineastas españolas de la década de los 90.* Madrid: Ocho y Medio. CIMA (Asociación de Mujeres Cineastas y de Medios Audiovisuales). n.d. See www.cimamujerescineastas.es.

De Miguel, Casilda, Elena Olábarri, and Leire Ituarte. 2004. *La identidad de género en la imagen fílmica.* Bilbao: UPV/EHU.

De Miguel, Casilda, Elena Olábarri, Leire Ituarte, and Begoña Siles. 2005. *La identidad de género en la imagen televisiva.* Madrid: Servicio Editorial Instituto de la Mujer.

Doane, Mary Anne. 1987. *The Desire to Desire: The Woman's Film of the 1940s.* Bloomington & Indianapolis: Indiana University Press.

González Sinde, Angeles. 2008. Interview by Inma Flor, "En el cine español está en crisis el sistema de financiación." In *Público.es,* January 28.

Heredero, Carlos F. 1999. *Veinte nuevos directores del cine español.* Madrid: Alianza.

—— ed. 1998. *La mitad del cielo, directoras españolas de los años noventa.* Málaga: 1º Festival de Cine Español de Málaga.

—— 1997. *Espejo de miradas: entrevistas con nuevos directoras del cine español de los años noventa.* Alcalá de Henares: 27º Festival de Cine de Alcalá de Henares.

Informe anual de la profesión periodística. 2006. Madrid: Delegación de Publicaciones de la Asociación de Prensa de Madrid.

Irazabal, Martin C. 1996. *Alice, sí está. Directoras de cine europeas y norteamericanas (1896–1996).* Madrid: Horas y Horas.

Ituarte, Leire. 2007. *El imaginario posmoderno de la feminidad en la filmografía de Juanma Bajo Ulloa y Julio Medem.* Bilbao: UPV/EHU.

Jordan, Barry, and Rikki Morgan-Tamosunas. 1998. *Contemporary Spanish Cinema*. Manchester: Manchester University Press.

Labanyi, Jo. 1995. "Postmodernism and the Problem of Cultural Identity." In *Spanish Cultural Studies: An Introduction*, edited by Helen Graham and Jo Labanyi. Oxford: Oxford University Press.

Martin-Márquez, Susan. 1999. *Feminist Discourse and Spanish Cinema*. Oxford: Oxford University Press.

Merino, Azucena. 1999. *Diccionario de mujeres directoras*. Madrid: Ediciones JC.

Paris, Inés. 2007. Interview, "Lo importante es que haya cine e imágenes creadas por mujeres, y que cada una cuente lo que le dé la gana sin ser excluida por ser mujer," Ameco Press (July 17). At www.amecopress.net/spip.php?article210.

Parrondo, Eva. 1996. *Feminidad y mascarada en "Lo que el viento se llevó" y "Jezabel"*. Valencia: Edit. Episteme.

Pohl, Burkhard, and Jörg Türschmann, eds. 2007. *Miradas glocales: cine español en el cambio de milenio*. Madrid: Iberoamericana Editorial / Vervuert.

Siles, Begoña. 2006a. *La mirada de la mujer y la mujer mirada (En torno al cine de Pilar Miró)*. Bilbao: UPV/EHU.

———. 2006b. *Pilar Miró, creadora audiovisual (1940–1997)*. Colección Biblioteca de Mujeres, nº 72. Madrid: Ediciones del Orto.

8

Matriarchy versus Equality:
From Mari to Feminist Demands

Carmen Díez Mintegui and Margaret Bullen

Translated by Jesus Sepúlveda and Jeffrey M. Petrie

Various analyses (del Valle et al. 1985; del Valle 2002; Diez Mintegui 1999b) show changes in the gender system and the situation of women in Basque society since the Franco decades, when conservative ideology relegated the feminine collective to the domestic realm. However, the social facts and figures show that Basque society is still clearly a male-dominated society in all spheres of power and social prestige. In this context, it is remarkable that the notion of a Basque matriarchy survives and is defended, especially in the realm of nationalist ideology. This chapter studies the reasons for this persistence through a study of the relationship between the myth and a mythical figure, Mari; its possible interpretations; and the role that the myth plays in the elaboration of Basque nationalism and culture. We start from the basis that matriarchy is one of the fundamental and differentiating myths of "Basqueness" that, in relation to other myths—such as that of being a specific race, which has been questioned throughout the twentieth century—remains a basic building block of national identity.

The survival of this belief in a matriarchal order that ultimately does not question the establishment is the reason why many women of all ages defend traditions that only allow them prominence at the margins of real and symbolic power, but provides them a certain prestige. In this sense, the main characteristics of this myth, which are fundamental pillars of Basque culture, can be more attractive to many women than other newer alternatives.

The image of a supposed goddess, Mari, is built on the basis of mythology mainly gathered by the Basque ethnographer, Joxemiel de Barandiarán. These myths concerned the Mother goddess and the Earth, which were present in the origin of a prehistoric Basque religion. This goes along with the representation of the strong Basque woman, connected to the idea that women endure through time, like caryatids who sustain the social structure, whose base is firmly set in the soil and who are one with the Earth itself.[1] This representation has two cultural pillars common to the Basque Country: *ama lurra*—Mother Earth—and *etxea*—the house as a physical home and as a metaphor for the people.

All these topics have been the object of a number of analyses in traditional Basque ethnology, among which those of Barandiarán (1889–1991) and Julio Caro Baroja (1914–95) stand out, and there is important ideological and theoretical support to maintain this myth.[2] Moreover, the existence of a Basque matriarchy is defended in public and private circles, especially whenever the topic of women's inequality comes up and during moments of crisis and calls for change.

Matriarchy: Origin Myth, Justification of the Present

European industrialization and new models of the social and sexual division of labor, as well as the modern nation-state were already consolidated by the second half of the nineteenth century. These developed simultaneously with racial theories from the new fields of physical and cultural anthropology and evolution that reconstructed the origin and history of humanity. These perspectives served to legitimize supposed Western superiority and its colonial imposition, as well as social orders and Western family models based on monogamy and patriarchal authority (considered a superior form of organization resulting from Western progress). Moreover, most evolutionist authors defended the matriarchal order as the primordial form of family social organization The Basque context was also one of significant industrialization where physical anthropology had selected the supposed "Basque race" as one of its topics of study. As anthropologist Joseba Zulaika (1996) has shown all these aspects had a marked effect on the elaboration of Basque nationalism and identity.

---

1. Anthropologist Dolores Juliano (1993) utilizes the image of caryatids to refer to how in many analytical models women are structural supports, without being the object of any questioning or explanation.

2. In English, see Barandiarán (2007) and Caro Baroja (2009).

The role gender has in the process of nation-building has been discussed by several women authors,[3] and it had already been taken into account in the first anthropological study to use a critical feminist approach regarding the situation of women in the Basque Country (del Valle et al. 1985). This research confirmed that Basque nationalism had "coined an image of Basque women that has had great historical influence" (226). By exploring "historical nationalism," from its beginnings with Sabino Arana (the founder of Basque nationalism) during the second half of the nineteenth century until 1936—when the Spanish Civil War broke out—and following the emergence of the radical nationalism of ETA (Euskadi Ta Askatasuna, Basque Country and Freedom) in 1958, there were both ruptures and continuities within these two versions.

In historical nationalism, the concept of woman was traditionalist and influenced by Catholicism: "the role of the mother stands out, the strong mother capable of holding everything together and sorting everything out, an organizer mother capable of keeping the house in order and having everything ready, but also a mother who looks after the faith of her children and the maintenance of traditional and moral order" (del Valle et al. 1985, 253). In the case of ETA, which defined itself as a secular movement, many religious elements disappeared from nationalist thinking and even, in its first documents, any explicit allusions to the image of women. It was not until 1965, in its "Letter to Basque intellectuals," that this image appeared in an ambivalent declaration. This reinforced a line of continuity from the original nationalism, linking women to their role of wife and mother, yet it also stated that Basque women should "enjoy the same rights and possibilities as men in all sectors of political, social, economic and cultural life."[4] However, this declaration was censored in the second edition of the letter, showing that it was a controversial and difficult topic. ETA's nationalism was more concerned with social changes than with its own internal dynamics. It also existed in the unconditional support and emotional balance linked to affective and family ties, where women played a fundamental role, always in the private or symbolic realms (del Valle et al. 1985, 226–56; Aretxaga 1988).

Women's attributes constitute a fundamental pillar in the origins of nationalist thinking and its relationship with the myth of matriarchy.

---

3. A review of this literature can be found in Bullen and Diez (2008).

4. "Carta a los intelectuales vascos," first edition, published in *Documentos* (1979) vol. 3, 279–87. The second version is found in vol. 3, pages 501 et seq. This is also cited in del Valle et al. (1985, 235n3).

Maternity, and the mother's transmission of language and culture, plays a central role in both traditional and radical nationalist thought. However, contrary to traditional societies under male power—whose origin myths allude to a remote time in which women had power but lost it because they did not know how to manage it (Bamberger 1974)—in the Basque version the myth stresses that the change toward a patriarchal order was a consequence of an exterior imposition, and that women continue having power, although this is domestic rather than public. In short, real women control and organize the life of men who are under their "protection," although not on equal terms with men.[5]

We can thus see how this myth has played a role supportive of Basque nationalism. We can also begin to understand its persistence in a modern and advanced society where the idea of gender equality exists. Because nation-building is a dynamic process, our hypothesis is that in being confronted by modern, industrialized, and developed Basque society, it remains more or less hidden. It is an ideal based on a romanticized model of a rural society where egalitarianism, lack of conflict, and harmonious family and neighborhood relationships are the main identity markers. In modern Basque society, then, there is a tension between reality and what no longer exists but seems to be recoverable for the defence of certain ideas. Women are crucial, under the supposition of the survival of a matriarchal order, in the nation-building process and the Basque ideal. Linked to that, the figure of Mari seems to be a key element because of her versatility and possible interpretations.

The Matriarch Mari versus the Transgressor Mari

Barandiarán was the main compiler, between 1918 and 1925, of narratives related to the character Mari (1972). In these stories, it is interesting to note how the similarities between the representations of genies such as *laminak*, *sorginak*,[6] and the figure of Mari disappear. Little given to interpretation in his work as a whole, the author establishes a hierarchical relationship in which Mari appears in mythology as a *numen* or main chief, an Earth goddess, a complex figure, "a thematic nucleus of or point of convergence for numerous mythic themes of different origins . . . a symbol—perhaps a

---

5. See Oscar Terol (2009) for more on this "power."
6. *Laminak* are mythological female characters. On these, see Xamar (2006, 54). *Sorginak* are also mythological figures, midwives and healers, later seen as "witches." See Bullen (2003a, 146).

personification—of the earth" (Barandiaran 2007, 107) that he attributes to a supposed pre-Christian Basque religion—a kind of "Matriarchalist" religion. Barandiarán, who besides being an anthropologist was also a Catholic priest, even coined the name "Mari." He himself indicated that he had chosen that name to facilitate understanding of his argument, faced as he was with the multiple names she had, typically Madame, Lady, or Anderea, together with the toponym of the place she was associated with.[7] For Barandiarán, this myth and the characteristics surrounding it is the paradigm for discovering past Basque culture.

After Barandiarán, many and varied interpretations have been made that are too many to be presented here; instead, we will focus on some of the most important in terms of our thesis.[8] Caro Baroja dated the legends and myths of Mari and the other female figures in the context of European social change and the Basque Country between the fifteenth and eighteenth centuries, taking into account that the ancien régime had lasted more or less time in specific places. According to Caro Baroja, at this time "Satanism" dominated, but after centuries of persecution, by the nineteenth and twentieth centuries, the image of Satan had faded away and witches had emerged presided over by a female being identified with different names as noted above.[9]

Nevertheless, and using the same materials, the philosopher and hermeneutical scholar Andrés Ortiz de Osés (in collaboration with Franz Karl Mayr, 1981) elaborated—from a Jungian perspective, in a moment of upheaval and crisis in Spanish and Basque society after the end of Franco's dictatorship—an explanation that situated the existence of a matriarchal culture in the Paleolithic. This culture would have disappeared because of strong acculturation triggered by the penetration of power forms with patriarchal characteristics belonging to the Neolithic. For Ortiz de Osés, the survival of this matriarchal substrate—a female archetype—in the collective unconsciousness was a continual source of conflict in the Basque psyche. According to this, matriarchal culture became reality personifying itself through the figure of the *etxekoandre* (woman of the house in Euskara), a Basque woman related to the rural world and the home (*etxe*). This perspective was, however, challenged and criticized as much because

---

7. For more on this topic, see Anuntzi Arana (1996).

8. See Diez Mintegui (1999a and n.d.). For an English commentary on Diez Mintegui's article (1999a) see Bullen (2003a, 146–150).

9. See Caro Baroja's essays, 'El mundo mítico del campesino vasco-navarro" and "La imagen del mal" (1972, vol. 2, 289–307, and vol. 3, 393–415; 1985).

of its theoretical implications as its "political" opportunism (Aranzadi 1982; del Valle et al. 1985).

From a very different perspective, the anthropologist Teresa del Valle analyzed the situation of Basque women through their use of distinct spaces (the home, the festival, and death.) Observing mythic space through the figure Mari, she points out that "we need to find the meaning of Mari beyond her being female and beyond being the Earth symbol" (1983, 264).

Another interesting argument is that of Jakue Pascual and Alberto Peñalva (1999), who focus their interpretation on continuous rebellion (including both Mari and the punk subculture, which was an important feature of Basque society in the 1980s[10]) against the imposition of empire (Rome, Spanish Catholicism, or the New World Order). They insist on the necessity of analyzing Basque history and culture within the framework of relationships of conflict and bonding, both within the community as well as externally. These frameworks and contexts must be situated in relation to the consolidation of the European state-building process, from the late fifteenth century to the present. For Pascual and Peñalva, the early sixteenth-century Inquisition (charged with the persecution of witchcraft in the Basque Country) was an instrument to stop domestic dissidence. In other words, men and women accused of witchcraft could have easily been groups of "refuseniks"[11] opposed to the dogmatic moral commandments of the Catholic Church and of the monarchy on the Spanish side of the border (or French judiciary on the other), which clashed with a communal and unitarian mentality vis-à-vis work, ritual life, family care, and sexual practices.

Historian Gustav Henningsen (1980) underlines the importance of understanding the context in which seventeenth-century witches were hunted in Zugarramurdi and Urdazubi (Urdax), two small Navarrese towns near the French border. Although it is difficult to reconstruct the mentality of the time because it was basically an illiterate society and the elites did not record the events, we know the persecutions were real. It seems logical, therefore, when analyzing the information at hand, to speculate about the meaning of female figures who permanently transgressed societal norms.

Along these lines, we believe the myth of Mari contains all possible forms of real or imaginary contradiction and tension, and that the differ-

10. See Juan Porras Blanco (2005).

11. Noncompliance movements have appeared in distinct historical moments in the Basque Country. The most recent took place during the 1990s with regards to obligatory military service.

ent legends are responses to human and social problems connected with religion, medical practices, labor activity, and sexuality. In this feminist reading, the main characteristics of Mari are negation, disobedience, the adoption of multiple forms, the union of male and female, a capacity to be both inside and outside of the home, and the ability to perform many and very different activities. Such characteristics resemble the most radical forms of some feminist proposals.

The hegemonic model of the "bourgeois woman" that emerged in twelfth-century Europe but was not consolidated until the nineteenth century gave rise along the way to antimodels such as "witches, sorceresses, prostitutes, and other women who live badly" (Varela 1997, 125). As Varela points out, persecuted and controlled women have had—especially in the collective imagination of the lower classes—both positive and negative powers. Thus, the oral narratives compiled by Barandiarán could easily have been examples of reinterpreting or inventing a reality that differed from that imposed by the cultural mandates of the time.

In an earlier work (Diez 1999a), a parallel was drawn between Mari and the androgynous protagonist of Virginia Woolf's novel *Orlando* (1923). Orlando, crossing various centuries from Elizabeth I's time to the twentieth century, had lived first as a man and then as a woman. Despite the transformation, Woolf points out that Orlando is the same person and the sex change modifies his/her future but not his/her identity. In this same sense, the myth of Mari can be interpreted as a challenge to the dualistic proposals and cultural mandates that restrict the multiple possibilities of being a person.[12] However, societies as a whole do not easily accept revolutionary proposals. In the following section we study the controversy surrounding gender participation in the *alardes*[13] of Irun and Hondarribia as understood conflict whose complexity demonstrates the interplay between tradition and change and their specific influence on gender relationships and roles.

The *Alardes* of Irun and Hondarribia

A recent gender-based study on Gipuzkoa's festivals shows the difficulties and obstacles women have in participating in the main events of tradi-

---

12. We agree with Donna Haraway (1991), who observes that two genders are too many, and one not enough.

13. *Alardes* are festivals based on military-style parades.

tional celebrations in many places (Farapi 2009). However, the *alardes* of Irun and Hondarribia have provoked the greatest festival-related controversy in the Basque Country since 1995.

The ritualized acts of festivals are a symbolic condensation on many levels. The parenthesis that festivals imply supposedly produces a break with existing norms and values in everyday life and thus hinders an appreciation of what happens there in terms of discriminatory and unequal relations. This is how women's demands for equal participation in the central acts of the festivals—the parades—has been interpreted in these towns from a conservative point of view, popularly known as *betiko* (literally "always"); a reference to supporters of Irungo Betiko Alardearen Aldekoak/Defensores del Alarde Tradicional de Irun (Defenders of Irun's Traditional Alarde).[14]

Alardes consist of parades of companies from different neighborhoods or organizations. People dress in simple outfits that recall former local militias, traditional marches are played and gun salvos are fired at given moments. In Hondarribia's display around four thousand people participate, divided in twenty companies, and in Irun's display there are around eight thousand participants, who form nineteen companies. Each company chooses a *cantinera* (historically, a serving girl who accompanied troops on their campaigns, serving them from the canteen), a role that can only be played once in a lifetime. This was the only female role until 1995, when a group of about fifty women, supported by a few men, demanded the right to participate as "soldiers." At first there was a formal petition, but when this was denied mixed groups tried to participate in 1996, infiltrating the parades. In both municipalities the opposing reaction was severe; physical and verbal violence broke out during the celebration, and it continued via different forms of harassment for months and even years later.[15] The controversy created an internal social conflict of unforeseen proportions, which has lasted until 2010.

A key explanation of why the majority traditionalist position has been so strong in both towns can be traced to the rulings of the Basque Supreme Court and of the city halls and their respective mayors. The two towns have eluded all responsibility for the matter by privatizing this publicly funded celebration, thus avoiding any legal obligation to not dis-

---

14. For an English summary of events to that date, see Bullen (1999).
15. On this conflict's violence, see Bullen and Diez (2002).

criminate on the basis of gender when organizing public acts. Further, in July 2008 the Basque Supreme Court ruled that, according to the Law of Public Shows and Recreational Activities, the traditional *alarde* is not discriminatory, since it is a private rather than public act, and is therefore not required to include women. Between legal rulings and political to-ing and fro-ing, in 1997 Irun began celebrating two *alardes*: a traditional one (with only one woman as the *cantinera* in each company) and a mixed one (with the same number of women and men). In 2009 the mixed *alarde* included around one thousand people distributed in nine companies, and a woman, for the first time, occupied the post of general. Similarly, the mixed company Jaizkibel is also demanding integration into the traditional *alarde* of Hondarribia.

The vehement reaction to the inclusion of women in the *alardes* is multifaceted and has to be analyzed as a "total social fact" in order to capture its complexity. The explanation rests as much in the relationship between the gender system and the symbolic and cultural system, as with the intersection of the structural axes within politics and socioeconomics. Writing when the conflict first broke out, Carmen Diez (1996) underscores the importance of perceiving this controversy as an "ethnographic emergency," an event that shines light on an aspect of social reality that has been hidden or overlooked. In this way, the adverse reaction toward women's participation in the *alardes* reveals resistance, at a profound level, to women's access to all power positions in our society.

As far as the analysis of the confluence of social, economic, and political structures is concerned, del Valle (1997, 89–94) sees the outbreak of the conflict as a consequence of Spain being part of the European Union and the subsequent elimination of the border with France, and specifically the effect of this on Irun. In short, a period of economic transformation, employment loss, and social insecurity coincided with a call for change in the most emblematic event of the city's festivals. Del Valle argues that the climate of instability in everyday life had provoked attachment to tradition, to "the old way" and to "that which is ours" in the face of globalizing and homogenizing forces coming from abroad.[16]

This controversy has been studied from many perspectives: historical (Estornés 1996; Kerexeta 2001) and sociological (Moreno and Kerexeta 2005) for example. All shed light on understanding the conflict, as well as

---

16. See Bullen (2003b).

the political and power interests that have managed to continue to deny female participation. A significant majority of people in Irun and Hondarribia are against women's participation as soldiers, including women of all ages and social levels whose positions are among the most belligerent. This is one of the most difficult issues of the conflict to explain (Bullen and Egido 2004, 228–34; Díez 2003). However, if we recall the myth of matriarchy, we may find an important clue to understanding women's resistance to change in the *alardes*.

The defense of the traditional *alarde* is based on extolling the role of women from Irun and Hondarribia as the true "Basque woman": powerful, the head of her house and kitchen, independent and autonomous, whom nobody can tell what to do or how to do it. She is the matriarch, the mother who not only keeps the house and her family, but the spiritual and social order. The *betiko* women defend their decision to remain out of the parade and take a place with the public on the sidewalks applauding; to be—in Virginia Woolf's words—the "flattering mirrors" of their men. They defend a social order that gives them prestige and honor, but without access to the power of the public space nor inclusion in the symbolic center. The *cantinera* is also the traditional model of a woman who accepts a position created by a hegemonic and androcentric society. She is the woman as object, the woman desired, molded according to the precepts of beauty decided on by men and honored by all society.

Women who participate or defend the mixed *alarde* are socially punished or ostracized. They are branded as everything that is seen as the anathema of the matriarch or the beautiful and submissive woman: they are "ugly," "bitter," "lesbians," or "whores." They are disobedient, transgressors, they are "different" and given to wearing a man's uniform and doing the same things men do as much in everyday life as during the festivals. These women are accused of not having emotions, of not "feeling" the *alarde*; otherwise it is inexplicable why they would want to change it. They are accused of being coarse, subversive, ready to destroy the celebration and step on others' feelings to please their own whims.

Different interpretations of the Mari myth are embodied in these diverse models of women and they conflict with each other. However, while one model confronts the establishment, the other one accepts it. Thus, both groups function as active subjects that demand a particular way of being and participating in society. From the beginning of the conflict, traditionalist women have been key players in the consolidation of what they consider "their *alarde*" (resistance strategies, preparations for the privatized parade, fundraising). They also demand their recognition as women, with the right to decide where they want to be in the festival and in society. They have known how to engage with current narratives about women's empowerment and have acquired a new impetus. They have mobilized to organize celebratory dinners for former *cantineras* and tributes to the female veterans, creating their own associations in connection with the traditional displays while fostering new traditions. One of the most notable activities this collective undertakes is the "torch parade," organized by the Pagoki association since 1997 to represent the peripheral participation of women in the history of the *alardes* without usurping the central role of men in the main parade.[17] Here, the organizers emphasize the Irun women's initiative, authority, and control as a clear response to the image conveyed in which traditionalist women remain submissive and reactionary. They argue that while men were fighting the war, women were at home managing their duties, thus refuting the notion that women who defend tradition are under men's control (Bullen and Diez 2008, 91). The conflict over the *alardes* reflects different potential interpretations of the myth of Mari and its models of social formation: Mari the matriarch, capable of recovering lost power, defending a threatened tradition, and a hierarchical social order, or Mari the transgressor, ready to overcome imposed limits and increase her powers, in order to create a new system where gender and other differences are no longer the basis upon which unequal relationships are sustained.

In Irun and Hondarribia, confrontations continue—along with the analyses—since it remains a challenge to keep looking for explanations that might help understand the reasons behind attitudes that maintain androcentric gender relationships. In reality, we need to understand that women are not at the center of real and symbolic power, as the festive celebrations want us to believe. The relegation of women is the result of their inclusion in gender systems that serve to regularize hierarchical relationships, which are accepted because they have been normalized. This analysis is valid not only for these localities, but can also be extended to other places and contexts, both in their festive and symbolic aspects as well as in the everyday life of labor, chores, and leisure. In this case, any

---

17. The story goes that, faced with a combined Franco-German invasion, the men of Irun distributed torches to women and children and sent them to march by night along the Camino Real (the main highway) so that the invaders would believe that the army of Irun was going in that direction, thus allowing the men a surprise attack that routed the invaders. This nocturnal march takes place the night before the main parade.

reinterpretation of the myth of Mari, in the light of current contexts and conflicts, reinforces arguments against the immutable character of certain traditions. If on the other hand, one accepts that the myth is a representation of rebellion, its facility to condense social and historic situations is very interesting.

References

Arana, Anuntzi. 1996. "Mari, mairu eta beste." *Bulletin du Musée Basque* 146: 161–66.

Aranzadi, Juan. 1982. *Milenarismo vasco.* Madrid: Taurus.

Aretxaga, Begoña. 1988. *Los funerales en el nacionalismo radical vasco.* Donostia-San Sebastián: La Primitiva Casa Baroja.

Bamberger, Joan. 1974. "The Myth of Matriarchy: Why men Rule in Primitive Society." In *Women, Culture and Society*, edited by Michelle Zimbalist Rosaldo and Louise Lamphere. Stanford: Stanford University Press.

Barandiarán, Joxemiel. 1972. *Obras Completas. Diccionario Ilustrado de Mitología Vasca.* Volume 1. Bilbao: Editorial La Gran Enciclopedia Vasca.

———. 2007. *Selected Writings of José Miguel de Barandiarán: Basque Prehistory and Ethnography.* Translated by Frederick H. Fornoff, Linda White, and Carys Evans-Corrales. Introduction by Jesús Altuna. Reno: Center for Basque Studies, University of Nevada, Reno.

Bullen, Margaret. 1999. "Gender and Identity in the *Alardes* of Two Basque Towns." In *Basque Cultural Studies*, edited by William A. Douglass, Carmelo Urza, Linda White, and Joseba Zulaika. Reno: Basque Studies Program, University of Nevada, Reno.

———. 2003a. *Basque Gender Studies.* Reno: Center for Basque Studies, University of Nevada, Reno.

———. 2003b. "Transformaciones socio-culturales y la recreación de una fiesta." "Las culturas de la ciudad 2," *Zainak* 24: 937–52.

Bullen, Margaret, and Carmen Diez. 2002. "Violencia y cambio de culturas androcéntricas." Barcelona: Actas del IX Congreso de Antropología de la FAAEE, September 4–7.

———. 2008. "Fisiones / fusiones. Mujeres, feminismos y orden social." In *Feminismos en la Antropología. Nuevas propuestas críticas*, edited by Liliana Suárez et al. Donostia-San Sebastián: Ankulegi.

Bullen, Margaret, and José Antonio Egido. 2004. *Tristes espectáculos: Las mujeres y los Alardes de Hondarribia e Irún*. Bilbao: UPV/EHU.

Caro Baroja, Julio. 1972. *Etnografía Histórica de Navarra*. Volumes 2 and 3. Iruña: Aranzadi.

———. 1985. *Mitos vascos y mitos sobre los vascos*. Donostia-San Sebastián: Txertoa.

———. 2009. *The Basques*. Translated by Kristin Addis. Introduction by William A. Douglass. Reno: Center for Basque Studies, University of Nevada, Reno.

Del Valle, Teresa. 1983. "La mujer vasca a través del análisis del espacio: Utilización y significado." *Lurralde* 6: 251–70.

———. 1997. *Las Mujeres en Euskal Herria. Ayer y Hoy*. Hernani: Egin.

———, et al. 1985. *Mujer vasca. Imagen y realidad*. Barcelona: Anthropos.

———, ed. 2002. *Modelos emergentes en los modelos y relaciones de género*. Madrid: Narcea.

Diez Mintegui, Carmen. 1996. "Emergencias etnográficas." *El Diario Vasco*, October 20.

———. 1999a. "Mari, un mito para la resistencia feminista." "Generoaren inguruan – En torno al género," *Ankulegi* 3: 63–72.

———. 1999b. "Sistemas de género, desigualdad e identidad nacional." In *Sociedad vasca y construcción nacional*, ed. Pedro Albite. Donostia-San Sebastián: Gakoa.

———. 2003. "Conseguir la igualdad. Un proyecto inacabado." *Kobie*, Serie Antropología Cultural, 10: 41–56.

———. N.d. "La voz Mari. Antropología." In the *Enciclopedia Auñamendi*, online at www.euskomedia.org/aunamendi/78310/114643?op=7.

Estornés, Idoia. 1996. "El Alarde de San Marcial o la recreación torticera de una fiesta." *El Mundo*, May 21.

Farapi. 2009. *Análisis de las fiestas del territorio histórico de Gipuzkoa desde una perspectiva de género*. Donostia: Gipuzkoako Foru Aldundia/Diputación Foral de Gipuzkoa.

Haraway, Donna. 1991. *Symians, Cyborgs and Women: The Reinvention of Nature*. London: Free Association Books.

Henningsen, Gustav. 1980. *The Witches' Advocate: Basque Witchcraft and the Spanish Inquisition 1609–1614*. Reno: University of Nevada Press.

Juliano, Dolores. 1993. "Las pobres mujeres del mundo pobre." In *Sistemas de género y construcción (deconstrucción) de la desigualdad*, edited by Carmen Diez Mintegui and Virginia Maquieira. VI Congreso de Antropología. Santa Cruz de Tenerife: Federación de Asociaciones de Antropología del Estado Español; Asociación Canaria de Antropología.

Kerexeta, Xabier. 2001. *Dime de qué Alardes*. At www.alarde.org/a6/dimedeque/alardeas.htm.

Moreno, Gorka, and Xabier Kerexeta, eds. 2005. *Bidasoa Alardeak: Herria versus Hiria*. Bilbao: Udako Euskal Unibertsitatea. In Spanish: 2006. *Los Alardes del Bidasoa. Pueblos versus ciudadanía*. Irun: Argazki Press.

Ortiz de Osés, Andrés, and Franz Karl Mayr. 1981. *El matriarcalismo vasco. Reinterpretación de la cultura vasca*. Bilbao: Universidad de Deusto.

Pascual, Jakue, and Alberto Peñalva. 1999. *El juguete de Mari*, Bilbao: Likiniano Elkartea.

Porras Blanco, Juan. 2005. "Negación" punk en la sociedad vasca: Investigación socio antropológica de un simbolismo liminal." Ph.D. Diss., Universidad del País Vasco/Euskal Herriko Unibertsitatea.

Terol, Oscar. 2009. *Técnicas de la mujer vasca para la doma y monta de maridos*. Madrid: Santillana Ediciones Generales.

Varela, Julia. 1997. *El nacimiento de la mujer burguesa. El cambiante desequilibrio de poder entre los sexos*. Madrid: La Piqueta.

Xamar [pseud. Juan Carlos Etxegoien]. 2006. *Orhipean: The Country of Basque*. Translated by Margaret Bullen. Iruña: Pamiela.

Zulaika, Joseba. 1996. *Del Cromañón al Carnaval*. Donostia-San Sebastián: Erein.

9

Identity, Memory, and Power Games

TERESA DEL VALLE

Translated by Jennifer R. Ottman

One prominent twofold contribution of "new history" is that it both rescues women from oblivion and incorporates them as subjects into the narrative of time's passage. It confers visibility on them by categorizing them, thereby granting them identity through acknowledging their rightful members-hip in society, both as individuals and as a group. Cultural anthropology situates women within an analytical framework in which the relationships expressed by gender systems communicate each culture's specificities in a differentiated way, enabling one to critically discover the avenues along which cultural mandates, role assignments, and symbolic contents circu-late; and that frequently, by highlighting differences, generate inequalities, a field of reflection introduced into anthropology by feminist criticism.[1] Cultures are not atemporal, even if they move in accordance with measu-rements of time different from the standards established by the humani-ties and social sciences. They shape their own times and spaces.

Within the totality of the historical and anthropological processes, memory stands out as a key element in which the flow of past-present-future actively influences the creation of gender identities. It encompasses the apprehension of time and space, since memory fixes, engraves, and embeds. I have become fascinated by this process as it relates to women within the system in which relationships studied by feminist anthropol-ogy are structured, and more specifically, relationships that interact with

---

1. Maquieira's critique of the reification of culture (1999) is important in this regard.

the exercise of power, and hence, of equality or inequality. There are two reasons for this: the memory activity women engage in and the social way in which memory is exercised or avoided, making it possible to situate memory at the confluence of time, space, and power: aspects to which I have devoted a good part of my research over the last two decades.[2]

I distinguish social memory, individual or personal memory, and tangential memory. Tangential memory refers to the memory of alternative and marginal groups and most of what is encompassed by women's existence falls into this category. The broadest of the three is social memory, which stores up the elaboration of humanity's memory and is in most cases identified with the groups holding power. Ideally, it would gradually incorporate the stories told by tangential memory, in such a way so as to be representative of the diversity and richness of human experience. A country's degree of civilization might thus be measured by its memory, in that every time a country reworks its memory as a result of questions raised by tangential memory or it incorporates previously neglected knowledge, it takes a step in the direction of progress. The study of the incorporation of social memory and especially of tangential memories as part of the analysis of the progress of a society or of the different collectivities within one nation is a theoretical and methodological step that has only recently been embraced. Social memory has been described as a domain from which to define and to question some of the existing indicators in order to broaden the measurement of progress.[3]

Memory as a Temporal Process Encompassing the Individual and the Collective

Memory is like a wind that moves things to different places and simultaneously rescues them from the places where they happen to be. With age,

2. See "Bibliografía de Teresa del Valle" (2008, 179–86). With regard to influences on this chapter, I have drawn on reflections shared with Virginia Maquieira and Mari Luz Esteban. The seminar led by Amelia Valcárcel in 1994 as part of the master's degree program in "Women's Studies and Gender Systems" at the Women's Studies Seminar at the Universidad del País Vasco/ Euskal Herriko Unibertsitatea (UPV/EHU, the University of the Basque Country) led me to the reflections on solidarity to which I will refer later on. I thank Luz Maceira and Lucía Rojas for their suggestions.

3. On these, see del Valle and Pavez (2008) and the issues discussed at the seventeenth Conference of Basque Studies, where nine domains appropriate for measuring progress were defined: innovation, justice, globalization, revaluation of the public sphere, gender systems, quality of life, social tension, social memory, and solidarity society (www.eusko-ikaskuntza.org/ en/congresos/xvii/).

time gets switched around, and the distant past draws near to the present, in an attempt to overcome the fear that the future will be cut short. Yet how do people and places become filled with memory? How is this sediment of life created that will later serve for the weaving of memory? It is like looking at a sideboard that is gradually becoming covered with dust or at a desk where the former locations of books and papers are marked by phantom outlines. In this case, the dust is made up of miniscule particles of pleasant sensations, of feelings of fear and horror, of the fevers and chills of falling in and out of love. Strident notes and events wrapped in deafening noise raise a stir in the moment, but only time's retina gradually selects the lived experiences hidden within them in order to transform them and bring them to light.

How much do we retain of all that we experienced as small children? Of the games, the excursions, the initiation into friendship, the caresses of first love, how much survives? The same applies to the traces we have left on the roads, the trains, the beaches and mountains on which we have felt the wind and the caresses of sun and rain.

Here we find the sounds and cadences we have stored up: the sounds of our first language, of tender expressions, of angry shouts, of emotions, the sounds of streams that never cease, of bells, clocks, a neighbor's radio, blaring sirens, televisions in bars, children shouting in parks, telephones that will not stop ringing, and so on until we have filled bottomless vessels with sounds that remain latent until bursting forth at the slightest evocation.

Bodies receive traces that appear like notches tallying the impact of weather and age. The lines around our lips store up past smiles and difficulties and engrave on our faces much of what has happened in our personal histories. With the current effort to return skin, faces, and hands to their lost suppleness, we blot out a past that has crept up on us almost without our noticing and that many would prefer not to have always in view.[4]

How much language there is in hands! There is a beauty that can only be appreciated when we value the memory left by work. Wrinkles from the daily effort to grasp a tool or hold a basket, gradually traced into being with scarcely a thought to measuring what is today a faint sketch, will become deep lines with the passage of the years. They are a part of memory that holds deep feelings, some directed within and others shared.

---

4. In order to examine individuals' relationship to age and especially how women perceive age, I have distinguished among real age, felt age, and attributed age. Memory is present in all three categories (del Valle 2002).

For this reason, in my research on memory I have been collecting and analyzing photos of women that appear in printed news media and that show the traces of the passage of time, as well as photos of women who eliminate those traces.

In women's memories, there is a field that encompasses the transmission of knowledges generally related to the domestic and family sphere. Feminist analysis enables us to consider this field from three different angles. The first is the angle of difference, where we consider knowledges that are used as a means to highlight the being and status of women in opposition to men: in many cultures, these knowledges are assigned a differentiated being, and it is stressed that since they are characteristic of and belong to women, only women can properly transmit them. The second angle is that of equality, analyzing the extent to which these differentiated knowledges respond to a situation of oppression and whether continuing to set limits on them contributes to their devaluation. The third angle has as its principal referent the solidarity that situates all knowledges on the broader level of universal experience. Set within this global context, women's knowledges are analyzed across cultures, with the aim of weighing the nature and consequence of the contribution they make to knowledge in general. An integrative approach is sought that safeguards the individuation and valuation of each knowledge, but does so within a symbiotic relationship between particular knowledges and more all-encompassing ones. It is a task of painstaking attention to detail that at the same time requires familiarity with the broader contexts within which these knowledges should be inserted, and so with tangential memory.

I use the second angle of analysis in this chapter, with a brief foray into the domain of the third. I argue that there are knowledges associated with the domestic arena that have a differentiated field of valuation and memory. However, they are not incorporated into social memory as fully and consequentially as they deserve to be; what is more, in many cases, and primarily here in the case of those knowledges that are related to maternity, they remain outside it, without being appreciated to the degree corresponding to their intrinsic worth. It will be the strategies of a new, inclusive memory that will incorporate them in such a way that they will come to be part of our universal inheritance.

The Presence of Absence

Frequently, women appear in Mediterranean cultures as the depositories of the memory of events linked to the domestic circle. It falls to them to remember the birthdays, the difficulties, the moves from one house to another, and the celebrations. They should evoke the dead and those who have left for various reasons, such as conflict, work, or education. They are the archive of the days of exile and of the miseries of war. In short, they have the task of making absence present.

In traditional Basque culture, tied primarily to the rural environment and present in many areas until the 1950s, women activated the memory of the dead. The symbolic representation of this memory was the occupation of a place in the church that corresponded symbolically to the *sepulturia* (grave), where through the light of the *argizaiola*[5] they personalized the link between past and present. This evocative protagonism by women also appears in connection with the ritual events of certain ETA militants' political funerals held between 1980 and 1985, as analyzed by Begoña Aretxaga (1988). In these funerals, mothers and wives played an important public role. The mothers' task was to express social continuity by their presence, in the midst of the absence of their children. Continuity was expressed through symbols taken from nature and through reference to the maternal role.

In all these processes of bringing the past into the present, by activating the memory of others, transmitting knowledges about tasks, things known, and bodily experiences, women draw on memory, their own memory, in order to insert the past into the present. This is a vital memory that in many cases is marked by varied emotions and reveals itself in a luxury of subtle details. It is manifest in many cases with great narrative richness and abundance and constitutes a knowledge that in most cases is not incorporated into what is identified as recognized knowledge, but left to wait for someone to rescue it and grant it prestige.

In many cultures women are endowed with the capacity to transform absences into presences through the act of remembering loved ones and events related to the family circle: a paradox if we take into account the fact that one characteristic of world History has been to immortalize women's absence—an act of blindness to their constant presence.

---

5. A candle wick rolled around a piece of wood that the woman placed over the sepulturia and that remained lit during the mass or ceremony in memory of the deceased. The custom is still followed in some places, such as Amezketa (Gipuzkoa). For its place among the funeral rites more broadly, see Douglass (1969).

Social Memory's Mechanisms of Exclusion

All societies, over the course of time, gradually elaborate a corpus of knowledges that are considered sufficiently important to transmit to subsequent generations and that I call social memory. These knowledges are communicated in a wide range of forms. Some are committed to writing, others are transmitted by the media, and some are incorporated into space in the form of monuments or street names. Even the simple announcement of an occurrence entails a selection; the award of a prize or a tribute are public markers of something chosen to be highlighted as significant. Social memory, constantly in a process of elaboration and reelaboration, needs to be examined in order to discern both what is selected and what is silenced. This is why I stress the importance of paying attention to silences when we analyze tangential memory. Hence, I want to highlight street names, where women scarcely appear; historical monuments that memorialize a locality's "representative people" and events and yet in which women or aspects of daily life are mostly absent, and finally, the empty space indicated by the minority presence of works of art produced by women, to mention a few fields of silencing.[6]

At the same time, and within this general process of silencing that affects women directly, I have focused on the procedure for selecting knowledge manifested in a number of mechanisms—of which I have identified five—that act to the detriment of an inclusive social memory, that is, of a memory that would incorporate the narratives of tangential memories. I identify these mechanisms of exclusion as usurpation, devaluation, silencing, interested transformation, and genealogical lapsus.

Usurpation

Knowledge that is rescued and preserved is transmitted fully, but is done so as if its recipients were its originators. A clear example is the usurpation by men of the culinary tradition in Basque culture, which has gone from being the cooking of mothers and grandmothers to being elevated into a source of economic and social prestige under the label of "new Basque cuisine."[7] Usurpation occurs when the genealogy of a given knowledge

---

6. I address this primarily in del Valle (1997a, 101–32, 150–55).

7. For a discussion of Basque culture's embracing of and resistance to culinary knowledges and of the process by which those knowledges are being displaced from the domestic kitchen to locations outside the home, especially the traditional gastronomic societies, see del Valle (1997a, 65–79).

(one that, in this case, belongs to women) is left unmentioned, making it possible, in turn, to highlight changes and innovations.

Devaluation

Knowledge that is rescued and preserved is devalued when it is not assigned the status it deserves, but instead is valued in relation to the more general category to which it belongs, in this case, the category of women. Many activities, skills, and tastes are lumped together as "women's things," as if they were irrelevant forms of knowing. This categorization is also applied to knowledges and behaviors that are not connected to the domestic sphere and about which belittling generalizations are made. It is a simplifying mechanism that hides the real worth of what is included in the devalued category.

Silencing

It is known that a given knowledge or knowledges exist, but they are not given sufficient being to enable them, in their particular details, to be incorporated into and articulated within the context of general knowledge. This is the case of many activities linked to the daily life of the household, knowledges bound up with socialization, especially all those that have to do with maternity, the care of the body, and health. The spectrum runs from domestic practices to natural medicine and folk healing, as well as other contributions made by women.

Interested Transformation

Knowledge of the contributions made by women in the various fields of scientific and scholarly activity is frequently taken as the point of departure for an elaboration of the field to which they belong, but without acknowledging their origin. To the extent that the field of women's and gender studies and feminist criticism is gradually becoming consolidated and acquiring prestige for a variety of reasons (such as, perhaps, the innovative perspectives put forward), men's interest in the field may bring with it a differentiated positive valuation, as well as opportunities for promotion, especially through government-sponsored financing of projects that promote this sphere of knowledge. Furthermore, in some milieus this is judged positively as a progressive activity. For this reason, it is important that men take up the legacy of this knowledge and that—from the perspective of feminist and gender studies—they contribute different currents of thought, through interdisciplinarity and through articulations and

synergies with differentiated spheres of knowledge. This does not eliminate the critical stance that should taken by both men and women, which
is fundamental to progress of any kind.

Genealogical Lapsus

The same can be said of those who, ignorant of all the work that has already
been done, discuss women and gender without situating these topics critically within the tradition to which they belong, a tradition that has been
the work, primarily, of women. No one would dare to talk about Marxism
without being familiar with its origins, contributions, and most important
debates. If anyone tried, criticism from specialists in the area would serve
to discredit that scholar's work.

In criticism of this kind, it is necessary to disentangle what is entailed
in silence, inaccurate discussion, and scholarly silencing from the exclu-
sivist claim that only women should talk about women. As Henrietta
Moore (1988) notes, critiquing Edwin Arderner and drawing on a contribution by Judith Shapiro, this would mean renouncing the study of the
other from the necessary distance, something that is central to anthropology. The stage of defending studies carried out only by women was
characteristic of the beginning of the anthropology of women and was at
times effective in providing the impetus for excellent work. However, this
stage has now, at least in theory, been left far behind. At present, a study's
quality and its connection to recognized genealogies of knowledge, and
hence to their contributions already inserted into broader memory, are of
greater interest than the exclusivity of its authorship.

Maternity as Marginal/Tangential Memory, in contrast to Scholarly Knowledge

Many women elaborate their identity and exercise their personal memory
through maternity, as one of the body's key knowledges. This persona-
lization of experience can be traced in two directions: on the one hand,
it confers protagonism and prestige on the mother in the family circle,
where everything related to maternity is conceptualized as particular and
concrete, and on the other hand, in the broader context, it is frequently
contrasted to the universal and the scientific. It is blatantly obvious that
despite the almost infinite number of maternities that have occurred in the
most unusual times and places, maternity is not granted a separate chapter
in either history or scholarly activity. Subjects like wars, natural disasters,

political agreements, and the spread of different religions are raised up as milestones marking era changes or analyzed in depth in order to measure their significance. Maternity, despite being a key element in the survival of the human species, has not been elevated into the focus of important scholarly contributions. Even in the accounts that I consider most barbarous, like those of war, there is discussion of bombardments, of the victims of one side or the other, and of conquests, but rarely is there any mention of the maternities of war, that is, of how war affects the process understood in all its being and consequence.

Maternity is a complex field, since it encompasses the bodily experience of gestation, childbirth, and the care given and received, a process that involves the expectant mother's emotions about sons and daughters, as well as the relations established within the family and social structure. Its complexity encompasses structure and symbolism, and all this is in turn permeated by the varied ways in which different cultures value, interpret, and assign significance to maternity; nor does it escape from the influence of its contextualization within the evolution of socio-historical processes.[8]

There still subsists the strongly rooted belief that maternal instinct causes women to link suffering with the experience of biological maternity. Women should face it stoically, in a display of internal and external fortitude, while their expectations and desires about something that concerns them so closely are silenced. I recall detailed commentaries from young women that leave no room for doubt: what other women had told them turned out to be limited when compared with the experience of childbirth, especially in everything having to do with discomforts, uncertainties, anxieties, surprises, and contradictory sensations. In many cases, the memory of pain remained vivid long afterward.

Frequently, one hears it said that, despite the pain of childbirth, the experience of seeing the baby makes up for everything and even erases the suffering of the preceding hours. With this lack of differentiation, a predisposition to confusion is attributed to the category of "woman," such that women appear incapable of distinguishing between pleasure and pain, between the fear of not knowing what they can endure and the sensation of relief at having lived through it. Something else is happening when women are heard describing the way they lived each moment with an intensity of perception that clearly separated the limits of suffering

---

8. For a more in-depth discussion of maternity, see Imaz (2007).

and the choice in favor of pleasure. Nevertheless, despite all this wealth of perceptions, reflections, and experiences, the memory that emerges from maternity does not enter into the processes of social memory, and still less of history, except in exceptional circumstances: the cases of famous women or those whose daughters or sons have become famous.

My proposal to highlight the relevance of bodily knowledge leads me to focus on the perpetuation (memory across time) of women through their children. Given that in many cases women are going to link their temporal transcendence to their maternity, in principle, this is going to situate them in a social arena where their behavior and values are going to be interpreted as if they were based in an immutable interpretation of biology. Everything linked to maternity maintains its worth so long as its traditional parameters are preserved: endurance in childbirth despite pain, the inevitability of naturalized maternal love, the differentiated priority of one's identity as a mother, to mention a few. This is a knowledge in which the value of a physical and emotional experience, instead of being transferred to the level of other, similar human experiences, is particularized in such a way that there is no room for its universalization. The same occurs with the entire process of the memory of maternity and its possible incursion into social memory. Rarely are global approaches found that establish parallels between maternity and other key, habitual occurrences, or between the complexity of filial relationships and familiarity with the intricacies of autonomy and power. In most cases, the experience of maternity is presented as a distinct and exclusive path that can lead to conflict if combined, for example, with the creative process, professionalization, or a passion for the world outside the home. In contrast, the contents of the objectifiable knowledges that are identified with creation and scholarship are presented as part of a general knowledge with the capacity to branch out and manifest itself in the specificity of particular disciplines, discourses, and methodologies. This is a knowledge that draws renewed value from its changing nature, which can be differentiated and personalized and simultaneously viewed from the perspective of its influence on the redefinition of progress.[9] Maternity's knowledges are presented in more particularized form in many cases, situated within the kind of stability provided them by their anchorage in tradition.

---

9. The incorporation of the memory of maternity would enter fully into the domain of social memory, and that domain is understood as a referent when the time comes to measure progress (del Valle and Pavez 2008, 66–68).

In this way, important knowledges have come to cluster around reproduction, but they have not been incorporated, so that upon being exercised, they separate women from those axes of social life where the knowledge that confers transcendent prestige is elaborated.

Many of the knowledges recognized as having universal value and associated with masculine contributions had their origins in daily activities related to survival and the organization of basic production: hunting, fishing, agriculture, and industry. The difference is that these knowledges appear related to humanity's social organization or development across time and linked to the idea of progress. They form part of periods characterized by change and by its consequences for humanity's advancement. The lived experience of maternity is a woman's chief possibility for perpetuating the memory of her "present," what she understands as her personal history. The impediment is the insertion of this individualized occurrence into broader history. The unilateral importance that has been assigned to women's perpetuation of their memory in their descendants (daughters/sons), as a concrete aspiration expressed linearly across generations, appears in contrast to a general construction of knowledge. The latter is presented as something external, changing, subject to rules defined by the disciplines of scholarship and on which it is possible to act directly: a knowledge that, due to its separation from the biological, is changing and malleable, and hence expansive and multiplicative. Nevertheless, through a broader vision of scholarly knowledge, maternity could come to join and enlarge a changing and simultaneously accumulative process that would gather genealogies, universal contributions, and multiple memories of varied maternities. This would be a knowledge encompassing the spectrum of the quantitative and the qualitative.

At the base of these contrasting experiences of the value of the knowledge associated with maternity and the scholarly knowledge that is incorporated into social memory, there lie several premises nourished by the oppositions inside-outside, proximity-distance, and continuity of the biological-transcendence of the creative, in which the objectifiable is interpreted as the standard of value, and subjective knowing is minimized. This entails a reification of difference. Hence, for women, it entails maneuvering through fields of often opposed orientation, each of which has different status and assigns prestige in different ways, such as subjective experience and intergenerational communication. In scholarly knowledge, many of the characteristics that enter into maternity are devalued and left out of scientific quantification. Moreover, an entire knowledge is accumulated in individual memory, but is in turn part of the collective memories of countless maternities, into which each woman who chooses to become a mother is inserted, and that is to be understood in the broad sense of concept while lived experience, as seen above, is scarcely recognized as valid universalizing knowledge. These memories are not seen as contributions that can join and enlarge social memory. The most immediate and obvious class of knowledge, the physiological difference between the sexes (Handman 1993), is a knowledge equally open to all.

Marie-Elisabeth Handman discusses Françoise Héritier's (1994) hypothesis that it is from observing the physical differences of the human body that the essential and basic categories of all discourse arise, necessarily influencing the conceptual categories of that discourse, the world of the imaginary and the symbolic, the sexual division of labor, and consequently, women's and men's knowledges. At the same time, this is the knowledge that, in principle, presents the greatest opportunities for maintaining the possibility of equality, since it is a knowledge accumulated in the personal experience of every human being. It is transmitted in differentiated form and elaborated through social and cultural forms of expressing sexuality and reproduction. Each person can reflect on this knowledge of the body on the basis of his or her own experience. What is surprising is that, as Handman (1993) points out, these knowledges are passed down across the centuries in distinct lines of transmission for women and men, and rarely join or mix. The situations in industrial societies in which these lines tend to converge act as an indicator of change, and we should pay attention to discerning them. Handman and Heritier situate in bodily representations the sexual division of those knowledges that encompass the fields of economy, politics, and subordination. This centrality of the body, about which other authors (both male and female) have also written, leads one to propose the necessity of transcending maternity in order to establish the shared points of contact from which to conceptualize gender relations in an egalitarian way.

How can maternity be brought out of its private sphere? How can it be given a being that will enable it to be valued as a social good? This is not solely a question of solutions for making maternity compatible with work, something that may be achieved with time. Rather, it is more an issue of valuation and prestige. If maternity is to come out of its dark corner, it is necessary to break with the idea that maternity is women's distinguishing option. The more that women are separated, together with children, from men and their activities, the more those activities and the separation between nature and culture will be naturalized, at least in those societies in which such a dichotomy exists. It is not a universal, but it is a dominant concept and experience. In practice, a greater separation between the biological and the social functions of maternity would have a positive impact on diversifying the tasks characteristic of motherhood, in such a way as to transcend their traditional attribution to women.

The New Memory: The Experience of the Body as Shared Knowledge

Above and beyond maternity, there exist the experience and the referential memory of the body, for both women and men, not in divergent lineages, but rather as part of the variability of human beings' bodily experience.[10] Without trying to take the body as a generalized point of departure, but rather as one valuable approach, I stress the importance that this experience, closer at hand than any other, has for establishing the richness of certain knowledges. This vast spectrum includes the memories of pain and of pleasure, erotic games, the creases of tenderness, and the lines of time. I also value this approach because it highlights the repercussions that ignorance of the lived body can have for the experience of health and sexuality. And I believe that it is important to pause to consider what links the experience of the body through maternity to memory and power, for the purpose of seeing the extent to which identification of the cultural with the biological is maintained and how it functions to perpetuate women's exclusive identity.

In addition, this personalized emphasis on the body that incorporates felt experience as knowledge breaks with the biologicist woman-man binary. From this perspective, gender can be seen as a spectrum, with the most differentiated categories at the extremes and a gradual arc curving between them until it reaches an undifferentiated point where being a man or a woman is not what matters, but rather the degree of concordance between felt identity and identity as socially attributed. All this is located in turn in the cultural and socio-historical contexts within which

---

10. In subsequent articles I have highlighted the importance of corporeality, of the state of having been incorporated or incarnated, when one situates memory in feelings, emotions, pleasures, rejections, and sexuality. I have designed a methodology centered on the structural axes of memory: nodes, intersections, articulations, and interstices (del Valle 1995). In del Valle (1997b) I also apply this methodology to the bodily memories of an adult woman and an adolescent girl.

it exists, and with special attention to the inequalities generated. This perspective also insists on a reading of the body as lived experience that makes it possible to locate changes in discourse and alternative discourses in relation to the reinterpretation of physiological differences, in shifting configurations that lead to varying results. In some cases, they serve as support for the emergence, preservation, and transmission of inequality; in others, they lead to recognition of the capacities of the physiological and the social and cultural expressions of gender relations. This alertness to changes in discourse and to the critical detection of fixations on the biological entails a mental and emotional posture more inclined to the fluidity of individually and socially ascribed sexual categories than to a rigidity based on physiological differences.

Both women's and men's bodies can be taken as the point of departure, instead of thinking only about women's maternity. The body in turn stores up individual memory and can be a subject of social memory, since it accumulates areas of human experience.

This globalizing vision seeks to incorporate both the knowledge that identifies the biological part of maternity (and hence women's right to the memory of the body), and the social dimension that surrounds maternity and that, as noted, incorporates a spectrum of maternities. Social memory would be enriched if it were to recognize that the knowledge accumulated in the experience of billions of maternities could represent a multidisciplinary contribution to humanity, since it encompasses knowledges about emotions, health, pain, identity, relations of love and dependency, to mention a few, and the body in general. But what would it mean to recognize the value of a knowledge that is scarcely taken into account?

With the separation between procreation and knowledge presented in the way that it is, to the extent that women become involved in that task of procreation-creation in an isolated way, they experience whatever is outside that sphere as external and peripheral. This does not mean that procreation implies isolation, and in fact, the tasks of socialization bring women into relation with others: teachers, friends, health professionals, and so on. Closeness and exclusion are constructed as definitive. Breaking this isolation is more than sharing the project of one's children with a man and with others. The reference is to the fact that living this perpetuation of oneself through time by means of one's children is categorized socially as something separate and of lesser value. Memory in this case is seen as the fixation of a physiological experience in time, one that can only be neutralized by taking the step of transcending the biological and generalizing about the experience of maternity, placing it on a social and general plane. Women's perpetuation through what is interpreted as the biologization of memory is construed as a process that can serve the purposes of personal identification, but that will rarely be able to be incorporated into the elaboration of memory as a constructive cultural force.

It is precisely this vision of separation, and hence of incompatibility, that has influenced the division established between the reproductive sphere and the sphere of scholarly activity. This affects women more negatively than it does men. I argue that the effort a society makes to establish a continuum, rather than a separation, between the spaces, times, tasks, assignments of prestige, and relationships that link reproduction to production (in this case, production of knowledge) will result in an increase in the quality and quantity of knowledge. If at a moment of economic crisis like the present, the decision were to be taken to start a mental and practical restructuring of these spaces, it is to be hoped that this would have a positive impact on many levels: the management of resources and the presentation of alternatives for solving problems of demographic density, mobility, sexual violence, and how to exercise parenthood, to mention only a few.

The creation and development of new forms of memory could facilitate rethinking maternity as a response to a broad conceptualization of the body and of pleasure, above and beyond fixed biological and social-naturalization assignments. The conceptual separation between the biology and the social dimension of motherhood, as well as the division between reproduction and sexuality, provide a framework within which we can work toward the incorporation of significant expressions of individual and tangential memory into social memory. In contrast, the fixation on maternity as something distinctive of women and separate from the experiences and visions of paternity is, in my understanding, a path that by leading us again and again to the same destination, leaves us in a perpetual no-man's-land, outside of categorization and lacking the prestige it is due.

References

Aretxaga, Begoña. 1988. *Los funerales en el nacionalismo radical vasco.* San Sebastián: La Primitiva Casa Baroja.

"Bibliografía de Tersa del Valle." 2008. *Ankulegi* 12: 179–86.

Del Valle, Teresa. 1991. "Género y sexualidad aproximación antropológica."

In Teresa del Valle and Carmela Sanz Rueda, *Género y sexualidad*. Madrid: Fundación Universidad Empresa.

———. 1995. "Metodología para la elaboración de la autobiografía." In *Actas del Seminario Internacional "Género y trayectoria del profesorado universitario"*, edied by Carmela Sanz Rueda. Madrid: Instituto de Investigaciones Feministas/Universidad Complutense.

———. 1997a. *Andamios para una nueva ciudad. Lecturas desde la antropología*. Madrid: Alianza.

———. 1997b. "La memoria del cuerpo." *Arenal* 4, no. 1: 59–74

———. 2002. "Contrastes en la percepción de la edad." In *Mujeres mayores en el siglo XXI. De la invisibilidad al protagonismo*, edited by Virginia Maquieira D'Angelo. Madrid: Ministerio de Trabajo y Asuntos Sociales.

Del Valle, Teresa, and Amaya Pavez. 2008. "Una visión social del Progreso Sostenible para el siglo XXI en Euskal Herria." *RIEV. Revista internacional de los estudios vascos* 53, no. 1 (January–June): 45–81.

Douglass, William A. 1969. *Death in Murelaga: Funerary Ritual in a Spanish Basque Village*. Seattle: University of Washington Press.

Esteban Galarza, María Luz. 1993. "Actitudes y percepciones de las mujeres respecto a su salud reproductiva y sexual. Necesidades de salud percibidas por las mujeres y respuestas del sistema sanitario." Ph.D. Diss., Universitat de Barcelona.

Héritier, Françoise. 1994. *Les deux soeurs et le mère*. París: Éditions Odile Jacob.

Handman, Marie-Elisabeth. 1993. "La division sexualle des savoirs." In *Esruturas sociais e desenvolvimento. Actas do II Congreso de Sociologia*. Volume 2. Lisbon: Associaciao Portugesa de Sociologia; Ed. Fragmentos.

Imaz Martínez, Elixabete. 2007. "Mujeres gestantes, madres en gestación. Representaciones, modelos y experiencias en el tránsito a la maternidad de las mujeres vascas contemporáneas." Ph.D. Diss., Universidad del País Vasco/Euskal Herriko Unibertsitatea.

Maquieira, Virginia. 1999. "Antropología, género y derechos humanos." *Anales del Museo Nacional de Antropología* 6: 13–48.

Moore, Henrietta. 1988. *Feminism and Anthropology*. Minneapolis: University of Minnesota Press.

10

Three Decades of Reproductive Rights: The Highs and Lows of Biomedical Innovations

Itziar Alkorta Idiakez

Translated by Jennifer Martin

The increase in reproductive technologies is a phenomenon affecting many women. Delayed motherhood for social and economic reasons forces many couples and women to face age-related infertility problems. In this situation, reproductive medicine appears to be a last hope for those couples that consider it important to have their own children. Only once assisted reproductive methods fail, do these couples consider adoption. However, the use of such technology carries significant health risks, and moreover, does not seem to have boundaries.

This chapter begins with a contextualized analysis of the subject by focusing on the legalization of contraceptive methods, the change in the birth rate trends with the decline in fertility since the 1980s, the appearance of fertility clinics, and the early regulation of assisted reproduction techniques. Once the phenomenon of delayed maternity in Basque society is introduced, the first problem concerning reproductive medicine as a cure for the unexpected infertility associated with the delay in having children arises. Here, issues such as the risk of the techniques, reproductive tourism, and the implications of preimplantation genetic diagnosis are addressed.

The First Advances: The Legalization of Contraceptive Methods

In three decades, European women made the transition from a traditional family model to a more open-minded model in which they gradually became more aware of their reproductive rights.[1] In particular, medical and pharmacological innovations were crucial to achieving the right to contraception.

Contraception was legalized later in Spain than other European countries. The contraceptive pill, for example, was prohibited until 1978,[2] yet Spanish women became accustomed to using it very quickly, even before its legalization. A survey conducted in 1971 on Spanish women's attitudes concerning family planning methods reveals that the great majority of those surveyed (68 percent) wanted more information on contraceptive use and greater freedom in deciding if they wanted to have children or not (Díez Nicolás 1973). Presently, contraceptives form part of everyday life for the majority of Basque and Spanish women (Ruiz-Salguero 2000; Delgado Pérez 2001).

Clearly, then, the transformation of Spanish women's reproductive behaviors occurred at an extraordinary speed. In the span of one generation, mothers and daughters followed completely different behavioral guidelines: the mother used contraception in the later years of her fertility to avoid having more children, while the daughter used it to reduce or delay maternity (Arregi Gorospe and Dávila Legerán 2005).

Presently, the use of contraceptive measures is a daily feature of life for European women, to the extent that birth control is not what concerns them today (except the struggle for abortion rights), but rather the difficulty to have the kind of children desired. In Spain and the Basque Country, three decades after the legalization of contraception and coinciding with the transition to democracy, many women lament the difficulties that they have to overcome to form a family at certain ages.

Trend Change: The Drop in Fertility

Complex social factors have led couples to drastically reduce the number of their offspring and to have children later. Spain now has one of the lowest fertility rates in the European Union (EU). In 2008, after a slight recuperation with respect to previous years, the number of children per woman was 1.46 in Spain (Eurostat 2008).

---

1. See Alkorta Idiakez (2003, 2006a, 2006b).
2. Law 45/1978, of October 7, 1978, reformed articles 343 and 416 of the Penal Code, permitting the sale and use of contraceptives. Its use was regulated by decree 3033-1978, of December 15, by the Department of Health and Social Security, on the issuance and advertising of contraceptives.

In a country where having children is valued and women say that they would like to have more than they do, the low birth rate is explained by a set of interrelated social factors. An improved cultural level and economy have had the double effect of reducing the number of children per couple and pushing back the age of having children in the population as a whole, except in the case of economic immigrant groups, whose first generation tends to maintain the reproductive patterns of their native cultures.

The average age of maternity for Spanish women is older than thirty: the highest in Europe, along with Italy. Around forty thousand children are born in the Spanish state each year to women who are over thirty-five.[3] Female fertility rapidly diminishes after this age, but despite that, the tendency of Spanish women to delay motherhood is increasing over time and reaching such dimensions that we might speak of infertility as a social cause among the Spanish female population.

Public policies adopted in the face of this situation have not been able to counteract the declining birth rate trend. Legal and economic measures to promote family and work reconciliation have had little effect on the continued trend of delaying motherhood, so that many affected women find themselves destined to seek the help of assisted reproduction. Proof of this is that the majority of women who turn to assisted procreation programs are older than thirty-seven and do not present any physical condition that would explain their infertility, except for age.[4]

Early Regulation of Assisted Reproduction Techniques

In Spain, reproductive medicine in general has been aided by tolerant legislation that, from the late 1980s on, authorized the use of almost all known medical methods up to that time: the anonymous donation of gametes and embryos was accepted, women could use anonymously donated sperm whether they had a partner or not, and the parentage of a child conceived with sperm frozen after the death of one's husband was recognized; the only thing prohibited was surrogate motherhood.

---

3. In 1965, only 12 percent of births were registered to mothers older than thirty-five. Mothers older than thirty-five now account for 39.17 percent of births, while those aged between thirty and thirty-five account for 34.39 percent, and those between twenty-five and thirty, 29.28 percent (Instituto Nacional de Estadística 1999; Delgado 2002).

4. Generalitat de Catalunya (Government of Catalonia), see http://www.gencat.cat/salut/depsalut/html/ca/dir1934/fivcat2005.pdf.

The first Spanish law on medical reproductive assistance (one of the first in the world) dates back to 1988.[5] The singularity of this law is explained in part by the legislative tendency of the time and by the liberal nature of the first post-Franco Spanish legislatures, both of which contributed to progressive regulation in both medical matters and in family law. There had been a democratization of family structures in Spain following the impetus stemming from the 1978 Constitution and from the 1981 laws regarding marriage and the family. Further, the fact that Spanish society at that time was immersed in a modernization process also encouraged change. The "biolaw" enacted during the 1980s showed a clear resolve, then, to promote research into and development of biomedical sciences in the country (Méndez Baiges 1998).

However, more complete regulations concerning human reproduction did not occur until the mid-1990s. These specified the authorization and operation requirements for the centers that practiced assisted fertilization; information, donor, and user study protocols; the creation and organization of a national donor registry; and the creation and organization of the Comisión Nacional de Reproducción Humana Asistida (CNRHA, the National Commission on Assisted Human Reproduction). The same regulations also included three more provisions: the creation of a list of hereditary diseases that are detectable through prenatal diagnosis; requirements for authorizing experimentation with gametes; and the transport of gametes and of pre-embryos.[6] However, only three of the six planned decrees were ultimately enacted.[7] The first two were published seven and a half years after the law came into effect and the last after eight

---

5. Law 35/1988, of November 22, 1988, concerning the regulation of assisted reproduction techniques. The law was the object of an unconstitutionality appeal by the conservative Partido Popular (PP, People's Party). The Constitutional Court's ruling (STC 116/1999, June 17), after thirteen years, rejected the appeal and proved the appropriateness of all the rulings on the Constitution, with the exception of a statutory empowerment for the government that it considered expired. Unlike the rest of the Spanish state, the Catalan Autonomous Community had regulated the operation and control of centers offering assisted reproduction techniques by means of an earlier decree in 1999. It also regulated, through law 7/1991, of April 27, on parentage, complemented by the Code of Succession (inheritance law) that same year, the establishment of derived parentage in assisted reproduction.

6. Law 35/1988, of November 22, on assisted reproduction techniques, first, second, third, and fourth final provisions.

7. Royal decree 412/1996, of March 1, which establishes the compulsory protocols for the study of donors and users connected with assisted human reproduction techniques and regulates the creation and organization of the national registry of gamete and pre-embryo donors for purposes of human reproduction; royal decree 413/1996, of March 1, which establishes the technical and operational requirements for the authorization and approval of the centers and

years. As of 2010, the last three provisions mentioned lack statutory regulation. However, the Spanish government has announced, for the first half of 2010, the enactment of a law for regulating the donor registry for egg and sperm (Prats 2009).

The 1988 law was reformed in 2002 at the initiative of the conservative PP government, in order to prevent the fertilization of more than three eggs per cycle.[8] Nevertheless, subsequent regulations expanded the exceptions to such a point that they justified the fertilization of a higher number of eggs, so that the resulting enacted law resulted in being poorly effective. Eventually, in May 2006, the new law 14/2006 on assisted human reproduction techniques was passed. This is the current law in force today, and repeals the two previous laws. This new law introduced few substantial changes with respect to previous regulation. However, among its novelties, preimplantation genetic diagnosis is now authorized for third party therapeutic purposes (those termed "savior babies"), as well as to detect any hereditary genetic diseases in the embryo.

The law allows for the possibility, denied in most European countries, of anonymously donating eggs to infertile women. However, this authorization is accompanied by a warning that any advertising that promotes donation for profit will not be permitted and that donor remuneration should be limited to compensation for expenses and trouble caused. Moreover, it establishes a limit on the number of times that hormonal stimulation can be carried out for donation purposes, which should not, in any instance, put the donor's health at risk, although the earlier law 14/2007 on biomedical research expands the authorization of egg donation by extending it for the purpose of biomedical research (Dickenson and Alkorta Idiakez 2008).

Finally, the CNRHA, which is empowered to interpret the law, has allowed an exception for anonymous egg donation in the case of lesbian couples. Based on the argument of avoiding gender discrimination in the case of same-sex couples, the CNRHA has authorized that a woman can gestate the egg of her partner so that both may be mothers, one the biological and the other the gestational mother of the future born child.[9]

medical services connected with assisted human reproduction techniques; and royal decree 415/1997, of March 21, creating the CNRHA.

8. Royal decree 1380/2002, of December 2002.

9. In Spain, law 13/2005, of June 1, authorized same-sex marriages by amending the Civil Code on the subject of the right to marry.

Delaying Having Children: Assisted Reproduction as Cure?

The early regulation of assisted reproduction techniques and the liberal application of the regulatory laws have favored the proliferation of fertility clinics in Spain, where the number of authorized clinics greatly exceeds the average number of assisted reproduction centers per inhabitant of EU countries.[10] Nine out of every ten Spanish clinics that offer this type of treatment are private.

In 1988, fourteen centers practiced in vitro fertilization (IVF), and four of these were public hospitals that operated pilot programs for assisted reproduction (Congreso de Dipuatados1988, 129). On February 1, 2003, a census from the Registry of Assisted Reproduction Centers of the Department of Health registered 203 centers authorized for the practice of reproductive medicine, 38 of which that were public and 165 that were private.[11] In the Comunidad Autónoma del País Vasco/ Euskal Autonomia Erkidegoa (CAPV/EAE, Autonomous Community of the Basque Country) there were three public and ten private centers. In the *Foral* Community of Navarre, meanwhile, these services were only recently offered in public centers. In the absence of a recent update from the Registry of Assisted Reproduction Centers, other non-official registries note that there are more than three hundred assisted reproduction centers in Spain; the majority of them concentrated along the Mediterranean coast.[12] By means of comparison, in 2000 the French association FIVNAT reported that there were eighty-three centers authorized to practice several reproductive medicine techniques.[13]

Medical studies show that the infertility rates of Basque and Spanish couples are on the whole similar to those in other Western countries: namely, around 15 percent of couples of child-bearing age. Why then is there such a big market for reproductive medicine in Spain? The answer to the question could have, in part, something to do with the patient's

---

10. In 1998, on average, there were 209,424 inhabitants per center in Spain, while in France this number was 698,795. Data taken from the Spanish registry of centers, FIVNAT (the French association for assisted reproduction), and the American Registry.

11. Despite the fact that, by legal mandate, the Department of Health must make public the data concerning Assisted Reproduction Techniques from the Registry of Centers and Health Services (RCTTRA) in Spain, the information dates back to February 1, 2003. For Catalonia, a registry of centers may also be consulted.

12. See information on the Spanish Fertility Society (Sociedad Española de Fertilidad, SEF) website, at http://nuevo.sefertilidad.com/index-en.php.

13. See http://perso.wanadoo.fr/fivnat.fr.

age (and termed a social cause of infertility). A second explanation of the extent and amount of business that assisted reproduction has attained in Spain is found in the foreign demand for these techniques, a point that I will refer to later.

The Toll of Assisted Reproduction: Technique Risks

The most frequently employed assisted reproduction techniques are artificial insemination and IVF. Artificial insemination consists of introducing the male partner's or a donor's sperm into the woman's uterus through a catheter. In order to facilitate this process, fertility clinics count on sperm banks where the sperm is submitted to numerous screenings and then frozen until used.

The current legislation comprehensively regulates the screening to which the donated gametes should be submitted in order to avoid disease transmission, and requires the creation of registries so that there is a record of origin and use of the germ cells.[14] It also prohibits the birth of more than six children from the same donor, in order to avoid future couplings that could produce accidental inbreeding.[15] To avoid this outcome, the creation of a centralized donor registry was planned that would be fed with the data previously gathered by the autonomous communities where the donations were made.[16] This registry, although in an advanced stage of regulation, has still not been set into motion, so that at the present time, controlling births from the same donor is impossible in Spain.

The second most frequently used technique for infertility treatment is IVF. It involves removing eggs from a woman's fallopian tubes after the patient has undergone hormonal treatment to induce maturation of more than one egg per cycle. Once the eggs are removed from the body, the female gamete is artificially inseminated by means of the ICSI (Intracytoplasmic sperm injection) technique. This involves making an incision in the zona pellucida in order to mechanically inject the selected spermatozoon. After one or more viable embryos are obtained, they are kept in a culture for several days before being placed into the patient's uterus,

---

14. Royal decree 1301/2006, of November 10, which establishes quality and safety standards for the donation, procurement, testing, processing, preservation, storage, and the distribution of human cells and tissues, and establishes the coordination and operation standards for their use in humans.

15. Article 5.7 of law 14/2006, of May 26, on assisted human reproduction techniques.

16. Article 21 of law 14/2006, of May 26, on assisted human reproduction techniques.

to which hormones are administered to facilitate the implantation of the zygote.

In the early 1980s, when the technique first emerged, specialists transferred up to five pre-embryos to the uterus per cycle in order to increase the odds of becoming pregnant (Kerin et al. 1983). As a result, the first cases of multiple pregnancies (of three, four, and up to five embryos) made news shortly thereafter.[17] It has been claimed that the use of out-of-body fertilization produces notable psychological stress in the patient and her partner, who are facing a procedure that does not guarantee more than a 30 percent success rate per attempt.[18] Only one out of every three IVF-ET (embryo transfer) patients has a full term pregnancy by means of this technique. There are also risks involved in a multifetal pregnancy and the derived effects from ovarian stimulation.

In all cases, these techniques require that the patient undergo prior hormonal stimulation so that more eggs than normal can be produced. In this process, drugs are usually administered that can produce (among other secondary effects) severe ovarian hyperstimulation syndrome (OHSS), which may lead to serious consequences in 0.5 to 5 percent of cases (Delavigne and Rozenberg 2002). In addition to these effects, administering hormones may cause liquid retention, arthralgia (acute pain), dyspnea (breathing difficulty), nausea, depression, vision loss, loss of pituitary gland function, hypertension, tachycardia, asthma, generalized edema, and abnormal liver function (Norsigian 2005). Cases of bone density loss of up to 7.3 percent have even been recorded (Lazar 1999).

Spain, the Country of Destination for European Women in Need of Reproductive Treatments

The extraordinary growth of assisted reproduction services in Spain is due to favorable legislation, delayed motherhood, and an exponential growth in foreign demand (on the latter, see France 2006). Spain is one of the

---

17. Carrying twins is connected with preterm pregnancy: between 11 and 35 percent of IVF-ET pregnancies terminate prematurely. The French IVF National Registry records twin pregnancies at 23 percent and triplet pregnancies at 4 percent in 1986 (FIVNAT 1995).

18. Some observers have argued that the aforementioned odds are close to those of naturally occurring pregnancies. There is now significant controversy over how to measure IVF success and failure rates. Some hospitals have been accused of inflating their numbers to present more favorable results. In order to achieve reliable results, an agreement was made to calculate the rate of successes by dividing the number of pregnancies by the number of women that have gone through at least one complete cycle of IVF-ET. See Page (1989).

preferred destinations for thousands of European women (ahead of others such as Crete, Kiev, Slovenia, Romania, and even India) in need of assisted reproduction techniques that are prohibited or difficult to obtain in their own countries (for either legal or financial reasons). Egg donation is prohibited in EU countries like Germany, Austria, Switzerland, and Italy; and is considered to be a dangerous procedure for the donor's health in Denmark and Sweden, where they only allow the use of excess gametes from patients who undergo IVF for their own needs. Yet anonymous non-IVF patient egg donation is allowed in Spain and in other European countries, although there are significant differences in how this is regulated.

In Great Britain, for example, a legislative change that permits those born to know the identity of the donors has caused a considerable reduction in available eggs. Different kinds of legislation and varying costs have led many women to go to other countries in search of treatment. This is a recent phenomenon, encouraged by internet marketing, a greater availability of cheap flights, and the opening up of borders within the EU.

In December 2004, the German media reported on a Romanian clinic specializing in egg donation to British couples. The clinic had established an agreement in which it would fertilize the eggs received from Romanian donors (who were paid 250 euros, approximately $335 at the then exchange rate of $1.34 to 1 euro) with the client's sperm sent from Great Britain. Once fertilized, the eggs were sent back to a British clinic so that they could be implanted in the patient. The practice continued until several donors reported the clinic after suffering from severe OHSS that almost killed them. The complaint led to a decision in 2005 by the European Parliament that condemned the trade of eggs (European Parliament 2005).

Since the anonymous donation of female gametes was authorized in Spain in 1988, the number of donations has grown steadily, and lately, has increased significantly as a result of the financial crisis. In view of the growing demand, private clinics have chosen to recruit donors by offering them compensation that varies between 700 and 1,000 euros (approximately $890–1,270 according to the exchange rate, $1.27 to one euro, at the time of writing, July 2010).[19] However, public hospitals that cannot pay these amounts to their potential donors use extra eggs from IVF cycles or,

---

19. In 1998, the CNRHA established a limit of 600 euros (100,000 pesetas), or approximately $660 at an exchange rate of $1 to 150 pesetas, on the compensation. However, clinics argue that the consumer price index increase has to be applied to this amount, and offer up to 1,200 euros or just over $1,500 per donation.

alternatively, have chosen to offer a better position on the waiting list to patients that provide a donor. In any case, the compensation offered to volunteers has been enough of an incentive to ensure that private clinics are much better supplied with eggs than public clinics. The most common donor profile is that of a university student between the ages of twenty and twenty-five. Lately, immigrant women, mostly from Eastern European countries, have also become typical donors. Some of these donors are asked to undergo three and up to four ovarian stimulations in one year. The Spanish practice is, without a doubt, safer and offers more guarantees than its Romanian counterpart. Nevertheless, the growing urgency to recruit donors may be causing pressure to be applied and advantage taken of some women.

The voluntary donation of human organs and tissues is an ethic principle codified by the European legal system.[20] This principle means that commercial trade in body parts is contrary to human dignity. Just as EU directive 2004/23/EC on tissue donation warns, excessive financial payments may unduly influence the consent of young women who donate, since the profit incentive may lead them to underestimate the physical and psychological risks of ovarian stimulation and egg extraction.

However, despite such legal precautions, the Donor Registry and Donor Activity Registry are still not functioning. This poses a risk for the children born from these techniques because they may unknowingly find themselves in relationships with blood brothers or sisters. The absence of official data on these procedures raises a significant problem when it comes to exercising regulatory control over the use of reproductive medicine, and at the same time, prevents the public from accessing basic information on the techniques.

The demand exerts great pressure on clinics to recruit donors with karyotypes similar to those of the women seeking the treatment. This means that clinics fight over Slavic and Eastern European donors whose physical appearance is similar to the British or German patients seeking treatment. This group of immigrant women thus becomes especially vulnerable in a time of financial crisis such as the present when the number of foreign donations has increased exponentially.

---

20. The Convention for the Protection of Human Rights and Human Dignity with regard to the application of Biology and Biomedicine, passed by the Committee of Ministers of the Council of Europe, on November 19, 1996. 686.96.CON. DIR/JUR (96) 14 of the Council of Europe.

The question of donor anonymity can also lead to international private or civil law issues when, for example, after using eggs obtained in Spain, a child is born in Germany or Great Britain, where legislation recognizes the right to research one's origins.

Finally, it is necessary to think about the criterion for allocation and distribution of this biological resource that depends almost completely on the established protocols of each private center. This is important when public centers that lack the means to pay donors have to create waiting lists of up to three years. For example, according to data in the voluntary registry of the Spanish Fertility Society, 55.7 percent of the women who have received oocytes are older than forty.

Preimplantation Genetic Diagnosis

This technique entails first bringing about the hormonal maturation of many eggs in only one cycle, removing them from the fallopian tubes, creating an in vitro embryo and, finally, extracting a cell for genetic analysis. This way, embryos affected by disease can be ruled out in order to only implant healthy ones or those that lack disease. The current assisted reproduction law establishes that couples who carry the risk of passing on a serious hereditary disease to their descendents may use preimplantation genetic diagnosis (PGD). The law does add, though, that this technique may also serve as "the detection of other alterations that may compromise the viability of the pre-embryo."[21]

With this second approach, embryos that present chromosomal alterations because of the patient's age are ruled out as a precaution against this causing the technique to fail. Once sorted, the embryos that do not show chromosomal alterations are selected in order to increase the chances of pregnancy. In a 2005 study it was reported that this second legally sanctioned approach accounted for more than 50 percent of the PGD practiced in Spain (López de Argumedo González de Durana et al. 2005).

After several years of employing this practice, scholarship on the topic has placed doubt on its effectiveness in leading to pregnancy. The evidence accumulated in available clinical trials shows that the manipulation of embryos for chromosomal selection seriously compromises their viability (Goossens et al. 2008). In short, the technique shows little effec-

---

21. Law 14/2006, of May 26, on assisted human reproduction techniques.

tiveness, especially in women with poor prognoses: those older than forty and couples who have had repeated abortions.

Regarding the first approach sanctioned by the law, the prevention of serious hereditary diseases, the CNRHA analyzed nineteen requests to use preimplantation genetic diagnosis in 2009. Of these, thirteen were considered for the purpose of selecting healthy embryos in couples that were carriers of serious genetic diseases. The CNRHA authorized the use of the technique in ten of these cases (two cases of facioscapulohumeral muscular dystrophy, six cases of Huntington's disease, and two cases of cancer: one of colon cancer and the other breast cancer). The other six cases concerned genetic selection of embryos for therapeutic purposes (having a child to cure a sibling) that were also permitted.

Among these decisions, authorization of PGD for colon and breast cancer cases stood out. Until now, genetic selection had been considered for diseases in which the cause is only one gene and where the connection is direct and certain: whoever has the corresponding gene will develop the disease. Unlike diseases such as cystic fibrosis or Huntington's disease, in which the child is born with the illness and will die at an early age, cancers are a group of diseases in whose etiology (although it does influence the genetic load) there are other environmental factors that determine its manifestation and development. In other words, the carrier of the gene does not always develop the disease. In the two cases authorized by the CNRHA, the disease is not early-onset, but usually appears after the age of forty and is treatable.

Between the time this diagnostic technique was first authorized and the decision to allow it to rule out embryos that are carriers of breast cancer and other cancers with low-level penetration, the CNRHA shifted to more lenient positions regarding its use. In view of this shift, the CNRHA has responded by promising that it will develop a list of authorized diseases as an important means of aiding the genetic localization of hereditary and congenital diseases.

Nevertheless, certain interests opposed to the notion that diagnostic capacity should be limited to certain diseases will become more and more important (insurance companies or preventative medicine for example). Besides, any list can be accused of being subjective and arbitrary. One might say that it imposes unnecessary and excessively rigid restrictions, when the decision should be left in the hands of the doctors and couples whose perception of the seriousness of a disease may differ from that of the CNRHA.

In any case, PGD is now offered at private clinics to women who have a family history of breast or colon cancer. These women face the dilemma of either undergoing these techniques (with the associated physical risks and high failure rates) or leaving it to nature. In the latter case, they may later feel themselves responsible for bringing children into the world that may be prone to cancer when they could have avoided this.

Conclusion

When one looks at the reproductive phenomenon in the Basque Country and Spain, one is first struck by the speed with which women assimilated contraceptive methods and, thereafter, over the course of two generations, completed the transition toward a better understanding of their reproductive rights. Pharmacological innovation played an undeniable role in gaining contraception rights. However, there is now a paradoxical situation in that the recognition of positive reproductive rights for women has led to a growing dependency on the use of another kind of medical-pharmacological technology: assisted reproduction.

There is no doubt that reproductive medicine has made very important progress in the fight against infertility and has allowed couples with physiological conditions that prevent procreation to have children. However, data indicate that technology may have gone beyond the limits of fertility therapy to become an alternative response to fundamentally social problems.

A significant portion of these techniques' users are women who have set out to have children at an advanced age. As a woman's age is one of the primary reasons for turning to assisted reproduction: women who can afford it can have children much older than they could naturally. It is unlikely that the compensated donors in Spain have the rights accorded by the principle of ethical voluntary donations noted earlier. However, this practice sheds light on the risk of exploiting groups that are especially vulnerable to an economic downturn, such as young women and immigrants. Spain is one of the few European states, though, where anonymous egg donation is practiced, and that guarantees treatment without a waiting list for national and foreign patients through the numerous private fertility clinics that have opened up in the country.

The medicalization of infertility reaches extreme levels through some applications of PGD techniques. Some Spanish fertility clinics offer women older than forty who have unsuccessfully undergone different treatments to become pregnant the subsequent possibility of subjecting themselves to techniques of dubious effectiveness, like genetic screening to detect chromosomal alterations in embryos. Such activity constitutes a case of excessive overtreatment, which questions the principle of proportionality that all medical treatment should abide by.

Yet the new genetic diagnostics to avoid passing on congenital diseases goes further still. Should a woman whose sister has breast cancer undergo a PGD in order to select embryos free of the disease? The argument for a patient's freedom of choice favors the diffusion of reproductive technologies but does not solve the problem of the social and familial pressure to which a growing number of women find themselves subjected.

Spain enacted lenient laws covering assisted reproduction as a form of major social progress. However, there has been no social debate on the issue. Discussion over the application of reproductive technologies has been reduced to steadfast opposition from the Catholic Church and its supporters, without other social groups or representatives having any say on the matter. Moreover, these laws have not been fully applied, which has led to a proliferation of fertility clinics and, ultimately, the creation of a fertility industry that increasingly resembles that of the United States in scale.

It is therefore not enough to enact supposedly progressive laws. What is needed is a profound social debate over the new reproductive technologies. That debate should address social infertility, delayed motherhood, and the effective practice of the reproductive rights granted to European women.

References

Alkorta Idiakez, Itziar. 2003. "Los derechos reproductivos de las españolas. En especial, las técnicas de reproducción asistida." *Derecho y Salud* 11: 165–78.

———. 2006a. "Los derechos reproductivos de las mujeres vascas en el cambio de siglo: de la regulación de la anticoncepción a la reproducción asistida." In *VIII Jornadas de Historia Local: Discurso y prácticas de género. Mujeres y hombres en la historia de Euskal Herria, Vasconia*, edited by Begoña Gorospe Pascual. Donostia-San Sebastián: Eusko Ikaskuntza.

———. 2006b. "Nuevos límites del derecho a procrear." *Derecho Privado y Constitución* 20: 9–61.

Arregi Gorospe, Begoña, and Andrés Dávila Legerán. 2005. "Geopolítica de la fecundidad a fin del siglo XX." In *Reproduciendo la vida, manteniendo la familia, reflexiones sobre la fecundidad y el cuidado familiar desde la experiencia en Euskadi,* edited by Begoña Arregi Gorospe and Andrés Dávila. Bilbao: UPV/EHU.

Congreso de los Diputados. 1988. *Informe de la Comisión Especial de Estudio de la Fecundación in vitro y la inseminación artificial humanas.* Madrid.

Delavigne, Annick, and Serge Rozenberg. 2002. "Epidemiology and Prevention of Ovarian Hyperstimulation Syndrome (OHSS): A Review." *Human Reproduction Update* 8: 559–77.

Delgado Pérez, Margarita. 2001. *Las pautas anticonceptivas de las españolas a fines del siglo XX.* Madrid: Aula Médica.

——. 2002. *Estudio sobre la evolución de la maternidad en España entre 1975 y 2000,* Madrid: CSIC.

Dickenson, Donna, and Itziar Alkorta Idiakez. 2008. "Ova Donation for Stem Cell Research: An International Perspective." *International Journal of Feminist Approaches to Bioethics* 1, no. 2: 125–44.

Díez Nicolás, Juan. 1973. "Actitudes de la mujer española hacia los métodos de planificación familiar." *Revista Española de Opinión Pública* 31: 23–54.

European Parliament. 2005. "Resolution on the Trade in Human Egg Cells: Planned Egg Cell Trade." *Official Journal of the European Union* P6_TA, 0074, C320 E/251 (March 10).

Eurostat. 2008. *Population in Europe, 2008.* See http://epp.eurostat.ec.europa.eu/tgm/table.do?tab&init=1&language=en&pcode=tsdde220&plugin=1,2009.

——. 2009. *Mean Age of Women at Childbearing.* See http://epp.eurostat.ec.europa.eu/tgm/table.do?tab=table&init=1&language=en&pcode=tps00017&plugin=1.

France, Louise. 2006. "Passport, Tickets, Suncream, Sperm ..." *The Observer,* January 15. At observer.guardian.co.uk/woman/story/0,,1684149,00.html.

FIVNAT. 1995. "French National IVF Registry: Analysis of 1986 to 1990 Data." *Fertil Steril* 59, no. 3: 746–56.

Goossens, Veerle et al. 2008. "Diagnostic Efficiency, Embryonic Development and Clinical Outcome after the Biopsy of One or Two

158

Itziar Alkorta Idiakez

Blastomeres for Preimplantation Genetic Diagnosis." *Human Reproduction* 23, no. 3: 481–92.

Instituto Nacional de Estadística. 1999. "Encuesta de fecundidad de las mujeres españolas de 1999." At www.ine.es/daco/daco42/analisoci/fecundi/notafecun99.htm.

Kerin, John F. et al. 1983. "Incidence of Multiple Pregnancy after In Vitro Fertilization and Embryo Transfer." *The Lancet* 322, no. 8349: 537–40.

Lazar, Kay. 1999. "Wonder Drug for Men Alleged to Cause Harm in Women." *Boston Herald*, August 22.

López de Argumedo González de Durana, Miguel, et al. 2005. *Diagnóstico preimplantacional de portadores de cromosoma X frágil y otros trastornos hereditarios en técnicas de fecundación artificial*. Vitoria-Gasteiz: Servicio Central de Publicaciones del Gobierno Vasco.

Méndez Baiges, Víctor. 1998. "Bioética y Derecho." *Tribuna* 21: 24–45.

Norsigian, Judy. 2005. "Egg Donation for IVF and Stem Cell Research: Time to Weigh the Risks to Women's Health." In *Our Bodies, Ourselves*, edited by the Boston Women's Health Book Collective. Boston: Boston Women's Health Book Collective.

Page, Hilary. 1989. "Calculating the Effectiveness of *In Vitro* Fertilization: A Review." *British Journal of Obstetrics and Gynaecology* 96, no. 3: 334–39.

Prats, Jaime. "Un registro evitará la donación sin control de semen y óvulos." *El País* (online edition), November 10, 2009. At www.elpais.com/articulo/sociedad/registro/evitara/donacion/control/semen/ovulos/elpepisoc/20091110elpepisoc_4/Tes.

Ruiz-Salguero, Magda. 2000. "La anticoncepción en España según la encuesta de fecundidad de 1995." Paper presented at the *XXII Simposi de la Societat Catalana de Contracepció*, l'Acadèmia de Ciències Mèdiques de Catalunya i de Baleares i per la Societat Catalana de Contracepció. Published by the Centre D'Estudis Demogràfics, at www.ced.uab.es/publicacions/PapersPDF/Text176.

11

Love and Violence in Learning about Relationships

MILA AMURRIO AND ANE LARRINAGA

Translated by Robert Forstag

Feminist theory and research (Miguel 2003) has shown that gender violence is the result not only of power disparities that exist between men and women in society, but also of specific ways of understanding sex and sexual relationships, along with the meanings of being a man and a woman within such relationships. These meanings are constructed on the basis of different ways of understanding, behavioral norms, and social practices that have been learned and internalized by most members of a social group at an early age and reinforced by the development of a secondary socialization process intrinsic to the daily life of every individual.

Currently, many more people are aware of the origin of such violence, and many more still are trying to find ways to prevent it from occurring. There are, however, both social practices and ideologies that make it difficult to deal with the problem and there are even myths that continue to legitimize and justify violence—myths that are lent credence by a significant proportion of young people who, during their school years, have had the opportunity to learn and internalize new forms of understanding about relationships between men and women. This has been shown in social research concerning the relationship between young peoples' attitudes and gender violence that has been conducted in other autonomous communities of the Spanish state.[1] The research presented here also

---

1. As well as research conducted in other countries, as shown by Ana Burgués et al. (2005).

shows how models of egalitarian relationships coexist, among adolescents and young adults, alongside models of unequal relationships that are reinforced by deeply rooted sexist stereotypes. This coexistence, which is the result of contradictory messages, leads to tolerant attitudes toward situations involving the risk of psychological violence, and enables the cycle of violence to continue unabated until it is expressed in its most extreme manifestation: physical and sexual violence.

Gender Violence and Popular Ideas of Love

In the broadest sense, violence can be understood as an action that involves the "abuse of power" in which at least one or two fundamental human rights are violated: the right to determine what we can do with our own body, as well as what is done with it, and the right to make our own decisions and face the consequences of our own actions (Flores 2005).

Violence is generally viewed in terms of those who hold power recognized on the basis of their holding authority that is socially legitimated, following Weber's definition of power (1978, 942) as "possibility of imposing one's will upon the behavior of other persons." He adds that, within the social and political arena, the more correct term is "domination," understood as the probability of observing obedient behavior in response to orders, based on the belief in the legitimacy of domination.

Gender violence is a form of violence that reflects the asymmetry of power in relationships between men and women, because it is violence that is exercised by those who hold a power that has been legitimated by their position of domination. This power asymmetry in relations between men and women is defined by gender. This is socially constructed and constantly affected by a social power that imposes types of femininity and masculinity that in turn both define differential behavior and attitudes and affect the entirety of social existence. Thus, gender violence is any activity, action, strategy, behavior, display, or conduct that results in either damage or in physical, psychological, or sexual suffering—including those involving fatal consequences—on the part of a person acting in both the public and private sphere. Gender violence is expressed simultaneously, consecutively, or in an escalated manner, and its occurrence may be either consistent or sporadic. It is expressed through psychological violence, physical violence, and sexual violence.

Eliminating this social disease involves addressing gender violence at its root, which means confronting the disparity of power between men

and women. Until recently, the social "norm" upheld the superior position of men in terms of the power division within society, and was legitimated on the basis of nature, a source of legitimacy refuted by feminist
theory, whose delegitimation has laid the groundwork for the beginnings
of change in the Western patriarchal order. However, there continues to
exist in society an entire symbolic order that reproduces a male domination that is maintained by our basic social institutions—family, state,
church, and school—and is represented in a cultural production that,
through the socialization process, is introduced into the personality structure of men and women.

One fundamental element of the reproduction of male domination
is the "cultural norm" regarding popular ideas of love, affective relationships, and sexual relationships. Socialization processes have inculcated in
us the idea that the origin of love is something "biological" or "magical":
nobody knows why it occurs and why it disappears (Flecha, Puigvert, and
Redondo 2005, 110). Thus, the education of women has empowered emotions and romantic feelings at the expense of physical attraction, and has
inhibited desire; an emotional empowerment has only one purpose: the
finding of true (eternal) love. And because it is love rather than pleasure
that justifies sexuality, it is up to women to place limits on a man's primitive impulses, which are "naturally" stronger. This kind of education leads
to girls seeing consenting to sex not as an unimportant momentary activity but as a kind of commitment and proposition with future implications.
Taking care of, giving and devoting oneself to others are demands of the
female role, and life only makes complete sense in the process of falling
in love, the highest expression of unity with the man who is loved. This
is a unity that, moreover, makes the understanding of one's own space
difficult: Women find it easy to combine spaces, but find it difficult to
differentiate spaces (they do not have a "room of their own" or their own
time).

For men, love and sex are separate entities. Men are taught to consider
sex as something physically necessary and important, and sex is even seen
as something that confirms one's masculinity in the eyes of both women
and one's male peers. Brought up to take action, the script of a man's life
is not geared toward union but rather separation: they are solitary heroes
whose lives are driven by some important task that needs to be carried out,
and love becomes something of secondary importance. Beacuse the script
of a man's life calls for separation, his social identity (work, hobbies) will
be considered important and necessary independently of his mate.

The relationship models that men and women aspire to are related to the way space is experienced. For women, the three different spheres of personal space are interior space (what we experience, feel, and think through fantasies, sentiments, fears, memories, and hopes); relational space (which we occupy in relation to another person); and social space (the place or places that we occupy at any given moment as defined by profession, social status, or the role of mother). These three spheres are actually experienced as if they comprise a single sphere. Thus, women aspire to an intimate relationship model that is *unifying* in nature, and where sharing everything is expected. The typical male model is, however, one of interdependence, with one element of social space that is shared and another that is one's own.

In order to be emulated, these models require the acquisition of qualities (attributes of the generic male and female roles) and attitudes/behavioral learning (role components), all of which need to be introduced from the outside, via socialization, into the personality structure. For women, one such model is Aphrodite/Venus, a symbol of the woman who is focused on asserting her feminine charm in order to succeed in society. Making a display of erotic appeal is a weapon that a woman can use. Yet, such a tactic also represents a submission to the male definition of what it is to be female—a subjection to the devices of patriarchal power. In contrast, the goddess Hera, the consort of Zeus, represents a woman whose life revolves around the roles of wife and mother, both within and outside of the home, although this role is at the same time invested with dignity and social recognition. Finally, Athena, the goddess of war, science and art, portrays the image of a woman who throws herself into her professional work, meets the challenges of this work, and in a general sense operates according to rules imposed by men.[2]

Men also have to properly fulfill the responsibilities of their role in patriarchal societies in order to assure that their virility is recognized, and often the punishment for those who deviate or who do not make the grade can be quite harsh. The three masks that represent the public male role are that of hero, patriarch, and monster; alternative and ambivalent personas that coexist in every patriarchal ego. Portraying the hero involves a man displaying daring and courage in social and competitive

---

2. Note also Judeo-Christian patriarchy, and its traditional image of woman as mother or as helpmate of man, with the goodness of the Virgin Mary contrasted with the paradigm of evil, represented by Eve.

activities. The patriarch represents male roles of normative or beneficent responsibility (father, minister, ruler, and economic provider for the family). The monster symbolizes the excessive expression of the passions or of the irresponsible quest for individual fulfillment (violent, perverted, and unpredictable). These masks are used to earn recognition—of both men and women—for being a man who is by turns worthy of admiration; respectable and fearsome; daring and competitive; heterosexual and the antithesis of any kind of effeminacy (Taberner 2008, 134–35). It is easy to guess which of these emerged as models to be emulated for each gender with respect to "normal" emotional and sexual relationships: for women, it was the beauty represented by Aphrodite/Venus and for men it was the force represented by Ares/Mars, the god of war.

Gender violence is inextricably woven both into popular ideas of love, and into those models of love and attraction according to which we have been, and continue to be, socialized. Culture and the context of our daily lives sometimes conveys an idea of love that is connected to suffering, while at the same time making a point of teaching us that violence and love are two concepts that are mutually exclusive.

In this regard, preventing gender violence means contributing to the evolution of a new socialization in which we bring forth new ideas and values about love, models of loving, and models of masculinity and femininity, that we consider more desirable and appropriate (Flecha, Puigvert, and Redondo 2005). Among those institutions previously mentioned as responsible for reproducing structures of masculine domination in our environment, only schools seem to have made some attempt to transform current models of socialization. The family, influenced mainly by economic structural changes in societies with respect to the social construction of gender (for example, regarding the sexual division of labor), has begun the process of transformation. Yet it has not yet undertaken a new process of socialization regarding emotional and sexual relationships that is capable of transforming the reigning symbolic order. The family's inhibition in this regard enables the continuing reproduction of this very order. Both the media and social interaction among individuals—especially among peers—reinforce the reigning symbolic order.

Education in values is the foundation of the Basque educational system at the primary and secondary levels, and this has made possible the implementation of different (although not yet widespread) educational innovation projects throughout the system. However, most efforts addressing the issue of emotional and sexual relationships have perhaps suffered from a lack of focus. This is because feminist research and educational practice has shown that what increases risk and leads to bad experiences in emotional-sexual relationships is not so much ignorance of contraception methods. Rather, it is the existence of a range of ideas regarding what it is to be a "real man" and a "good girl" (Sanchís 2006, 11–12).

The point of departure of this research has been the hypothesis that children and adolescents have been socialized within a cultural context that reproduces ideas and values about love, models of loving, and male and female models of attractiveness that reflect structures of male domination, and these ideas serve as a compass for emotional and sexual relations, as well as committed relationships.

This study's quantitative element sought to diagnose the degree to which gender violence is present in affective-sexual relationships among university students aged eighteen to twenty, by means of a closed structured questionnaire.[3] The subjects of the study were freshman students enrolled in the Universidad del País Vasco/Euskal Herriko Univertsitatea (UPV/EHU, University of the Basque Country) in Bilbao during the 2007–8 academic year. A total of 2,303 students participated. The confidence level of the sample design was set at 95.5 percent, with a sampling error of plus or minus 3 percent, p = 40, and q = 60. A sample was established of seven hundred individuals. The actual sample used was 832 individuals: 701 were eighteen to twenty years old and 131 were twenty-one to twenty-eight years old. The survey was administered in April and May, 2008.

The main purpose of the study's qualitative element was twofold: to explore interpretations of gender violence among young adults and adolescents and to analyze the ways these individuals construct meaning based on their experiences and lifestyles with respect to feelings and affective relationships. The data-production technique utilized for this purpose was a discussion group. Six discussion groups were formed that were composed of: fifty adolescents in the fourth year of compulsory secondary education (twelve to sixteen years old), in the first year of high school (sixteen to seventeen years old), or in comprehensive educational programs (sixteen to seventeen years old); and five discussion groups involving university students, in which forty students of the UPV/EHU in Bilbao took part. Fieldwork was conducted during the months of April and May, 2008.

---

3. Only overall results are presented here. For a complete version of the study, see Amurrio et al. (2008b).

Family Socialization of the Social and Symbolic Gender Order

The adolescents and young adults who took part are mostly from families where the issues of the division of labor within the family and home are in a process of transition toward more egalitarian relationships. Yet these relationships continue to feature very important inequities that have their origins in gender stereotypes that define particular activities as either male or female. These are families in which there are household rules, and that look to the couple as a unit that has the ultimate authority within the home. However it is usually the mother who insists that the rules in question be applied, with the majority seeing this as being applied equally among brothers and sisters within a family. Only 16 percent of participants saw the rules as being applied in a discriminatory manner. Here, the participants felt that different standards were applied to males and females that reflected traditional stereotypes. This group felt that there was a greater emphasis for girls and young women on protecting/providing security, along with the expectation of both a higher level of responsibility, both in general terms and with respect to participating in domestic chores, all of which reinforce the traditional female model. In addition, age difference as a criterion for granting a higher degree of freedom to boys and young men reinforces the traditional male model.

When it comes to the socialization process of the symbolic order, which serves as the foundation upon which affective relationships are constructed, the arena of feelings has traditionally been the province of mothers. Young women indicate that they have more confidence in their mothers, as do boys and young men, although to a lesser extent. Boys and young men are also more likely to trust both their mothers and their fathers. As regards the affective relationships between these young people and their parents, even if an atmosphere of trust is important with both of their parents, it is more important with their mothers. Thus, they speak more with their mothers about feelings, relationships, and interpersonal conflicts with friends—and even regarding sexual relationships, a subject that remains taboo in the majority of families. Once again, this preference is more prevalent among females, but is also noted among males. This shows that learning about sexual relationships depends more than anything else on other socializing agents, in light of the fact that 59 percent of young women and 73 percent of young men indicated that they did not talk about sex with either of their parents.

Issues closely related to the sphere of rational thinking—models of presenting oneself to others, thinking, and behaving—are more varied among males and females than those traditionally assigned by gender stereotypes. This is because these are subjects that they more frequently discuss with their parents. All in all, the critical role assumed by the mother in fostering this climate of trust and communication shows a family model in which the mother continues to represent the sublimation of emotionality: taking care of others, giving and devoting herself, integrating the spaces that constitute the basis of women's construction of their social identity—without either a space or time to call her own. As for the father, he represents rationality, the separation of different spheres, the parent who assures that his social identity is based upon his work, his preferences, and his hobbies, independently of his wife or family.

In terms of the sexual division of labor and the relationships and roles derived from this division, the family model seems to be evolving toward more egalitarian relations. However, we cannot say the same as regards the transmission of values assigned to genders within the symbolic structures. Within the framework of the family, then, there is no deconstructing social agent of the dominant symbolic order, and thus the family does not transmit new forms of thinking and acting in the world when it comes to affective and sexual relations.

Values Education in the Non-university Basque Educational System

Nonetheless, Basque schools have attempted to undertake new socialization initiatives. The recollection of the group about their school years shows that 80 percent of both males and females remember programs they participated in concerning drug abuse, respect for the environment, expressing feelings, adolescent sexuality, and equality between men and women. Some 60 percent of subjects remembered having participated in programs addressing school violence, social violence, conflict resolution, and gender violence. More than 60 percent of subjects indicated that the school contributed "a good deal" or "a lot" to them with respect to the values of solidarity and commitment, responsibility, equality between men and women, and respect for those who are different. More than 50 percent conveyed the same opinion in reference to the values of personal autonomy, self-esteem, self-control, and a sense of justice. However, in this latter case, the proportion of females indicating this opinion was higher than that of males. These data seem to indicate that new socialization strategies have more influence upon females than males.

The Anonymous and Diffuse Socialization of Mass Media

Media consumption by the young people interviewed revealed a world of values that, in most cases, reinforces the dominant symbolic order of the society in which they live. There is often no difference between males and females when it comes to media consumption, and yet there are significant differences when it comes to the most stereotyped programming choices that they make, with 80 percent of males choosing TV sports and action films and 60 percent of females choosing show business publications or TV programming, 40 percent choosing reality shows, and 45 percent choosing fashion magazines and websites. This same tendency is observed with respect to publications purchased by 40 percent of those questioned, as well as in terms of the famous people they are able to name from the world of movies, television, music, sports, literature and, in addition, as regards what they can explain about what it is they most value about these people. Females most frequently choose the category of "physical attractiveness," while males express their preferences in terms of who they find "entertaining," "the money they earn," "creativity-brilliance," and "ways of thinking/ideas." These choices reveal a world of values where, for women, social success is based on physical attractiveness and beauty, and for men, on rationality and social abilities.

Daily Life as Seen through Social Activities and Interaction

We then asked these young people to make a short-term projection of their future daily lives with respect to interpersonal activities that have an impact on their intimate relationships and social life. Notably, 95 percent of all those interviewed said that they would like to spend more time with their partners. Relationships are thus important and such an overwhelming preference, expressed with equal force among both men and women, remains surprising. Perhaps what is most surprising is the gender symmetry of the response, specifically as regards adolescents who seem to reproduce to some extent the male stereotype that is constructed on the basis of separating intimate, relational, and social spaces—and especially the separation from one's partner. For adolescent girls, however, such a response is to be expected, in that it reflects the demands of the female role in the merged relationship, where spaces are integrated in a way that makes both the perception and management of one's own personal space difficult.

Affective and Sexual Relationships of Adolescents and Young Adults

Nearly half of all people interviewed were in some kind of relationship when we were conducting our research. A higher percentage of females than males were in a relationship, and female relationships lasted on average longer—more than one year. More than 70 percent of females in a relationship said that they felt the relationship was stable—with the rate of males making the same affirmation somewhat lower.

This type of relationship has been defined by the discussion groups as a long-term liaison that is lacking in responsibility and mutual commitment. It involves both physical attraction as well as an affective dimension. It involves no future plans and may involve an emotional relationship that lasts various days, weeks or months without involving any kind of commitment to regularly spending time with one another—either intimately or socially. In such a relationship there is, of course, the implicit commitment not to simultaneously have a similar emotional or sexual relationship with another person. It is evident that the people involved in such a relationship do not have much experience, and that those experiences which are most commonly shared are one-night stands or temporary hook-ups. We can therefore assume that the way they express ideas about love and understand relationships are based upon the values according to which they have been socialized more than on their actual experience. Thus, males and females both have a vision of love and of a romantic relationship in that 76 percent of respondents indicated that such a relationship is based on feelings toward and commitment to the other person. Further, in these relationships both males and females share the view that such relationships are not dependent but rather egalitarian in nature. However, it was revealed that the initial approaches in such relationships among adolescents and young adults, which are related to parties and alcohol consumption, are more notably sexual than romantic in nature, especially for males, who almost always take the initiative. Thus, male peer groups constitute an audience to whom they can exhibit the "trophies they have won" and that serve to enhance their status within the group. Female peer groups serve as an arena for expressing feelings, but also as a space of rivalry. Female behavior during courtship is almost always passive. They wait, and typically do not express their own desires (and if they do so, they are stigmatized and looked down upon). The typical behavior of both sexes conforms to stereotypes that encourage and legitimize abusive and violent behavior.

The Ideal Couple

Adolescents and young adults see being in a couple as an important component of emotional and affective stability, although, on an individual level, there are subtly different understandings of this relationship. They overwhelmingly think of a couple as implying heterosexual relationships, with 91 percent of females and 87 percent of males indicating that they have been in sexual relationships, and 1.1 percent of male university students reporting that they have been in homosexual relationships (no females reported having been in homosexual relationships). When identifying elements that favor a stable relationship, females listed more factors (sexual, sentimental, affective communication, and ethical) than males.

These adolescents and young adults characterized a "good relationship" as one where there is confidence, sincerity, and respect—a series of ethical principles that ensure a relationship of equals. However, females continue to maintain an image of the male as a protector of women. In fact, one of the most important differences between males and females is that while females are concerned with being loved, helped, and understood, males mainly look to be accepted for who they are.

As regards the characteristics of an ideal partner, there are no significant differences, with both sexes choosing characteristics typical of a relationship among equals. Yet, at the same time, there is a notable presence of elements indicating a dependent relationship, with young women expressing a need to be protected and provided security (90 percent) and young men wanting women to be sufficiently attractive to assure a satisfying sexual relationship (80 percent). However, females do not consider either a man's physical appearance or the sexual relationship as important factors.

We can thus observe in the socialization of these young male and female university students the rootedness of specific gender stereotypes that endorse differential behavior patterns typical of an unequal and dominant relationship. While it is true that the discourse of a relationship among equals continues to gain ground among young people, it is also true that the survival of gender stereotypes indicate that there is still quite a way to go in terms of avoiding situations involving the risk of psychological violence—a risk that continues to be tolerated.

Relationship Models and Men and Women's Behavior

As regards relationship models and the behavior of men and women within a relationship, 80 percent of young people reject the idea of the woman having to be submissive in order for a relationship to function well. Moreover, they also share the convictions that being the sole bread-winner does not grant anyone special powers within the household and that women are not required to satisfy their husband's sexual desire's. This level of rejection indicates a break with traditional visions of dependency and submission of women. In this regard, there is convergence with the discourses expressed by the young women in discussion groups in which they state and emphasize the importance of personal autonomy and self-realization, conveying the need to have their own secure place within a relationship. It is also significant that, even when they are essentially spea-king of the same thing, males and females express the same value in diffe-rent terms. Young women, for example, talk about the need for their own space and for companionship during their free time, as revealed in the following extract from a discussion group (Amurrio et al., 2008a, 53):

> So what does a good relationship with your partner mean to you?
> What would it need to include?
> Girl: Sincerity.
> Boy: A Little freedom.
> Girl: Space. You need to have space as well.

Respect for the other person, individual autonomy, and having one's "own" space seem to be considered indispensable elements of a healthy relationship by the younger generations. This implies an increasing level of demand within a relationship and a moving away from traditional family roles, since young women undertake life goals independently from their roles within a relationship, the family, and the home.

This break with tradition is also shown, although rather more subtly, when it comes to beliefs regarding people's character and attractiveness. However, the same rejection is rather less strong when a man's aggres-siveness is seen as part of his attractiveness. In fact, responses to the two questions regarding male aggressiveness showed that the stereotype con-tinued to be endorsed by one in every ten males. The big picture is some-what modified when differences between males and females are observed. Typically, males show a lower measure of disagreement and therefore a shorter distance from stereotypical images of men and women. Females, on the other hand, lead the way in deconstructing stereotypes, outdistancing males considerably in this regard. Yet it should also be noted that, in the case of the stereotype regarding male aggression, the difference in views is smaller, a phenomenon that shows the strength of this image for both men and women. The data obtained seem to indicate that aggression as a component of attraction is still considered a positive value.

Familiarity with Gender Violence

Young male and female university students regard abuse as something that exists on a continuum and, therefore, that can be tolerated to different degrees. The variation in the responses obtained for each situation that was posed confirms that, in the definition of a specific behavior such as abuse, different gradations of the concept can be recognized. The difficulty in recognizing particular kinds of behavior as abuse is greater when the component of physical violence is lacking, or when such a component is not clearly present. Yet it is also significant that, even when it comes to behavior that involves more explicit violence, the criterion for defining abuse is not uniform.

Thus, uncertainty abounds in situations where the aggression is not explicit; when harm is caused in a manner that is not obvious, as a result of acts of omission; and when the abuse is psychological. All of these circumstances constitute risky situations for the youth studied, since they involved different kinds of behavior that these young people have learned to tolerate, as a result of either their development or their actual personal experience. Contrary to what had been expected, there was no significant gender difference regarding familiarity with various manifestations of abuse. Our analysis does not allow us to conclude that young women in general are more sensitive, or that they have more definitive knowledge than young men—or that boys have a more relaxed view of things. Some small yet statistically significant differences[4] were observed that constitute evidence of distinct sensibilities regarding particular kinds of behavior. Females found *control of money, emotional withdrawal* and *rape* to constitute clearly abusive behavior, while men were more sensitive regarding *cutting off their partner during a conversation.* The subjective component of the perception of abuse also includes a gender-specific significance that varies as a function of the values and sentiments that have been internalized by men and women.

---

4. The mean difference is shown in Amurrio et al. (2008b, 89).

The Experience of Gender Violence: Abuse in Affective and Sexual Relationships

We also attempted to show the extent to which violent attitudes and behavior are present in the affective relationships of young people. When a person has revealed that he or she has suffered abuse by their partner, this inherently involves the recognition that particular kinds of behavior involve violence. The definition of abuse is not particularly clear among male and female university students, and the disconnection between an explicit rejection of violence and an implicit embracing of attitudes that defend the use of force in personal relationships is a constant element in the discourse of many adolescents and young adults. Consequently, force is perceived by males and females as an acceptable recourse in human relationships, under certain circumstances. In general, the recognition that one has been victimized involves a slow and painful process in which one's self-esteem and social image are at stake. The results of this study confirm the presence of violent behavior in relationships among young university students. This behavior involves abuse on the emotional-affective level, abuse that has a coercive component, and abuse that involves placing limits on personal autonomy and freedom. The abusive behavior most frequently experienced by young male and female university students (behaviors experienced between 14 to 27 percent of subjects) at the hands of their partners was lack of sincerity and hiding information (27 percent), perceived aggression (17 percent), and disrespectful treatment (14 percent).

The results obtained do not define either the level of tolerance or the frequency of occurrence for those who have experienced such situations. Yet the fact that such situations have occurred constitutes a clear indicator of risk, especially in situations involving behavior that is not identified clearly by young persons as constituting abuse, and that usually precedes or accompanies more explicit manifestations of violence. Being in a relationship is not something associated with experiencing abusive treatment, yet a specific type of relationship is associated with abusive treatment. The presence of particular kinds of behavior—demands concerning how one's partner should dress and behave, threats of abandonment, aggressive and nonconsensual sexual behavior—is significantly greater among those who define their relationship as "informal, or a hookup." A lower incidence of such behavior was observed in relationships defined as "stable" or as involving a "formal commitment." Exercising the caution appropriate in a study involving an analysis of such small subsamples, we believe that the data lead to a particular interpretation: namely, that there is a higher incidence of abuse within relationships that are characterized as more informal or sporadic.

Conclusion

Both male and female adolescents and young adults express ideas regarding emotional issues and their partners reflecting relationship models that include components of both mutual respect between partners as well as behavior that is reinforced by sexist stereotypes—behavior that, instead of respect, encourages and legitimizes conduct that involves abuse and violence.

The prevention of such abusive and violent behavior involves deconstructing stereotypes, thus contributing to a new socialization that allows for the introduction of more appropriate ideas and values about love, as well as male and female models of attraction—especially models of affective and sexual relationships. Even though schools seem to be the only socializing agent that has explicitly introduced new forms of socialization, they have not completely uprooted differential gender socialization—schools have not succeeded in providing an education in equality, or an education that is oriented toward equality. Sexism and androcentrism in schools produces women with low self-esteem and men with a "superiority complex." Employing this supposedly "neutral" model with regard to gender, the values education typically offered in our schools displays an all-too-frequent neglect of a coeducational practice that attempts to learn and teach equality, and to eliminate both the dichotomy of masculinity/femininity and the hegemonic model of masculinity. Coeducation and the teaching of the emotions most definitely constitute a true values education—an education that allows the introduction of changes in various spheres of life, and especially in the symbolic structures of male domination that provide normative models of affective and sexual relationships for adolescents and young adults. The introduction of a new model along these lines would contribute to avoiding risky situations that neither adolescents nor young adults identify as abuse—situations that usually precede or accompany more explicit forms of violence—and specifically, physical and sexual violence.

References

Amurrio, Mila, Ane Larrinaga, Elisa Usategui, and Irene del Valle. 2008a. *Violencia de género en las relaciones de pareja de adolescentes y jóvenes de Bilbao. Informe cualitativo.* At www.bilbao.net/castella/mujer/violencia_genero/informe_violencia_adolescentes_jovenes/informe_cuanlitativo.pdf.

———. 2008b. *Violencia de género en las relaciones de pareja de adolescentes y jóvenes de Bilbao. Informe cuantitativo.* Bilbao: Área de la Igualdad, Cooperación y Ciudadanía, Ayuntamiento de Bilbao; UPV/EHU.

Burgués, Ana, Esther Oliver, Gisela Redondo, and Maria Angeles Serrano. 2005. "Investigaciones mundiales sobre violencia de género en la universidad." Comunicación del grupo de trabajo de Género y Educación de la XI Conferencia de Sociología de la Educación, Santander, September 22–24.

Flecha, Ainoa, Lidia Puigvert, and Gisela Redondo. 2005. "Socialización preventiva de la violencia de género." *Feminismos* 6: 107–20.

Flores, Rosa. 2005. "Violencia de género en la escuela: Sus efectos en la identidad, en la autoestima y en el proyecto de vida." *Revista Iberoamericana de Educación* 38: 67-86.

Meras, Ana, and Cristina Laviña. 2002. *Adolescencia y Violencia de género.* Madrid. Federación de Mujeres Progresistas.

Miguel, Ana de. 2003. "El movimiento feminista y la construcción de marcos de interpretación: el caso de la violencia contra las mujeres." *Revista Internacional de Sociología–RIS* 35:127-50.

Sanchís, Rosa. 2006. *¿Todo por amor?. Una experiencia educativa contra la violencia de la mujer.* Barcelona: Octaedro.

Taberner, José. 2008. *Sociología y Educación. El sistema educativo en sociedades modernas. Funciones, cambios y conflictos.* Madrid: Tecnos.

Weber, Max. 1978. *Economy and Society: An Outline of Interpretative Sociology*, edited by Guenther Roth and Claus Wittich. Translated by Ephraim Fischoff et al. Berkeley: University of California Press.

12

Conciliation and Participation: Capacities that Affect Women's Well-being and Quality of Life

Idoye Zabala Errazti, María José Martínez Herrero,
and Marta Luxán Serrano

Translated by Julie Waddington

This chapter attempts to establish a methodological frame of reference with which to analyze changes in equality studies by means of a series of indicators. It is based on fieldwork carried out in 2009 by sociologists and economists from the Universidad del País Vasco/Euskal Herriko Univertsitatea (UPV/EHU, University of the Basque Country).[1] The purpose of this study was to compile a list of indicators (and even when appropriate to construct new ones) that we considered to be the most relevant for considering the position of women in Bilbao, and for identifying transformations or advances with regards to gender equality.

We have continued this analysis, developing a theoretical framework for observing different facets of life at local levels (municipalities, autonomous regions) related to well-being; particularly the well-being of women (Martínez and Zabala 2009). Here, we employ Amartya Sen's focus on capacities as a framework that allows us to reflect on the degree of people's well-being and quality of life, and we attempt to extend our reflections by introducing qualitative aspects when selecting quality of life indicators. We begin this study by analyzing two capacities—conciliation between

---

1. The study (Zabala et a. 2009) was carried out at the request of the Bilbao City Hall. The research group included Mila Amurrio, Maria Luz de la Cal, Yolanda Jubeto, Mertxe Larrañaga, Ane Miren Larrinaga, María José Martinez, and Elisa Usategi, with Idoye Zabala and Marta Luxán acting as project coordinators.

personal, family, and work life, and political and social participation—although we also take into account the importance of extending this frame of analysis to other basic capacities.

Well-being and Quality of Life: The Need for a Framework of Evaluation

Concern for the quality of life and well-being of a society is a key theme in philosophy and social sciences. This concern has led to the search for a way of measuring quality of life by means of indicators that reflect distinct conceptions of what well-being is. Sen principally employs the utilitarian and the means approach. Here we will briefly survey these two approaches, and examine critiques of them from the framework of capacities.

The neoclassical school's utilitarian philosophy, the most widely accepted line of thought in this discipline, holds that the well-being of a society can be measured in relation to the degree of satisfaction obtained by its members. From this perspective, then, happiness or the fulfillment of desires are the indicators that would need to be applied.

Utilitarianism is an approach based on efficiency that pursues the maximum aggregate utility regardless of how unequally this sum of utilities is distributed; meaning that equality in the distribution of benefits is of little concern. What is of concern is the achievement of utilities, which are considered to be pleasures and satisfactions in perceived preferences or in existing desires. As Sen argues, this does not take into account the fact that traditional and persistent inequalities may mean that desires and preferences are adapted to these inequalities, given that people adjust their desires to what they believe to be achievable. "One of the features of traditional inequalities," he emphasizes, "is the adaptation of desires and preferences to existing inequalities viewed in terms of perceived legitimacy" (Sen 1995, 262).

He also points out that the unequal treatment that women and children receive, particularly within the family, may be considered "acceptable" according to certain social norms that affect both men and women's perceptions of their respective levels of well-being. "The presence of objective deprivation in the form of greater undernourishment, more frequent morbidity, lower literacy etc. cannot be rendered irrelevant just by the quiet and ungrumbling acceptance of women of their deprived conditions" (Sen 1990, 52). Utilitarianism does not question the role of social prejudices that affect and influence preferences. The fact that someone does not have basic human capacities is important in itself, regardless of whether they suffer or complain about it.

Utilitarianism, as Sen criticizes, thinks that utility should be "the variable" par excellence given that, in the end, any other could be reduced to satisfaction or happiness: "The victory of utilitarianism not only suppressed the claims of rival theories, it also corrupted and deformed the intellectual basis of the claims underlying these theories by making their advocates opt for a subsidiary route to influence via their effects on utilities" (Sen 2000, 20). This implies denying the possibility of using other variables (liberty, equality, participation) for evaluating quality of life. However, the advantage of focusing on capacities is that it has transcended this monothematic vision by adopting a more plural conception of well-being and development.

Recognizing the insufficiencies of the utilitarian focus is not to imply that satisfaction with life itself, happiness or the fulfillment of desires are not important; rather, it implies questioning whether this satisfaction is the only valid indicator of well-being or quality of life.

A second approach focuses either on the means available for satisfying human needs, or on primary goods as requisites for the development of individual benefits. The study coordinated by Paul Streeten (1981) involves an analysis where basic needs are defined as the need for a minimum quantity of goods that are essential for covering the requirements of food, clothing and housing, alongside other nonmaterial needs such as participation. Meanwhile, John Rawls (1971) discusses an idea of primary social goods that encompasses everything a rational being desires, such as rights, liberties, available opportunities, income, wealth and the social bases related to this.

For Sen, the problem with this lies in the fact that the satisfaction of basic needs, as well as the acquisition of primary goods, is focused on the means of acquiring value-laden ends, but "the usefulness of the commodity-perspective is severely compromised by the variability of the conversion of commodities into capabilities" (1990, 47). Yet not all human beings can turn primary goods into benefits, capacities or liberties in the same way. In some cases the differences are biological or physical; pregnant women, for example, will not attain the same level of nourishment as men of the same age with the same provision of food supplies, or a person with a disability will require more primary goods or means in order to achieve the same mobility.

The social differences that influence what people can do with their lives are as important as physical or biological differences. Behavioral limitations with regards to what is legitimate or proper in each society can, and in fact do, affect the relation between these goods and the liberties that they may generate. Sen argues that, "If women are restrained from using the primary goods within their command for generating appropriate capabilities, this disadvantage would not be observed in the space of primary goods" (1995, 265).

Despite the problems associated with focusing exclusively on the means that people have at their disposal, it is important to take into account that without the appropriate resources it is difficult to obtain either quality of life or well-being, and because of this it is also important to take into account the resources that we have. As Ingrid Robeyns indicates (2005, 94), "The capability approach is a broad normative framework for the evaluation and assessment of individual well-being and social arrangements, the design of policies, and proposals about social change in society. It is used in a wide range of fields, most prominently in development studies, welfare economics, social policy and political philosophy."

In Sen's initial focus on capacities, the constitutive elements of life are a combination of different functionings, and these achievements reflect what each person can do or be, thereby reflecting a part of their state of being. A variety of functionings exists ranging from the most elemental, such as being well-nourished, to the most complex such as taking part in the functioning of the community. According to Sen "The capability of a person is a derived notion. It reflects the various combinations of functionings (doings and beings) he or she can achieve. . . . Capability reflects a person's freedom to choose between different ways of living" (1990, 44). This freedom to choose between different options is what differentiates the concept of capacities from a mere list of achievements that any person could achieve with their functionings, emphasizing the importance of liberty in human life.

From a philosophical viewpoint, Martha Nussbaum (2000) indicates the importance of treating each individual as a person with the right to live a fully human life. She studies the importance of this approach in order to combat the oppression suffered by women all over the world and in the role that the family can play, given that it is an institution that can foster the capacities of its members. The family influences the formation of infants' internal capacities and enables the central capacities of all its members to be exercised, but it can also be an institution that fosters or perpetuates gender inequalities.

Each combination of capacities, as Sabina Alkire points out, represents a real opportunity for achieving what we value, but in addition to the achievements, it also shows us the alternatives that are not selected (2008, 5). Her goal is to place the evaluation of quality of life in the space of capacities and functionings. However, the data reflect the functionings and achievements attained more than capacities, which are more difficult to capture. Other writers, as Alkire points out, contend that a measurement of quality of life must include some functionings achieved; for if there is a systematic difference between groups with regards to the functionings achieved, one may conclude that the members of those groups have not had access to the same capacities, unless there are plausible reasons to explain why they systematically choose a different way. Furthermore, in the case of people with serious disabilities, of small children, or people in intensive care, for example, functioning is the best indicator available for evaluating quality of life. On the other hand, she suggests that "in many cases adults do not have a capability in isolation and it is in fact quite difficult to measure their capability set, because whether or not they have a capability depends upon choices of their life partner or a neighbor or another actor. In such cases functionings data alone are feasible" (Alkire 2008, 6).

From other fields, Naila Kabeer (1999) considers the difficulties of measuring qualitative aspects. For this reason, even though she focuses on the empowerment of women in India, her analysis might also be applied to measuring well-being and quality of life in the framework of capacities. She proposes incorporating resources, agency, and achievements, and develops a complex analysis on the basis of these.

In terms of resources, this concerns access and/or control not only of material resources (properties, income) but also human and social resources (to be able to count on family, to have friendships) that increase the capacity or possibility of choosing. This represents an attempt to analyze how these resources increase women's opportunities taking into account not only allocations in the present but also in the future. Control indicates more power than access because it enables decisions to be taken with regards to resources.

Agency means the power of decision-making and acting and is usually taken to be an exercise of power that contributes toward well-being;

however, women sometimes make choices even though these do not improve their situation. In India, women have interiorized the perception that they are people of lesser value. Because of this, they decide to have many children to satisfy their husband's desire to have male sons, even though this decision has a detrimental effect on their health. In this way, decisions emerge from and reinforce the subordinate status of women, and male power operates by means of the complicity of women. The existence of alternatives, or the awareness of these, enables different choices to be made.

Within the power of decision-making it is important to remember that not all decisions carry equal importance given that a hierarchy of decisions usually exists, some belonging to men and others to women. In many countries, decisions related to children's food or health belong to women, while decisions concerning the education and marriage of children or capital goods belong to men. It is important to note who makes the strategic decisions, whether new choices are made that could not have been made before, and to observe the degree of advancement or regression. However, all this is difficult to measure merely by way of statistical focuses because negotiations and informal decisions are undervalued.

Finally, when it comes to achievements, as regards results and functionings, we can distinguish between the attainment of different results according to whether they stem from different choices or of different opportunities for choosing. Agency, or women's decision-making power, is more significant with regard to achievements if women have escaped tradition and routine than when the results are molded to existing practices. Some achievements reflect women's efficiency within their traditional role and others are indicators of their capacity of transformation.

If an analysis takes into consideration these three aspects, one can see how different approaches contribute to measuring quality of life. Women's agency as regards their voice or role in decision-making in their families or in the community can indicate the control they have over their own lives, and their opportunities for choosing lives they consider to be value-laden as well as feeling satisfied with these. And analyzing the resources available to women highlights the importance of means in being able to exercise capacities. Ultimately, achievements reflect functionings that are in reality adopted, as well as transformation strategies that may be adopted.

An Analysis of the Chosen Capacities

As noted, we focus on two capacities: the conciliation between personal, family, and work life, and political and social participation; although we are aware of the importance of extending this frame of analysis to other capacities. The theoretical framework of capacities enables us to introduce a series of indicators that help to reflect upon these chosen capacities.

These indicators constitute an essential base that enables us to analyze gender, observe reality, recognize diversity, and detect inequalities; in short, to take into account the different economic, social, and cultural realities that men and women acquire, and they also allow us to carry out an evaluation of public intervention regarding the capacities analyzed. These gender indicators do not just comprise a disaggregation of information by sex, but also allow us to appreciate existing differences in people's conditions and quality of life, and to ascertain the advances that have been achieved concerning equality between men and women.

Feminist studies are now beginning to employ non-androcentric indicators more widely (Carrasco 2007). These indicators, constructed from different perspectives, are not ordinary gender indicators but rather advocate equality in difference. They advocate recuperating women's experiences in order to locate them in an analytical framework that is not centered in the male experience as a valid norm for both sexes. In this way, non-androcentric indicators attend to different social conceptions while gender indicators highlight inequalities in order to achieve equality, but often without altering the dominant model of participating in society.

Another obstacle to overcome is the difficulty of designing qualitative indicators that address the three aspects to which Kabeer (1999) refers: resources, agency and achievements. Disposing of a good set of qualitative indictors, and the information to be able to elaborate them effectively, would represent a significant advance in the measurement of quality of life.

Conciliation of Personal, Family, and Work Life and Their Respective Indicators

Within Sen's analytical framework, capacity is the freedom to choose between a combination of value-laden functionings, reflecting the freedom of the person to choose between different ways of living. In the real world, it is not easy for women to articulate a combination of functionings that they would like to achieve. In order to do this, conciliation is a relevant capacity that enables people's options to be extended, thereby increasing their freedom of choice.

A significant proportion of care-related jobs and work carried out in the home falls to women due to the traditional sexual division of labor. However, the incorporation of women into the paid workplace means that they are unlikely to be able to carry out all these tasks without excessively increasing their workload.

Conventional economics has ignored the existing relation between the process of producing goods and the process of reproducing work effort, with the latter including satisfying people's needs in all cycles of life, from infancy to old age, and not only when they are of working age. From this traditional view, the field of study is reduced exclusively to activities carried out in the market, identifying work as paid employment and forgetting that the commodity sector is supported by the domestic sphere. The reality is that women have had to assume a double working day and/or accept more flexible jobs in order to be able to cope with all the tasks they have. This is because the conciliation measures adopted up to now have been fundamentally oriented towards women, thereby contributing to the idea that the problem is one that belongs exclusively to them.

Conciliation policies must enable men and women to combine their work commitments with their family responsibilities and to have some time for themselves. Measures such as the establishment of a maximum time for finishing the working day, flexibility of working hours, individual and non-transferable parental leave, and care services for minors and dependents, encourage the sharing of social responsibilities. In this way, women will not feel forced to choose between family and work.

Addressing conciliation also implies taking into account other measures such as the promotion of personal autonomy and attending to people in situations of dependency, which means recognizing and financially supporting carers (85 percent of whom are women), and the professionalization of caring for dependents, freeing it from its traditional assignation to women in the family environment.

For all of this, it is essential to establish co-responsibility as a principle of equality policies beyond that which is usually understood by conciliation. Social co-responsibility is essential in order to tackle the problems of combining the time dedicated to care, paid work, and personal and social relations. Co-responsibility, whose meaning goes beyond that of increasing the involvement of people (especially men), extends to other social agents and to public and private bodies. For this, strategies of change need to be developed in order to combat cultural resistance toward the equal sharing of time (understood as a priority resource), and the sharing of tasks related to the upkeep of the home and care. In order to move toward co-responsibility of conciliation, it is important to take into account various fields of action:

- In the private sphere, promoting a more egalitarian model of cohabitation between men and women. A distribution of time is needed among family members in terms of domestic work and care work.

- In the labor market, promoting the development of a new model of work relations and quality employment that facilitates co-responsibility for the conciliation of personal, family, and work life. This requires the efforts of labor unions and business organizations to facilitate the conciliation of men and women by means of collective agreements.

- In public services, strengthening and fully developing legislation on leaves of absence, days off, and the network of care services for minors and dependents. A change in the design and functioning of urban infrastructures is also needed to facilitate the conciliation of men and women's different times.

If we want a society that increases the options and opportunities of everyone to lead a life that they consider to be, and have reason to consider, value-laden, then we need an agreement between all social agents to organize a response to the care needs that all people have in the best possible way, but especially those requiring more attention due to their higher dependency. This agreement should include social recognition for careers (better pay and working conditions).

Our goal is also to analyze the means and instruments that might lead enable conciliation between work life, family life, and personal life in the most satisfactory way possible. We thus need to observe the dedication and time that men and women invest in paid work, non-paid work, and leisure, as well as the means they have at their disposal and that they can use to carry out conciliation in the most satisfactory manner.

Within non-paid work (housework and care work), it is important to quantify the hours dedicated by women and by men to the production of goods and services within the home, as well as different domestic tasks, in addition to the care work carried out in order to attend to the needs of dependents, whether these be minors or elderly persons. Likewise, we must also quantify the hours dedicated to personal time, for leisure or for spending with others; time that directly affects people's well-being and quality of life.

Surveys on use of time quantify the time invested by people in different activities of daily life, whether or not they have a financial nature. Their goal is to quantify the duration of the tasks and daily activities that people carry out in both the public and private sphere; for this reason these indicators are considered to be the most appropriate ones for measuring inequalities generated between men and women resulting from the sexual division of labor. In this way we can observe the distribution of time between activities that are paid (and in this way register incomes), and those that are unpaid, as well as recognizing the time dedicated to leisure, cultural and community activities.[2]

Labor statistics will enable us to appreciate the degree of men and women's participation in paid work, the duration of the working day, the type of contract and reasons that lead men and women to reduce their working day, and even to give up work altogether. We are able to ascertain income levels obtained by means of salary statistics, as well as observing the differences in pay and participation in work.

We also need to know the means that we have at our disposal for carrying out conciliation. For this we will consult the data provided by social services, such as licenses, leaves of absence, and days off for family reasons, the infrastructure of public social services, as well as monetary allowances for family reasons or for dependence.

Once the best possible indicators available have been chosen, it is important to compile qualitative information that indicates the perceptions that men and women have of well-being and control over their own lives The quantitative and qualitative information available can be organized according to the aforementioned aspects of "resources, agency and achievements," and which are related to the level of satisfaction, the means available for well-being, and the options and functionings that they produce.

---

2. On the use of time in the methodological construction of these polls, see Legarreta (2008, 57).

Social and Political Participation and Their Indicators

The focus on capacities suggests that social and political participation is a key idea upon which quality of life and people's well-being can be measured, given that this enables integration in the community and can therefore be considered constitutive of human development (Nussbaum 2000). This focus, applied to the sociopolitical field, has contributed to the feminist critique of the concept of social and political participation in particular, and of politics and the political in general.

As in economics, classical definitions of the political and of participation have been tightly bound to the public/private liberal dichotomy; separate antagonistic spheres that, theoretically speaking, are totally unrelated. The public sphere—typically identified with social and political participation—is assigned to men, thereby making women's role invisible. In other words, this kind of definition excludes female experiences of participation and, furthermore, does not consider the existence of a relation between the public and the domestic. But what difference is there between privacy and domesticity and what has the role of feminism been in developing a different conception of the political and participation?

Feminism has contributed a fundamental critique to this classical liberal dichotomy, enabling us to overcome its limitations and embrace a new way of understanding social participation and politics, open to all the community and not just a part of it. This critique of participation models in liberal democracies—which after having excluded women from citizenship over a long period of time, accepts them as second-class citizens—highlights the need to recuperate and incorporate the female experience in sociopolitical definitions and practices (Zabala et al. 2009).

Furthermore, feminism suggests that an inclusive definition lies in an understanding of reality that is much more complex than a dual and antagonistic division. Moreover, besides claiming that the *personal is political*, that personal circumstances are framed by public factors (Patemen 1996), feminism also indicates that the private and domestic are not the same and that privacy refers solely to the male world. In effect, the private is a positive value that refers to ownership, to those spaces and times about which one can take decisions. In short, *male privacy* is a way of distancing oneself from the exterior world to achieve well-being. The complete opposite can be said for *female privacy*, which signifies a total renouncement of one's own time and space for the sake of others; a situation of service in which any attempt to be alone generates feelings of guilt (Murillo 1996).

Returning to the initial definition, as opposed to the pre-feminist approach that highlighted the disinterest of a large proportion of women towards conventional political activities, feminist thought has formulated the initial question in another way. For Judith Astelarra (1990, 8), "Instead of asking what is wrong with women that makes them not interested in politics nor willing to participate in them, we could ask ourselves what is wrong with politics that makes women not interested in them and question whether there is something in politics that stops them from participating." This new perspective, as well as questioning the reductionist and patriarchal conception of the current political model, also allows for recognition of the diverse manifestations of female participation in the sociopolitical community field.

It is not true that women have been absent from community life. Rather, they have participated in their own way and in a different way than men. In developed societies, women participate in different associations (consumer groups, schools, parents' and neighborhood associations) linked to daily life and their place of residence. A significant network of citizenship networks also exists in which they have always had an important presence, such as aid and support organizations and service providers' associations. Such organizations are not considered political according to classical definitions, but many of the objectives and problems that they address have a clear political sense and their members often attribute this sense to them (Luxán et al., forthcoming).

Highlighting these realities in relation to noninstitutional forms of collective action, a change in the conception of political participation is taking place in the academic world that includes expanding the object of analysis. Political participation is now conceived as an analysis of a wide variety of citizens' actions by which individuals transmit their demands and interests and attempt to influence the political system, regardless of the means that these actions adopt and of their legality or legitimacy. In this way, generating political conflict by way of mobilizations and social battles is understood as political participation (Revilla 2002).

However, the centrality of *conventional politics* in terms of guidelines and plans for equality continue to be patently clear. Therefore, lasting change requires redefining social and political participation in a way that incorporates the female experience and takes into account the fact that domesticity and the political are closely related questions. We therefore need to reclaim and value nonconventional ways of participation. It is interesting to note, for example, the existence of schools of empowerment; municipal initiatives that could be extended to wider areas. In any case, a wide and inclusive definition of social and political participation will not only help women to emerge, but also other social collectives such as "illegal" immigrants or transsexuals.

Meanwhile, it is essential to advance the study of social and political participation beyond that of quantifiable means. We want to find out how women participate in politics, but also how they perceive this participation and its effect on public life. From the focus on capacities, this subjective perception is important given that it often determines behavior, driving or inhibiting participation. Because of this, the pact we referred to when discussing the conciliation of personal, family, and work life—and the politics derived from it—must pay special attention to the perception that people have of the effect of their participation, building channels and implementing strategies that increase both opportunities for participating, as well as having a real influence on public life.

And how can perceptions, other kinds of participation, and the possible changes that occur be measured? What kinds of sources do we have and what indicators can we construct? We suggest a system of indicators that surpasses the public/private duality and, in addition to women's access to political rights and their participation in formal political organizations, incorporates other kinds of participatory experiences.

As regards access to and exercising of political rights, we can refer to the electoral register. Concerning women's participation in formal political organizations, systematic information is not available, which means that the data of parties and labor unions themselves will have to be consulted, as well as the results of different electoral processes. In this way we will be able to develop a set of indicators that report any increase in women's political participation in formal politics.

But how can the female experience be recuperated? How can the construction of non-androcentric indicators be advanced? When discussing conciliation, we referred to the potentiality of the surveys on use of time. In this sense, it would be immensely useful to include a section referring to sociopolitical activities in these same questionnaires. In addition to obtaining information on participation, this would also enable us to relate the time dedicated to political and social participation with that dedicated to the production of goods and services within the home or with paid work. Further, there are municipal registers of citizen associations that provide information on the structure of associative networks.

Finally, we believe that it is vital to generate information on the political competence of women that should pay particular attention to the perception that women have of their participation. As indicated with respect to conciliation, it is important to gather qualitative information that reflects the perception of well-being and control that men and women have over their own lives.

References

Alkire, Sabina. 2008. "The Capability Approach to the Quality of Life." Working Paper Prepared for the Working Group "Quality of Life," for the Commission on the Measurement of Economic Performance and Social Progress, Paris (October). At www.stiglitz-sen-fitoussi.fr/en/documents.htm.

Astelarra, Judith. 1990. *Participación política de las mujeres*. Madrid: Centro de Investigaciones Sociológicas.

Carrasco, Cristina. 2007. *Estadístiques sota sospita. Proposta de nous indicadores des de l'experiencia femenina*. Barcelona: Institut Catalá de les Dones/Generalitat de Catalunya.

Kabeer, Naila. 1999. "Resources, Agency, Achievements: Reflections on the Measurement of Women's Empowerment." *Development and Change* 30, no. 3: 435–64.

Legarreta, Matxalen. 2008. "El tiempo donado en el ámbito doméstico. Reflexiones para el análisis del trabajo doméstico y los cuidados." *Cuadernos de Relaciones Laborales* 26, no. 2: 45–69.

Luxán, Marta et al. (Forthcoming). "Propuesta de construcción de un sistema de indicadores de igualdad y no androcéntricos para el municipio de Bilbao: Una reflexión metodológica." *Actas del VIII Congreso Vasco de Sociología*. Bilbao: Asociación Vasca de Sociología y Ciencia Política.

Martínez, María José, and Idoye Zabala. 2009. "La conciliación y la calidad de vida de las mujeres: posibles indicadores para un análisis de situación en la CAE." *XVII Congreso de Estudios Vascos—Eusko Ikaskuntza*. Vitoria-Gasteiz, November.

Murillo, Soledad. 1996. *El mito de la vida privada. De la entrega al tiempo propio.* Madrid: Siglo XXI.

Nussbaum, Martha C. 2000. *Women and Human Development: The Capabilities Approach.* Cambridge: Cambridge University Press.

Pateman, Carole. 1996. "Críticas feministas a la dicotomía público/privado." In *Perspectivas feministas en la Teoría Política*, edited by Carme Castells. Barcelona: Paidós.

Rawls, John. 1971. *A Theory of Justice.* Harvard: Harvard University Press.

Revilla, Marisa, ed. 2002. *Las ONG y la política. Detalles de una relación.* Madrid: Istmo.

Robeyns, Ingrid. 2005. "The Capability Approach: A Theoretical Survey." *Journal of Human Development* 6, no. 1: 93–117.

Sen, Amartya. 1990. "Development as Capability Expansion." In *Human Development and the International Development Strategy for the 1990s*, edited by Keith Griffin and John Knight. Houndmills, Basingstoke, Hampshire: Macmillan in association with the United Nations.

———. 1995. "Gender Inequality and Theories of Justice." In *Women, Culture, and Development: A Study of Human Capabilities*, edited by Martha Nussbaum and Jonathan Glover. Oxford: WIDER; Clarendon Press.

———. 2000. "A Decade of Human Development." *Journal of Human Development* 1, no. 1: 17–23.

Streeten, Paul, with Shahid Javed Burki et al. 1981. *First Things First: Meeting Basic Human Needs in the Developing Countries.* Washington, D.C.: Published for the World Bank by Oxford University Press.

Zabala, Idoye et al. 2009. *Propuesta de selección de un sistema de indicadores de igualdad y no androcéntricos para el municipio de Bilbao.* Bilbao: Mimeo.

13

Anthropology of the Body, Corporeal Itineraries, and Gender Relations

MARI LUZ ESTEBAN

Translated by Lura Bunt-MacRury

Recent theoretical innovations in the social sciences place the body at the center of analysis surrounding social and cultural processes; converting it into an analytical object, but also into an empirical subject. In this new social theory, the body acts, "as agent in, and as locus of intersection of, both an individual psychological order and a social order . . . as both a biological being and a conscious, experiencing, acting, interpreting entity" (Lyon and Barbalet 1994, 63).

This theoretical-conceptual context allows for alternative readings of complex and multiple experiences that require a relational, performative, and dynamic view of gender. Such readings expand and transform what we call *being a woman, being a man,* or *being whatever we may become.*[1] These contributions are also intertwined with reformulations of frameworks such as power and sexuality arising in social, political, and scientific contexts—which due to their affinities affect and feed off each other.

Here, I outline this new focal point as well as show the potential of anthropological approaches to delineate such embodied, incarnate, and somatic analyses of gender relations. These approaches more concretely

---

1. By this, I mean that today there are many people who do not live as "women" or "men" in a hegemonic fashion. There are women who use the "seal of gender" in social circumstances as a form of vindication, yet in their everyday interactions they actually perceive life in less dualistic and more ambiguous, neutral, and multiple terms. At the other extreme are those people that are defined as "transgender," regardless of their physiology.

address the evolution of social equality and inequality, among other uses of how social change can be dealt with in general terms. Additionally, I detail a specific theoretical approach for the study of *corporeal itineraries* (Esteban 2004).

Differences in the Construction of Social Inequality: A Revision of the Boundaries of Sex, Gender and Sexuality

The 1980s were a turning point in feminist theory because a broad sector of feminism set aside the ascribed differences between women and men in order to focus on analytical models surrounding the construction of inequality. This in turn also allowed for a more circumspect examination of such differences. In disciplines such as anthropology, this was facilitated by second-wave feminism, launched the 1960s, "from [which] a static and synchronic analysis transformed into to a dynamic analysis of sociocultural processes in which human action, structures, and systems have a dialectical relationship" (Del Valle et al. 2002, 21). This process is highlighted in the work of Sherry B. Ortner (1984).

Given the assumption that not only gender, but also sex and sexuality were cultural constructions, the result of this critical revision set the stage in terms of maximizing the quintessential feminist agenda, or its anti-determinist and anti-essentialist mission. In this context, gender is always a polysemic concept and a defining principle of social organization (Maquieira 2001) that facilitates how people identified and socialized as women find themselves in situations where they have less power than those people designated as men. This is not to say that at the same time hierarchies are established among men and among women according to other factors such as social class, ethnicity, age or sexual orientation.

Yet, differences and inequalities do not take the same shape, nor do they have the same significance in distinct historical, social, economic, and cultural contexts. Later, I will address this issue of diversity through new concepts such as *gender system theory*, which is more suitable for tackling this variability than outmoded concepts such as *patriarchy* or *sex-gender system theory*. At this juncture, my aim is to understand *gendering processes* in their various institutional, normative, symbolic, ideological, relational, designative, and corporeal dimensions. Throughout the course of life, these dimensions turn people into *women and men* at biological, subjective, behavioral, and social levels. Moreover, as a result, they themselves become hierarchized beings.[2]

This questioning of gender boundaries (and sexual orientation) goes beyond the notion that *women and men* as groups are discrete, distinguishable, and separable from each other, so that the concept of gender can be comprehended in a relational and dynamic manner. This does not mean that change would be the same for all social groups. If this were the case, one could simply examine active contemporary dichotomies between men and women and ignore the historical reasons and motives as to why they exist. This perspective is indefensible, since it does not account for the influence of gender in the socialization process or in existential experience. Nor does it give importance to what it means to be socially designated as "male" or "female."

By way of example, statistics from various countries clearly reveal who are the poorest people in the world, who are disproportionately assaulted or murdered by their partners, and who are those that hold positions of power. Therefore gender is not finite, essential, or immutable. Moreover, critical examination of socially defined categories and taxonomies (including those by feminists), can be productive not just for the sake of knowledge, but also for social intervention.

Social Theory of the Body

Social scientific research on the body has proliferated in recent decades, addressing themes such as gender, health, sexuality, violence, power, memory, and old age. I will focus here on those works originating in the 1980s that follow a critical perspective in order to analyze social, political, and cultural reality, because such approaches "start from a phenomenological understanding the body as a material entity, considering the body as a place for the establishment of hegemony, inequality, and social control. Yet, the body is also an area of critical consciousness and resistance, as well as in a more generic sense it is a space for alternative worldly experiences" (Ferrandiz 2004, 23–24).

This theoretical model implies a distancing from other approaches in the social sciences and history in which the body is taken as a neutral surface and a reservoir of ideas—or as merely a set of representations and

---

2. On different dimensions or components of gender, see Scott (1986) and Maquieira (2001).

symbols, so that now the body has been transformed into an acting subject, into an agent. At present, then, it is located at the junction between
structure and agency, while still trying to rescue and mold the material
carnality of life.3

This approach, however, is deeply indebted to certain intellectual
efforts in the twentieth century where two authors in particular hold a
special place of merit. Marcel Mauss (1950; 1979), was the first person
to attempt a general socioanthropological theory of the body. Another
author, Maurice Merleau-Ponty (1945; 1962), argued that the world is
perceived through a certain localization of our bodies in time and space—
this being the very condition of existence. More recently, the study of the
body was influenced by Michel Foucault (1976; 1998), whose concept of
biopower, the political body in Western history, and the resilience of subjects have compelled us to align the body and sexuality with other broader
axes of analysis, such as the economy.[4]

Among the concepts that embrace this new perspective, that of
embodiment is especially noteworthy.[5] This term is commonly used in
Anglo-American academic circles and has now been reformulated by
authors such as Thomas Csordas (1994).[6] What is more, the use of this
concept is meant to surpass the notion that the body is socially inscribed,
and instead to speak of what constitutes "the body" as a genuine cultural
site; and to speak of a *material process of social interaction* that underscores
the body's potential, intentional, interactive, and relational dimensions.
Thus, "the interactive dimension of agency acquires a broader basis when
the social actor is understood as an embodied agent" (Lyon and Barbalet
1994, 55). Moreover, this perspective seeks to break with the fundamental dualities in Western thought (mind/body, subject/object, subjective/

3. Some foundational texts are Featherstone, Hepworth, and Turner (1991); Csordas
(1994); Grosz (1994); Conboy, Medina, and Stanbury (1997). In addition, see also the journal
Body and Society (Sage).

4. Scheper-Hughes and Lock (1987) offer a classification of the various theoretical and
empirical approaches to the body, which differentiate between the individual body, the social
body, and the body politic.

5. For a discussion of this concept in Spanish, see García Selgas (1994) and Esteban
(2004).

6. See also Bourdieu (1984) who, in his discussion of "taste" and the relationship between
body and class, breaks with a sociological tradition that situated the notion of embodiment
outside of the acting social subject.

objective, thought/judgment, passive/active, rational/emotional, and language/experience) or more importantly it calls them into question.[7]

Most studies of the body (and related issues such as sexuality, emotions, and love) in the social sciences have been—and continue to be—deliberately constructivist. However, this trajectory (that does not sideline corporeal agency in its analysis) has also resulted in acknowledgement of constructivist excess. R.W. Connell (1987) draws attention to the danger of treating the body as a machine that produces natural inequalities (typified by biological-determinism), while also highlighting the risk of seeing it as a mere vehicle of social ideologies (typified by extreme constructivism).[8] A general caution is warranted for an overly scientific view of humans as *robots* (or making them *mechanical information processors*). One should also try to overcome the limits of a dichotomous social analysis that both tends to lead to structural rationalizations and causes of social phenomena,[9] and to produce intentional and symbolic rationalizations, actors, scripts, and meanings (Berthelot 1991, 39).

From Being to Doing/Placing:[10] The *Somatization* of Feminist Analysis

The study of inequalities between women and men in the late twentieth century highlight three types of contributions that mutually feed off each other: gender systems theory; the analysis of practice, agency, hegemony, and subalternity; and performative embodiment of the concept of gender.

Gender system theory was developed by authors such as Connell (1987) and Janet Saltzman Chafetz (1991). Their research allows us not only to understand societies as systems that can take many different configurations with regard to relationships between women and men, but also with regard to kinship and the differences (including biological ones) that are constructed in specific and diverse ways in global frameworks and various localities.[11] There is a concurrence within those systems that

---

7. In this regard, Haraway's theorizations on the *cyborg* (1985).

8. In a similar vein, Reddy (1997) criticizes overly constructivist views of the cultural history of emotions.

9. See Lutz and White (1986) for a review of anthropological work on the emotions.

10. In Spanish the verb "to be" has a dual connotation: *ser* (to be someone) and *estar* (to place). I use these here to express different meanings and uses of the concept of gender. The verbs *hacer* (to do, make) and *estar* allow us to break this essentialist vision of gender and understand it in a more dynamic way.

11. For Connell (1987), gender is a structure of social relations that are in continuous interaction.

distinguish three autonomous, yet interrelated, subsystems: the relations of power and prestige, the relations of production and the sexual division of labor, and the construction of sexuality and emotions.[12] The situation of women and men in any of these areas can be variable and contradictory.

Secondly, two anthropologists, Dolores Juliano (1992) and Ortner (2006), stand out in studies of the subaltern and applied feminist theory. At this stage, re-examinations of the concept of power by authors such as Antonio Gramsci and Foucault are particularly relevant. Power here is understood not as something possessed by those in the upper echelons and unilaterally imposed on those below, but rather as a nexus where it circulates and is administered between individuals and groups. The hegemonic/subaltern axis allows us to move beyond overly simplistic views that make some groups (women) into mere victims of a system. As such, there is an increasing awareness of the importance of privileging the study of the social and individual actions of people against the cultural constraints and situations of inequality.

Thirdly, the systemic, relational, and dynamic definition of gender is also based on an alternative conceptualization of the body and the relationships between bodies and cultures. Additionally, the notion of performative gender is reinforced by authors such as Judith Butler;[13] although it has various influences.[14] In this vein, the concept of gender does not allow for an understanding of self-proclaimed, culturally determined, and stereotypical *essences of being a man and a woman* (namely, "being masculine" is to be active, tough, and aggressive versus the notion that "being feminine" is to be sensible, caring, and sensual). Rather, gender is *what one does* in social and individual actions where "the corporeal" is essential (Stolcke 2003; Connell 1987; Esteban 2004). Now, more that ever, authors call for a notion of gender as something not outside of the body, but rather as central to its construction (Connell 1987). This would lead to a potential vision of gender, identity, and inequality as *ways of doing* and *ways of being* in the world that are repeated continuously, but at the same time ever-changing. From this threshold, one only need take a step further in ascertaining gender.

---

12. This is according to the adaptation made by del Valle et al. (2002).

13. For Butler (1993; 1997), gender is a set of discursive and bodily acts that are repeated continuously, but are simultaneously processed.

14. Grosz (1994) classifies the main currents of feminism that deal with body and differentiates between the approaches of equality, difference, constructivism, and poststructuralism.

In other words, being or feeling like a woman, man, or transgendered individual (as well as a heterosexual, a lesbian, or whatever sexual mode), would consist of acts that are modified over time and composed of sensory experiences (both physical and emotional). These acts would occur within particular historical coordinates and cultural factors that make them possible, such as ways of feeling, walking, speaking, moving, dressing-up, self-adorning, touching (oneself), exciting (oneself), attracting companions, enjoying, and suffering in continuous interaction with others (Esteban 2004). Initial theorization should disregard whether or not these acts are conscious, and rather consider the reflectivity (in its varying degrees) as implicit in human action. Additionally, this "action" should be thought of in the same way as the material conditions of existence (gender, social class, ethnicity, and age) that are reflected in bodies and practices, in as much as body-reflexive practices (that are neither internalized nor individualized) occur as an interrelation constituting the social world (Connell 1995).

Ethnography and Corporeal Itineraries

For Francisco Ferrandiz, "the turn towards the body in social analysis involves an adaptation of our methods and analytical frameworks in order to decipher and interpret different types of human activity upon bodily practices—in all its complexity" (2004, 22). Lately, anthropologists have developed a kind of ethnography that could be labeled *corporeal ethnography*. One of the strategies implemented within this type of ethnography is founded in the definition and description of these so-called corporeal itineraries, which can be defined as

> Individual life processes except that they are always extracted from collective experience occurring within concrete social structures in which preference is given to the subjects' social actions, understood as corporeal practices. The body is therefore considered as a nexus of structure and action, the site where experience, desire, reflection, resistance, contestation, and social change meet at various points on economic, political, sexual, aesthetic, and intellectual crossroads (Esteban 2004, 54).

Spanish anthropologists use this concept to refer to sensory learning mediums; for example, Ferrandiz (2004) analyzes the cult of Maria Lionza in Venezuela from a phenomenological and critical position. And Iban Ayesta (2003) also uses this notion in his ethnography of Berlin, where he describes the experience of various socially and economically marginal individuals. For my part, I adapt and apply this concept in the Basque Country (Esteban 2004). Here, I analyze changes in gender identity and gendered practices in the corporeal itineraries of ten women and two men with varying backgrounds and social profiles (in sports, business, the arts, and so on).

This type of theoretical and methodological approach also enables an assessment of an individual's "subjectivity" in a manner not common to the social sciences. This includes anthropology, where (barring a few exceptions) research has tended to focus on "the group" and "the community." Now, however, discrete, unique, and individual cases (though extracted from collective and social spaces which are themselves culturally and historically particular) are the basis for an analysis of interrelationships. Equally, these cases form a basis for comparisons and conflicts on each side of a relationship (Esteban 2008).

Corporeal itineraries may include more or less extensive biographical timelines concerning the individuals being researched. This allows for a description of their unique trajectories that is at once fluid and permeable in its ability to register sensations, movements, gestures, and patterns of self-perception and self-knowledge. Although an examination into the real, inner-life of anyone is at hand, this kind of self-knowledge is usually achieved by people in certain personal or political circumstances (by profession, by having previous access to psycho-social knowledge and/or therapy, or by membership social movements and causes). For example, my research has shown that feminist-minded thinking had led some of my informants to become more conscientious about certain research topics such as nutrition, body image, and sexuality. In any case, the structure of the interview allowed an informant to articulate an account of their life and in doing so they instigate *making themselves conscious.*

There is a risk in understanding such biographies as corporeal itineraries, which might give the impression that these experiences are too consistent, rational, linear, and successive. Yet its main advantage is the ability to show lives and bodies in motion, while underscoring interrelationships and tensions between the actions (understood as corporeal), the ideologies, and the multiple contexts in which people operate. Further, this *corporeal interrogation* that guides the bodily practices of women and men is precisely a site that allows them to alter, resist, and counter such itineraries in social structures. Regardless of intention or impediment, it also contributes to their own empowerment in concrete situations and circumstances (Esteban 2004, 63).

Corporeal Itineraries, Identity, Relationships, and Change

One of the virtues of feminist ethnography is that it privileges an analysis of its subjects' corporeal actions that allows for a reformulation of social and self-definitions of gender. One example of this is the way in which one of my informants expressed what it meant to him "to be a man." In contrast to what would be expected, he believed that being a man meant lacking "man-speak" or a virile attitude: "Nor do I even like soccer, I don't even think that I'm the kind of person who spits on the ground, drinks beer, or pisses on street corners.... What does it mean to be a man? . . . It's who you associate with and in those circles you just don't ask certain questions.... Maybe some men are simply incapable of basic domesticity and civility" (Esteban 2004, 172).

The narrative of another interviewee, a weightlifting athlete, also allows a glimpse into the broad range of possible criteria when it comes to self-identify. In this case, gender is more fluid, dynamic, and open concerning the provisions of dominant discourses:

> I wasn't a girl that liked to play dolls.... Instead of making friends that were girls, I made friends with groups of boys where I as the only girl. We would go up to the mountains to make huts, to steal apples from the orchards, and to get into fights with other gangs.... Later on, I outgrew the stage where I hung out on the street and then started weightlifting.... In sports, you don't pay attention to differences [between males and females]. I mean, of course, I notice it when I get dressed up to go out, but when it comes to training, then no, I don't notice. When I train with men, there simply are no distinctions.... When I put on eye-liner, or go to dinner and dress up it's little different . . . I feel like a woman when I'm with him [her boyfriend], he is a man and I a woman, because it's obvious, but one only notices it there [in the gym]. Yet, when we're in the street with friends, then I don't feel that "I'm the woman and he's the man," but just like we are all one in the same (Esteban 2004, 155-56).

What is more, ethnography allows for a reflection upon the different modalities in which informants live, as demonstrated in another testimony:

A key factor is that I was socialized in a middle-class environment with parents who taught. Like all teachers of their generation, my parents had lived during the Franco regime. They held a rather complex professional status, tinged with a mixture of social prestige, especially in rural areas, and a socioeconomic status that was more precarious, although this improved with time. My parents had an immense perception of their responsibility as educators and maintainers of social order. . . . My family has always privileged intellectual pursuits over carnal ones. And this prioritization didn't take account of whether we were boys or girls (I had no brothers). It is consequently the omission—the silence surrounding anything sexual—that is characteristic not only this specific historical moment in the history of the Spanish state, but also of a particular class background. This would describe the atmosphere of my own family. This wasn't the best way to develop a healthy attitude towards one's body (Esteban 2004, 226–27).

Below, the following excerpt from another informant also illustrates the experience of individual and familial connections to a particular social class. In juxtaposition to the anecdote above, it clearly renders how power relations between people of different statuses are not always linear or unidirectional:

I went to school in the Women's Section [an official organization of the Franco regime]. It was obvious that I was not from the same social class as the rest of the girls. I was the daughter of a construction worker and a seamstress. This was apparent externally: I always came to school with the clothes my mother had sewn, in the way I spoke, and in the things I talked about. When we were about eleven or twelve-years-old, the gym teacher forced us to take a shower with the doors wide open. All the other girls freaked out, but truthfully, I didn't. Nevertheless, I acted like it bothered me. I remember the first time I noticed my incipient pubic hair and the other girls told me that I had a disease. "What do you mean a disease?! My mother also has hairs." "Well, maybe it's a genetic disease then." This would have meant that I was the only girl in my class of forty-six—I remember the exact number—who had seen her mother naked. I think that I somehow sensed that I had inside information that no other girl had. Seeing my mother's body gave me an advantage over them for the first time. That is, dressed or undressed, we were not equals; but now I had the power (Esteban 2004, 205).

These testimonies reflect specific aspects of socialization, gendered experiences, and sexual ideologies that correspond to class and historically particular crossroads. Taken as a whole, these elements allow us to more fully understand the social, political, and ideological channels that articulate bodies with mechanisms of basic social regulation.

In virtually all of the subjects studied, any changes were related to the institutions or groups (both social and professional) to which they belonged. Each presented an alternative to and a critique of hegemonic culture. "Membership" allows a person to rethink their experience and implement new knowledge, which in regard to gender becomes part of a new socialization process (del Valle 1992; 1993). On the other hand, informants who showed a greater and richer reflexivity (consciously or unconsciously) about their own gender position were engaged in areas where they mixed socially defined values and practices such as "acting feminine or masculine." Additionally, all these changes were produced within the contexts of social relationships. Nonetheless, they occurred outside of self-definition (which usually produces changes that much more polarized at an ideological level as opposed to the experiential level).

Corporeal theory and ethnography can also aid in rethinking the duality between subject and object. They can also help to reevaluate ourselves as individuals and as researchers, an excellent component of anthropological and feminist critique.[15] In sum, a *corporeal analysis of gender* that addresses social/individual action and change renders an understanding of both the micro and macro level of experience, while at the same time aiding understanding of the various nuances of human subjectivity and everyday practice—all without leaving aside historical, cultural, social, political, and economic factors. It allows us to examine experiences, negotiations, conflicts, and transformations of alternative modalities. Given that the body has become a major means of social control and regulation in Western culture, this corporeal analysis of gender also puts a finger on the pulse, as it were, of the detriment caused social inequality and the excesses of a body-centered culture.

References

Ayesta, Iban. 2003. "Berlin, fin de millennium: An Experiment in Corporeal Ethnography." Ph.D Diss., University College London.

Berthelot, Jean Michel. 1991. "Sociological Discourse and the Body." In *The Body: Social Process and Cultural Theory*, edited by Mike

15. In this regard, see Esteban (2001).

Featherstone, Mike Hepworth, and Bryan S. Turner. London. Sage Publications.

Bourdieu, Pierre. 1984. *Distinction: A Social Critique of the Judgement of Taste*. London. Routledge.

Butler, Judith. 1993. *Bodies that Matter*. New York. Routledge.

———. 1997. "Performative Acts and Gender Constitution: An Essay in Phenomenology and Feminist Theory." In *Writing on the Body: Female Embodiment and Feminist Theory*, edited by Katie Conboy, Nadia Medina, and Sarah Stanbury. New York: Columbia University Press.

Chafetz, Janet Saltzman. 1991. *Gender Equity*. Newbury Park: Sage.

Conboy, Katie, Nadia Medina, and Sarah Stanbury, eds. 1997. *Writing on the Body: Female Embodiment and Feminist Theory*. New York: Columbia University Press.

Connell, R. W. 1987. *Gender and Power: Society, the Person, and Sexual Politics*. Cambridge: Polity Press.

———. 1995. "Men's Bodies." In *Masculinities*. Oxford/Cambridge: Polity Press.

Csordas, Thomas J., ed. 1994. *Embodiment and Experience: The Existential Ground of Culture and Self*. Cambridge: Cambridge University Press.

Del Valle, Teresa. 1992–93. "Mujer y nuevas socializaciones: Su relación con el poder y el cambio." *Kobie-Serie Antropología Cultural* 6: 5–15.

Del Valle, Teresa et al. 2002. *Modelos emergentes en los sistemas y las relaciones de género*. Madrid: Narcea.

Esteban, Mari Luz. 2001. "Embodied Anthropology: Anthropology from Oneself." *AM-Revista della Società Italiana di Antropologia Medica*. Monográfico "Medical Anthropology and Anthropology." 11–12 (October):173–89.

———. 2004. *Antropología del cuerpo. Género, itinerarios corporales, identidad y cambio*. Barcelona: Edicions Bellaterra.

———. 2008. "Etnografía, itinerarios corporales y cambio social: Apuntes teóricos y metodológicos." In *La materialidad de la identidad*, edited by Elixabete Imaz. Donostia: Hariadna.

Featherstone, Mike, Mike Hepworth, and Bryan S. Turner. 1991. *The Body: Social Processes and Cultural Theory*. London: Sage.

Ferrándiz, Francisco. 2004. *Escenarios del cuerpo: Espiritismo y sociedad en Venezuela*. Bilbao: Publicaciones de la Universidad de Deusto.

Foucault, Michel. 1976; 1998. *The History of Sexuality*. Volume 1. *The Will to Knowledge*, translated by Robert Hurley. London: Penguin Books.

García Selgas, Fernando. 1994. "El cuerpo como base del sentido de la acción social." *REIS-Revista Española de Investigaciones Sociológicas* 68 (October–December): 41–83.

Grosz, Elisabeth. 1994. *Volatile Bodies: Toward a Corporeal Feminism*. Bloomington: Indiana University Press.

Haraway, Donna J. 1985. "A Manifesto for Cyborgs: Science, Technology, and Socialist Feminism in the 1980s." *Socialist Review* 15, no. 2: 65–108.

Juliano, Dolores. 1992. *El juego de las astucias: Mujer y construcción de modelos sociales alternativos*. Madrid: Horas y Horas.

Lutz, Catherine, and Geoffrey M. White. 1986. "The Anthropology of Emotions." *Annual Review of Anthropology* 15: 405–36.

Lyon, M.L., and J.M. Barbalet. 1994. "Society's Body: Emotion and the 'Somatization' of Social Theory." In *Embodiment and Experience: The Existential Ground of Culture and Self*, edited by Thomas J. Csordas. Cambridge: Cambridge University Press.

Maquieira, Virginia. 2001. "Género, diferencia y desigualdad." In *Feminismos. Debates teóricos contemporáneos*, edited by Elena Beltrán, Virginia Maquieira, Silvina Alvárez, and Cristina Sánchez. Madrid: Alianza Editorial.

Mauss, Marcel. 1950; 1979. Part IV, "Body Techniques." In *Sociology and Psychology: Essays by Marcel Mauss*, translated by Ben Brewster. London: Routledge & Kegan Paul.

Merleau-Ponty, Maurice. 1945; 1962. *Phenomenology of Perception*, translated by Colin Smith. London: Routledge & Kegan Paul.

Ortner, Sherry B. 1984. "Theory in Anthropology since the Sixties." *Society for Comparative Study of Society and History* 26, no 1: 126–66.

———. 2006. *Anthropology and Social Theory: Culture Power and the Acting Subject*. Duke: Duke Univesity Press.

Reddy, William M. 1997. "Against Constructionism: The Historical Ethnography of Emotions." *Current Anthropology* 38, no. 3: 327–51.

Scheper-Hughes, Nancy, and Margaret Lock. 1987. "The Mindful Body: A Prolegomenon to Future Work in Medical Anthropology." *Medical Anthropology Quaterly* 1, no. 1: 6–41.

Scott, Joan W. 1986. "Gender: A Useful Category of Historical Analysis." *American Historical Review* 91, no. 5: 1053–75.

Stolcke, Verena. 2003. "La mujer es puro cuento: La cultura del género." *Quaderns de l'Institut Catalá d'Antropologia* 19: 69–95.

Index

la palabra (Women and Words),
57–58; *Mujer Vasca. Imagen y
Realidad* (Basque Women: Image
and Reality), 55, 56
delayed maternity, 143, 148–49,
153
demythification, 56–57
devaluation, 133
Diez, Ana, 105, 106
Diez, Carmen, 121
Díez, Carmen, 59, 63–64n11
diputaciones or provincial
governments, 55n1
diputado general, 21
disobedience, 93–97
dissimulating, 76
divided love, 79
domestic work, 16–17, 21
domination, 160, 161
Donor Activity Registry, 152
Donor Registry, 152
double bind theory, 33

E
EAB. *See* Emakume Abertzale
Batza
ECAM. *See* Escuela de
Cinematografía
economics, 61–62
education, 14–15, 166
educational system, 163–64
egg donation, 147, 151, 151n19,
152
EHEA. *See* European Higher
Education Area
Ekimen Feminista, 44
El Mundo, 25–38, *34*
El País, 25–38, *33, 34*
Elizondo, Arantxa, 61
Ellis, Henry Havelock, 77

Emakume Abertzale Batza (EAB,
League of Nationalist Women),
88
Emakunde (Basque Women's
Institute), 9, 11, 50n31, 55n1, 61
embodiment, 194
emotions, 195n8
empowerment of women, 179
EOO. *See* equal opportunity office
equal opportunity office (EOO),
43–45
equality: co-responsibility as a
principle of, 182–83; effective,
41, 43; feminism of, 9; versus
matriarchy, 113–26; social
inequality, 192–93
equality politics, 39–53
Equipo Barañi, 62
Escuela de Cinematografía
(ECAM, School of
Cinematography), 106
Escuela Oficial de Cinematografía
(Official School of
Cinematography), 105
Esteban, Mari Luz, 59, 128n2
ETA. *See* Euskadi Ta Askatasuna
ethnographic emergency, 121
ethnography, 197–99, 199–200
etxea (house as home and people),
114
etxekoandre (housewife), 117
EUDEL-Berdinsarea, 55n1
European Higher Education Area
(EHEA), 39–40n4, 42, 50, 52,
64n13
Eurostat, 16n4
Euskadi Ta Askatasuna (ETA,
Basque Country and Freedom),
115, 131

Eusko Ikaskutza (Society of
  Basque Studies), 50n31, 56
Eve, 93–94, 162n2
exclusion, 132–34
executive authority, 21

F
family life, 165–66, 181–84
Fejerman, Daniela, 106n3, 107n4
female archetypes, 117–18
female athletes, 30
female fertility, 145
female identity, 25–38
female politicians, 30, 31
female press, 25
female privacy, 185–86
female soldiers, 31, 120, 122
female stereotypes, 29, 30–32
femininity, 196, 201
feminism, 9, 55–56, 77, 185–86,
  196n14
feminist academic production,
  55–70
feminist analysis, 195–97
feminist anthropology, 59
feminist film theory, 102
feminist knowledge, 56–57, 57–63
feminist movement, 8–9
feminist studies, 50–51, 181
feminist theory, 196
feminization of poverty, 19–20
Fernández, Idoia, 60
Fernández, Victoria, 63
Fernández de Larrinoa, Kepa, 59
Fernández Viguera, Blanca, 62,
  62n10
Fernández-Rasines, Paloma, 60
Ferrandiz, Francisco, 197
Ferreira, Patricia, 106
fertility, 144–45

festivals, 119–24
film, woman's, 108
film criticism, Spanish, 102
film studies, 61
film theory, feminist, 102
financial independence, 21
First Basque Feminist Forum, 9
First Conference on Feminist
  Economy (Bilbao), 62n9
Flores Silva, Beatriz, 106n3
foral system, 7–8, 8n1, 21, 88
Foucault, Michel, 75, 194, 196
Fourth Basque Feminist Forum, 9
France, 8, 48, 148
Freire, Díaz, 87n4
funeral rites, 57, 131, 131n5
future directions, 63–65

G
Galino Carrillo, María Ángeles, 48
games, 127–42
Ganzabal, María, 61
García Serrano, Yolanda, 106
Gardela, Isabel, 106n3
gender, 199; boundaries of,
  192–93; corporeal analysis of,
  201; definition of, 196, 196n13;
  as structure of social relations,
  195n11
gender gap: in academic
  performance, 15; in annual
  income, 18–19; in Basque
  Parliament, 20; in labor force
  participation, 17–18; in life
  expectancy, 13; in salary, 18–19;
  at university, 15–16; in use of
  health-related services, 14; in
  vocational training, 15
gender ideals, 71–83
gender order, 165–66

List of Contributors

For full biographical information about the contributors, links to their projects, and more, visit www.basque.unr.edu/currentresearch/contributors

Katixa Agirre

Itziar Alkorta Idiakez

Mila Amurrio

Nerea Aresti

Jasone Astola

Margaret Bullen

Casilda de Miguel

Teresa del Valle

Carmen Díez Mintegui

Arantxa Elizondo

Mari Luz Esteban

Maria Ganzabal Learreta

Jone M. Hernández

Elixabete Imaz

Leire Ituarte

Mertxe Larrañaga

Ane Larrinaga

Miren Llona

Marta Luxán

Flora Marin Murillo

María Jose Martínez Herrero

Ainhoa Novo

Idoye Zabala Errazti